How to Tan Animal Hides and How to Make High Quality Buckskin Clothing

Robert Wayne Atkins, P.E.
(Grandpappy)

Complete instructions for processing an animal hide into a soft buckskin so it can be converted into a beautiful article of clothing that will last many, many years.

Also included are instructions on how to create delicious smoked meat and how to preserve that meat for future consumption.

Instructions are also included on how to make ropes and primitive weapons and how to make parchment, ink, and a quill pen.

For more information please visit: https://www.grandpappy.org

How to Tan Animal Hides and
How to Make High Quality Buckskin Clothing
Robert Wayne Atkins, P.E. (Grandpappy)

Bible scripture verses are from one of the following translations of the Holy Bible:
Holy Bible, King James Version, KJV, 1611, Public Domain. Page 1.
Holy Bible, New King James Version, NKJV, Copyright © 1995 by Thomas Nelson, Inc. Page 1.

First Edition published by Grandpappy, Inc.

Complete and detailed instructions for processing an animal hide into a soft buckskin so it can be converted into a beautiful article of clothing that will last many, many years. A variety of different ways to make patterns for buckskin clothing are also explained so you can make your own high quality undergarments, bras, shirts, pants, skirts, dresses, jackets, caps, gloves, and moccasins.

Also included are instructions on how to create delicious smoked meat that has a normal shelf life of approximately one year. The meat can be smoked over a normal fire but instructions are also included that explain how you can easily build a simple efficient smokehouse.

Finally, instructions are also included on how to use some of the other parts of an animal to make ropes, whips, slings, and arrows.

ISBN: 978-0-9850358-0-8

Printed in the United States of America.
10 9 8 7

Preface to

How to Tan Animal Hides and
How to Make High Quality Buckskin Clothing

There are a variety of different ways to make high quality clothing from scratch, such as:

1. **Cotton Clothing:** Acquire some land to grow cotton. Plow the land. Buy some cotton seeds. Plant the seeds. Fertilize the plants. Water the plants when it doesn't rain. During the growing season frequently remove the weeds and spray for insect pests. When the cotton is mature harvest the cotton without destroying your hands. Separate the cotton from the stuff you don't need. Card and comb the cotton. Spin the cotton into thread. Weave the thread into fabric. Now you are ready to make some clothing.

2. **Wool Clothing:** Acquire some land to raise sheep. Buy some sheep. Make sure the sheep have adequate water, feed, and veterinary care. Protect the sheep from predatory animals. Sheer the wool off the sheep at the proper time. Clean and dry the wool. Card and comb the wool to align the fibers. Spin the wool fibers into thread. Weave the thread into fabric. Now you are ready to make clothing.

3. **Buckskin Clothing:** Acquire a wild deer (trapping, archery, or firearms). Skin and butcher the deer. Eat the deer meat. Tan the deer hide. Now you are ready to make clothing.

During really hard times which of the above three clothing production methods would you prefer to invest your time in? If you selected the third option above then this book will probably be of interest to you.

This book clearly explains how to tan animal hides and how to make high quality buckskin clothing. It also explains how to smoke meat to significantly extend its shelf life. It is not possible to survive without food and clothing so a prudent person should know how to provide these basic necessities from nature.

The time to start collecting animal hides is before you desperately need them. At the beginning of hard times most families will need food more than they will need clothing so they will butcher an animal and remove all its edible meat and fat, and then discard the animal hide because they have no immediate use for it. A better strategy would be to tan those animal hides and then put them away for a future date when your clothing wears out and you must make your own. If you were smart at the beginning of the hard times then you should have a really nice collection of tanned animal hides to select from to create almost any article of clothing that a member of your family might need in the future.

Although the process of tanning animal hides is thousands of years old there is no universal agreement on the best way to actually do this task. This is due to the fact that the vast majority of animal hides are processed each year using industrial equipment and chemicals. Only an insignificant number of hides are processed each year using the traditional methods of our ancestors. Although tanners share their knowledge relatively freely with one another, each tanner emphasizes the techniques that he or she has been using most of his or her life. Therefore, although each tanner is aware of other ways to do the same task, each tanner is pretty much set in his or her ways. And there is nothing wrong with this because each of the different methods achieves the same basic finished product, which is a soft flexible buckskin. The steps to get to that finished product may vary from tanner to tanner but the finished products are all very similar.

Some tanners may omit some steps and other tanners may add additional steps. And the order in which each of the necessary steps are done can vary from tanner to tanner, such as whether to scrape the hair side of the hide first or scrape the flesh side of the hide first. Both have to be done but different tanners have different opinions on which side of the hide should be scraped first. When you consider all the different necessary steps and the legitimate number of different ways that those steps could be done in a different order, then there are approximately 41,472 different ways to convert an animal hide into a nice buckskin by doing all the tasks that must be done but doing those tasks in a different sequence. Therefore most people will tan their first hide using the method that is taught to them by an experienced tanner or using a method that he or she learns from a book. But sooner or later a person will begin to experiment by doing things in a slightly different order, or adding a step, or deleting a step. This process continues during the entire career of the hide tanner and the process the tanner uses on the last hide that he or she tans will be noticeably different than the process he or she used on the first hide that he or she tanned. This is how the learning process works.

Since there are at least 41,472 or more different ways to convert an animal hide into a buckskin, it is not possible for any person (including myself) to experiment with all of these different options during his or her lifetime and then compare all the results in an unbiased manner.

However, it is possible to discuss all the different options that are available at each of the fifteen major steps in the hide tanning process and list the advantages and disadvantages of each option. This will give you the opportunity to carefully consider exactly how you wish to do each of the fifteen tasks based on the most likely outcome of each of the options for doing that task.

In this book a specific recommendation will be made for each of the fifteen major steps in the hide tanning process. But there is no reason why you could not achieve the same final results if you decide to use one of the other options for a specific step in the process. As time passes you will probably decide to experiment with a variety of different options and you will gradually settle on the combination of procedures that you prefer. However, for your first tanning project I suggest you follow the recommended procedures in each chapter in this book so that you will have a finished buckskin to use as a comparison when you experiment with some of the different procedures that are explained in each chapter. This will give you a benchmark, or a point of reference, with which to compare your final results so you can determine if the alternate procedure that you experimented with actually yielded a better buckskin, or an inferior buckskin, or a buckskin that is essentially no different from your benchmark buckskin.

The easiest way to get your first animal hide is from an animal that has been killed by a moving vehicle and that is lying dead on the side of the road (if it is legal in your state to remove road killed animals from the highway). The meat from this animal will probably not be fit for human consumption for a variety of reasons but its hide will usually be in almost perfect condition without any arrow holes or bullet holes. And since the animal is already dead a person who respects all forms of life should not have any moral problems salvaging the hide and the brain of the dead animal. The brains of all animals are big enough to properly tan the animal's hide. The only exception to this rule would probably be my tiny inferior brain (this is a joke).

Why should you be interested in my opinion on how to tan animal hides when there are already several good books available on this topic? The answer is simple. Those books do not agree on what should be done or the order in which things should be done. This book is not any different and the recommendations in this book do not match any of the other books that have been written on this topic. The reason my suggestions are different is due to my educational background as an Industrial Engineer. An Industrial Engineer's primary job is to determine the most efficient, the most practical, and the easiest way to make a product (or provide a service) while simultaneously achieving the highest possible quality. I have invested 40 years of my life working as an Industrial Engineer and I have now applied my years of experience to the task of converting an animal hide into a high quality buckskin using the minimum amount of manual labor along with the most practical tools and pieces of equipment that are available, or using tools you can make yourself. In other words, if you follow the hide tanning advice in this book then you will be able to produce a high quality buckskin with the least amount of work and effort because you will be using the methods and tools that an Industrial Engineer would recommend and you will be doing each of the steps in the hide tanning process in the most logical and efficient manner possible, from an Industrial Engineering perspective.

I also have six years of hands-on experience in the apparel and textile industries and I have shared my apparel knowledge in this book so you can easily and efficiently convert your buckskins into practical high quality articles of clothing for your entire family.

In conclusion, if you wish to create a high quality buckskin using the most practical tools and procedures while investing the minimum amount of physical labor then you should follow the recommendations in this book. This book will also explain how to convert buckskins into clothing, how to create delicious smoked meat, how to make buckskin ropes and primitive weapons, and how to make parchment, ink, and a quill pen. In my opinion, every one of these practical skills could be of timeless value to you and to your descendants.

Respectfully,
Robert Wayne Atkins, P.E. (Grandpappy)
May 1, 2012

Acknowledgements

Although the process of tanning hides and making buckskin clothing has a history that is thousands of years old, there have been some important enhancements to this ancient art during the past few decades.

One of the significant improvements to the traditional hide tanning process is the addition of vinegar to a water bath to enhance the softness of a finished buckskin. This enhancement was discovered by Matt Richards and he shared his discovery with the world in his classic book, **Deerskins into Buckskins, 2nd Edition,** Copyright 1997, 2004. The world of hide tanners owe Matt Richards their grateful appreciation for his willingness to share his knowledge with the rest of us, and Matt Richards should always be given the credit for discovering the benefit of adding vinegar to a water bath whenever his method is mentioned in the process of converting animal hides into buckskins. In his book Matt Richards gives Bob Kurasawe the credit for suggesting the use of ammonium sulfate fertilizer instead of vinegar in the water bath.

Another important improvement in the traditional hide tanning process is the use of Hog Rings to hold an animal hide inside a stretching frame. This simple inexpensive piece of metal significantly reduces the amount of time and work required to put a hide into a stretching frame, and to periodically tighten the hide while it is in the stretching frame, and to remove the hide from the stretching frame when it is finished. Paul and Victoria Dinsmore shared this idea in their Online Book, **Tanning the Infirm Way,** Copyright 1996.

The performance of a smoke pit can be enhanced by pushing a solid metal rod sideways through the ground at a 45 degree angle from the top of the ground down into the smoke pit and then removing the metal rod. This will create an air hole from the ground down to approximately six inches above the bottom of the smoke pit. This allows you to control the flow of air into the smoke pit by blocking or unblocking the end of the hole that is level with the top of the ground. This excellent idea was shared by Jim Riggs in his timeless classic, **Blue Mountain Buckskin, 2nd Edition,** Copyright 1979, 1980, 2003. Although Jim uses a solid iron rod to poke an air hole into the ground and I recommend that a metal pipe be inserted into the hole in the ground, I still wish to give the credit for this basic idea to Jim.

Acorn soup is very briefly mentioned in two sentences in **Buckskin, The Ancient Art of Braintanning**, by Steven Edholm & Tamara Wilder, Copyright 2001. In their book the authors mention that acorn soup is used by the Mountain Nisenan in California as an alternative to using brains to tan hides. This is a confirmation of the use of acorns as a legitimate hide tanning alternative. I provide detailed instructions for using acorns to tan animal hides in Chapter Seventeen of this book.

Safety Warning and Disclaimer

This book explains how to make buckskin clothing. This process begins with a live wild animal and it ends with a useful article of clothing that a member of your family can wear.

Every area has its own laws and regulations that protect the animal population in that area. Please learn and follow all of the hunting, trapping, and other laws in your area that pertain to the animals in your area.

All live animals can be dangerous and the appropriate safety precautions should be followed whenever you are in the presence of a live animal. Removing the hide and the meat from a dead animal requires the use of a sharp knife. The appropriate safety precautions should always be followed whenever you are handling a knife. The bodies of wild animals may contain germs, bacteria, and parasites. Therefore you should wear protective clothing and rubber, latex, or vinyl gloves whenever you are handling a dead animal.

This book briefly discusses bows and arrows and firearms and traps. This book also explains how to make primitive weapons. Any weapon, including a primitive weapon, can be dangerous and deadly. Therefore you should be extremely careful when using any type of weapon and you should follow all the safety rules for handling and using that weapon. A person who is qualified to teach you how to correctly and safely use a specific weapon should be present the entire time you are learning how to properly use that weapon.

For all the above reasons the author, publisher, printer, and distributor of this book all disclaim any liability for any damage or injury as a direct or indirect result of the use of the information in this book.

Table of Contents

Chapter One

The History of Hide Tanning and Buckskin Clothing

The Holy Bible says: **Genesis 3:21 (King James Version)** - *"Unto Adam also and to his wife did the LORD God make coats of skins, and clothed them."*

What does this one short sentence tell us? It tells us that God made the first clothes for Adam and Eve and that God made those clothes from the skins of animals. After God made Adam and Eve their first clothes there is no mention of God replacing those clothes when those clothes wore out. Therefore it is reasonable to assume that Adam and Eve eventually made their own clothes, and the clothes for their children, using animal skins. In order for Adam and Eve to be successfully at this task it is reasonable to assume that God allowed Adam and Eve to watch Him as He made clothes from animal skins for them to wear.

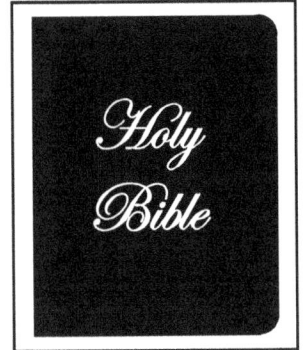

What else can be deduced from this one sentence in the Holy Bible? This one sentence tells us that God Almighty was the first butcher, skinner, tanner, tailor, and teacher. If God Himself skinned animals, tanned their hides, sewed those hides together into clothing, and showed Adam and Eve how to do these tasks, then it would be not be appropriate to criticize anyone who performs these same tasks today. Therefore the tasks of teacher, tailor, butcher, and tanner are honorable professions and any person engaged in any of these tasks should not be ashamed of following in the footsteps of God Almighty.

(Note: From a religious perspective that one sentence also tells us that God sacrificed the life of an animal and that its death and its blood temporarily covered the sins of Adam and Eve.)

Genesis 9:3-4 (New King James Version) - *"Every moving thing that lives shall be food for you. I have given you all things, even as the green herbs. But you shall not eat flesh with its life, that is, its blood."*

In the above scripture from the Holy Bible it says that God gave mankind permission to eat animals and fish and birds. Therefore there is no valid religious reason for a person to be a vegetarian. Anyone who is not allergic to meat has the right to eat meat without being condemned by other people.

The purpose of this book is to describe how to skin animals and how to covert their hides into soft useful buckskins that can be made into practical articles of clothing for your entire family. This book will also describe how to build a simple efficient smokehouse and how to smoke meat to extend its shelf life.

Buckskin Clothing

The **advantages** of buckskin clothing are as follows:

1. It will last longer than clothing made from most other materials, such as cotton, wool, and manmade synthetic fibers.
2. It has better insulation properties when compared to other materials of the same thickness.
3. It is more wind resistant and it will keep you warmer if the wind is blowing when compared to clothing of the same thickness that is made from other materials.
4. It will allow your skin to breathe and you will feel cooler and more comfortable in the summer.
5. It has a natural forest color and it quickly and easily blends into a wilderness environment.
6. It is almost silent when worn as clothing. This is important when moving through the wilderness.
7. It is less likely to collect burrs and stickers, when compared to clothing made from other materials.
8. It is less likely to tear or rip when it comes into contact with thorns or sticks or brush, when compared to clothing made from other materials.
9. It will stretch with your body as your body moves and bends.
10. It can be easily washed using ordinary soap and water.
11. It can be made in the wilderness because it does not require the application of any manmade chemicals.
12. It feels warmer against your skin compared to leather because leather feels cool or cold.

13. Buckskin clothing that is made from brain tanned animal hides is far superior in quality, softness, and flexibility than any type of leather, or tanned animal skin, that is produced by industrial processes and industrial chemicals.

The major **disadvantage** of buckskin clothing is as follows:

1. It absorbs water the same way as ordinary clothing that is made from most other common materials. On the other hand, buckskin clothing is warmer than cotton clothing when it is wet.

Definitions of Some Common Hide Tanning Words

1. **Pelt:** A pelt is the skin or hide of any animal but most of the time the word pelt is normally used in reference to the hide of a fur bearing animal.

2. **Hide:** A hide is the outer layer of skin of a large animal such as a cow or elk or moose.

3. **Skin:** A skin is the outer layer of skin of a medium size or smaller animal such as a goat or deer or caribou or pronghorn (antelope).

Most people associate the word "hide" with animals and the word "skin" with people. Therefore to be consistent with the current universally accepted meaning of these words, this book will use the word "hide" to refer to the outer layer of skin of all animals regardless of the size of the animal.

4. **Hair** and **Fur:** Hair and fur are synonyms and they both refer to the same thing. However, most people normally think of hair as being a human characteristic (getting a haircut) and fur being an animal characteristic (buying a fur coat). Generally people have less hair than most animals because most animals need their hair as protection from the weather and from the cold and people do not. In this book the word "hair" will be used instead of fur because the word "hair" has become universally accepted as the correct way to refer to the fur of an animal in almost all of the currently available hide tanning literature.

5. **Deer:** Deer will be used to refer to whitetail deer, mule deer, and black tail deer. It is relatively easy to distinguish between the different species of deer in the United States by looking at the rear end of the deer instead of its head:
   a. **White Tail Deer** (everywhere in the United States): It has a dark rear end. However, it does have a small white area that is just barely visible below its tail when its tail is lowered. Its tail is dark on the top side and white on the underside. When running the deer lifts its tail so it is erect and the white underside of its tail can be clearly seen.
   b. **Black Tail Deer** (west coast of United States): It has a dark rear with a clearly visible small white area on both sides of its tail and below its tail. But there is no white above its tail. Its tail is solid black and there is no white anywhere on its tail.
   c. **Mule Deer** (west coast and plains of United States): It has a white rear end. It has a huge white area above, beside, and below its tail. Its tail is almost all white except for a small black area on the very tip end of its tail.

6. **Buckskin:** Buckskin specifically refers to the skin of a male deer (a buck). However, in this book the word buckskin will refer to the hide of any animal whose skin has been tanned with brains, or a reasonable substitute, and that tanned hide may be used to make clothing.

7. **Leather:** In this book the word leather will be used to refer to animal hides that have been processed with manmade chemicals. Those hides will not be soft enough or flexible enough to be used to make clothing. But leather may be used to make belts or shoes or moccasins.

8. **Score Mark:** If a hide is cut during the skinning process then the cut area is called a score mark. A score mark is a knife cut on the inside of the hide. In most cases the cut does not completely penetrate the hide. However, it does leave a slice on the inside of the hide that cannot be removed during the tanning process. The origin of the term "score mark" is based on the way hide buyers would grade the hides that were offered to them for sale. Hides without any cuts received a higher price. But each and every cut in a hide reduced its final "score" or value.

Some General Characteristics of Animal Hides

1. Males have thicker hides than females.

2. Winter killed animals have thicker hides and longer hair than the same animal during the summer months.

3. Animals in the colder northern United States have thicker hides than the same exact animal in the warmer southern United States.

4. Elk and moose have the thickest hides, then mule deer, then whitetail deer, and finally pronghorns (or antelopes) have the thinnest hides.

5. **Pronghorns (or antelopes)** have thinner hides than deer but they are relatively strong and they make excellent lightweight buckskin clothing for summer use. They also make very nice dresses for a lady. Pronghorn hides should not be scraped as hard as a deer hide. They also require less pressure to wring the water out of them. A pronghorn hide will not stretch as much as a deer hide. Pronghorns have a gland on their lower back that makes that spot on their hide more difficult to convert into a buckskin that has the same characteristics as the rest of their hide. If you are aware of this then you can usually place your clothing patterns on the pronghorn's finished tanned buckskin in such a way that you can cut around that area so it can be discarded when you convert the buckskin into a useful piece of clothing.

6. **Elk hides** are thicker than a deer hide but they are weaker. Every step in the tanning process takes longer for an elk hide when compared to a deer hide. They require twice as much wood ash and twice as much brain tanning solution. They must be soaked longer, rinsed longer, wrung harder, softened longer, and dried longer. An elk hide needs to be stretched on a frame instead of using a cable. Elk moccasins do not last as long as moccasins made from deer hides.

7. **Moose hides** are thicker and stronger than deer hides. They make excellent moccasins. The hide will require more time at each step in the tanning process when compared to a deer hide. The hump of the moose is the most difficult part of the moose to convert into a useable piece of buckskin and many tanners will simply discard that area of the hide.

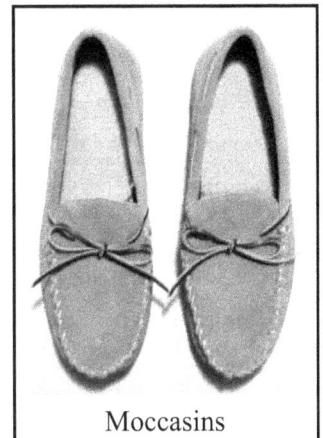

Moccasins

8. **Cow hides** do not make good buckskins but they make excellent leather.

9. **Pig hides** do not stretch well.

10. **Bighorn sheep** have skins that can be converted into good buckskins but the skins of domestic sheep are too thin to undergo the hide tanning process. However, sheepskins and goatskins are the preferred types of skins for making parchment. Chapter 38 has complete details on how to make parchment.

Some Basic Precautions

Wild animals almost always have ticks and bacteria on their hides. If you have a small cut or abrasion on your hands then it is possible for the bacteria and germs from a dead wild game animal to easily enter your blood stream and make you extremely sick (or those germs could kill you). Therefore you must wear rubber, latex, nitrile, or vinyl gloves when handling dead animals, their meat, and their hides in order to protect your body from becoming infected.

Never leave hides or brains where a dog or a wild animal can get to them. There is no difference between your dog, your neighbor's dog, or a stray dog. All dogs will eat brains and they can chew a hide into pieces in just a few minutes. You must constantly protect your hides and your buckskins from dogs. This includes freshly skinned hides, hides that are being soaked in a water bath, hides that are on a stretching frame, and exceptionally beautiful buckskin clothing that is placed outdoors to dry after it has been washed. Dogs, and any meat eating wild animal or bird, will destroy a hide unless you protect the hide and make it impossible for the hide to be eaten or torn to pieces. Most new tanners have to lose one of their hides, or an article of buckskin clothing, before they will take the appropriate steps to safeguard their investment in time and labor.

Chapter Two

The Fifteen Basic Hide Tanning Steps
and the Minimum Equipment and Supplies Required

There is no single best way to convert an animal hide into a soft, flexible buckskin. It is possible to create a high quality buckskin by omitting one or more of the fifteen basic steps, or by changing the order in which the steps are done, or by using more or less sophisticated equipment, or by using more or less physical energy.

When you compare good quality buckskins side-by-side that have been produced using different methods and equipment then you will probably not be able to detect any significant differences between those buckskins, nor will you be able to correctly guess the exact method each tanner used to produce the buckskin. On the other hand, if you wish to produce a high quality soft, flexible buckskin then you will probably want to minimize your investment in equipment, time, and human energy. That is the objective of this book. This book will explain how to produce buckskins of the highest quality while investing the least amount of your physical labor in the process. However, it may take a little longer to produce the finished buckskin but if that extra time is simply allowing the buckskin to soak in a water solution that contains some other chemicals then that is not a labor intensive step even though it does require a little more time to produce a high quality buckskin.

The fifteen basic steps for converting an animal hide into a soft buckskin are as follows:

1. Hide and Meat Acquisition.
2. Skinning and Butchering.
3. Soak One (clean water bath).
4. Scrape Flesh Side of Hide (membrane).
5. Soak Two (water bath with wood ashes added).
6. Scrape Hair Side of Hide.
7. Aging the Hide.
8. Soak Three (clean water or water with either ammonium sulfate or vinegar added).
9. Scrape the Residual Membrane.
10. Dyeing the Hide (optional).
11. Wring Dry.
12. Repair Holes and Cuts (sewing).
13. Tan Hide (use brains, or eggs, or oil and soap, or acorns).
14. Soften and Stretch (use a cable or a stretching frame or both, and sand the hide using sandpaper or a round stone).
15. Smoking.

When the above fifteen steps have been completed you will have a soft piece of buckskin that you can convert into an article of clothing, or some moccasins, or a blanket.

Minimum Equipment and Supplies

In order to convert an animal hide into a useable buckskin that can be sewn into clothing or footwear, you will need a few basic tools and supplies. The following list of items contains the **minimum equipment and supplies** you will need at each of the above fifteen steps in the hide tanning process from beginning to end.

1. Hide and Meat Acquisition: Some animal traps, or a bow and arrows, or a firearm.
2. Skinning and Butchering: A sharp knife. A knife that has a gut hook is preferred.

3. Soak One: Any plastic container that will hold between 5 to 10 gallons of water.

4. Scrape Flesh Side of Hide: A 6 inch diameter log (or plastic water pipe) and a used blade from an old lawnmower (or a drawknife).

5. Soak Two: Same as Soak One with some wood ashes added.

6. Scrape Hair Side of Hide: Same as Step 4.

7. Aging the Hide. A safe place to hang the hides.

8. Soak Three: Same as Soak One with some optional vinegar.

9. Scrape the Residual Membrane: Same as Step 4.

10. Dyeing the Hide: Tree bark or other dyeing materials (this is an optional step).

11. Wring Dry: A strong straight stick.

12. Repair Holes and Cuts: A handheld sewing needle and some strong thread or backstrap sinew.

13. Tan Hide: Some animal brains, or some eggs, or some oil and soap, or some acorns.

14. Stretch and Soften: A rope or steel cable plus some sandpaper or a round stone.

15. Smoking: Some matches or a butane lighter to start a fire and some dry decayed wood to make smoke.

The above items are the minimum items that are necessary to convert an animal hide into a high quality piece of buckskin clothing. There are also a variety of other items that could be used to help minimize the total amount of physical work involved. Each of these additional items will be described in detail in the chapter where that item would be needed.

Waterproof Gloves

In addition to the above items you will also need some waterproof gloves to wear each time you handle the animal hide until the hide has completed the smoking process (Step Fifteen). After the hide has been successfully converted into a buckskin then it may be safely handled without gloves.

1. **No Gloves:** Our ancestors did not use gloves while skinning animals or while tanning hides. However, today we know more about bacteria and germs. If you have a small cut or abrasion on your hands then it is possible for the bacteria and germs from a dead wild game animal to easily enter your blood stream and make you extremely sick or kill you. Therefore, if you do not have any gloves, then do **not** skin wild game animals or tan their hides if you have any type of cut on your hands, fingers, or near your fingernails where germs can easily gain access to your entire body.

2. **Hunter's Skinning Gloves:** These special gloves are available in the sporting goods department of many stores in their hunting, fishing, and camping section. These gloves are really big and the sleeves extend all the way to your elbows. This allows you to reach deep inside an animal to pull out its internal organs. These long gloves are not comfortable to wear because they slide down your arms. These gloves are normally good for one skinning session. In other words, if you are going to skin several animals at the same time then these gloves will allow you to skin several animals. However, if you wash the blood and other residue off the gloves when you are finished using ordinary soap and water, and then allow the gloves to dry, then the next time you use these gloves they will quickly develop small holes or tears in your predominant hand, such as your right hand. Therefore I do not recommend these gloves.

3. **Kitchen Dishwashing Gloves:** These kitchen gloves are a lot cheaper than hunting gloves and you can purchase kitchen latex gloves for about 99 cents at a dollar store, or between $1.59 to $2.97 at a grocery store. These vinyl latex gloves have a raised gripping surface on the fingers and the sleeve extends about 4 to 6 inches up your forearm beyond your wrist. The long wrists help to keep blood and guts off your forearms and/or long sleeve shirt. These gloves will last as long as the above hunter's gloves and the second time you wear them they will usually develop small holes or tears in the glove on your predominant hand which will make them ineffective at protecting your hands from bacteria and germs. Therefore these kitchen gloves are normally single use items.

4. **Medical Examination Gloves:** These gloves can be purchased in the medical supply section of almost any pharmacy or drug store in boxes of 50 gloves or 100 gloves. A box of 100 gloves costs about $9.98, or about 10 cents each or 20 cents for a pair of gloves. Medical exam gloves do not have a right hand glove and a left hand glove because all the gloves are identical and each glove may be worn on either hand. Before you put a new glove on your hand you may wish to place the wrist portion of the glove around the outside of your lips and then blow a gust of air into the glove to gently expand the glove. This will open the glove up and the glove will be easier to slide onto your hand. These gloves are disposable, thin, and smooth and they have no special grasping texture on the fingertips. Each glove will extend about 1 to 2 inches above your wrists. These are the gloves I recommend for skinning wild game animals and for the handling of the hides at each step in the tanning process. Because they are disposable you can toss the used gloves into the trash when you are finished each day. However, if you are on a budget then you could wash your gloves with soap and water before you take them off (the same way you wash your hands), and then throw the glove on your predominate hand into the trash but save the glove that is on your other hand. The glove on your least used hand will usually be okay for one more session of work before you will also have to throw it away.

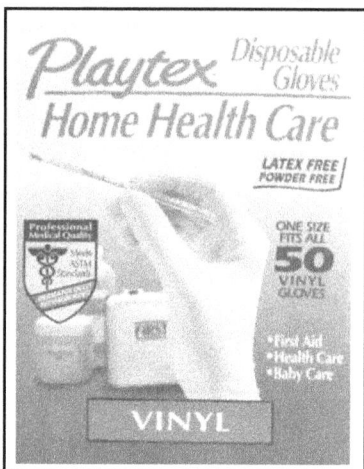

Wash Your Hands: Immediately after you remove your gloves you should wash your hands thoroughly with soap and warm water.

Chapter Three

Hide and Meat Acquisition and Meat Processing

Obey all the animal, hunting, and trapping laws in your area.

There are two questions that must be answered when processing a dead animal:

1. **Meat:** Do you intend to eat the meat of the animal?
2. **Hide:** Do you intend to use the hide of the animal to make something useful?

In many situations you will want to do both of the above. You will want to consume the edible parts of the animal and you will have a variety of potential applications for the hide of the animal.

But there are situations when you may only wish to eat the animal and you have no practical use for its hide. For example, many small wild game animals, such as squirrels and rabbits, are edible but their hides are too small to be useful for almost anything. Rabbit hides are usually too thin and they are easily ruined during the hide tanning process. Therefore the effort required to save and process small hides will usually exceed any value they may have because it requires too many of them to make anything useful. Another example would be a wild boar. You would probably want the meat and the fat from the wild boar but the hide of a wild boar is not as useful as the hide of other wild animals.

And there are situations when you may definitely want the hide of the animal but you have no desire to eat the animal. An example would be the hide of a three year old buck deer that has been killed by a moving vehicle and its internal organs and intestines have been ruptured and they have contaminated all the meat inside the animal with harmful pathogens. However, the hide of the animal may be in really good shape and if you are able to remove the hide within a few hours of the animal's death then you may be able to acquire a high quality hide with no bullet holes that you could use for almost any construction project.

Once you know the answer to both of the above questions then you will be able to plan exactly how you intend to skin and butcher the animal. If you only want the meat then you do not need to be extremely careful about how you remove the hide from the animal. If you only want the hide then you do not need to worry about any damage you may do to the meat of the animal. But in most situations you will probably want the meat and the hide of the animal and therefore you will need to keep both objectives in mind as you carefully skin and butcher the animal.

Now let's look at the advantages and the disadvantages of the different ways you could acquire the hide and the meat of a dead animal:

Farm Animals (goats or young calves): If you live near a rural farming area then you may be able to purchase a live animal from a rancher. Some ranchers will butcher an animal for you at an additional price but some ranchers will not butcher an animal for reasons that differ from one rancher to the next. If you negotiate with the rancher to butcher the animal for you then tell the rancher that you also want the hide and request that the rancher be careful when removing the hide so you can use it. The only way I know to encourage another person to be extremely careful when skinning an animal is to offer to pay extra for a usable hide without any knife cuts and to explain that no money will be paid for a hide that has been ruined with multiple knife cuts through the hide. Transporting a live animal to another location to slaughter and butcher the animal is generally not cost effective for most individuals. Therefore unless you can locate a rancher who will kill and butcher an animal for you then this will probably not be an option for you to consider.

Road Kill: In many areas of the United States it is not uncommon to see dead animals on the road or beside the road that have been accidentally killed by moving vehicles. Occasionally only the head of the animal was injured in the accident and the animal's meat and hide are both salvageable. But more commonly the animal was hit in its front, center, or rear body area and this usually results in the destruction of the animal's internal organs and intestines which dump their harmful contents inside the animal. Therefore the meat of the animal will be toxic and it should not be eaten. But the hide of the animal may still be in good condition. If this is the case then you could salvage the animal's hide, and its brains, and discard everything else. This may be done after you have dragged the animal at least 50 or more feet from the road. This assumes that your area allows you to travel with a skinning knife in your vehicle without being in violation of some law. This also assumes that your area also allows you to butcher "road kill" within some reasonable distance of the road. In addition to a skinning knife you will also need a pair of waterproof gloves. On the other hand, if the animal is not too heavy for you to lift and you have some large heavy-duty 55-gallon plastic bags with twist ties, or some large plastic tote containers in the rear of your vehicle, then you could put the animal inside one or those bags or tote containers and take the animal home and process it there. This method requires that you be prepared ahead of time so that you can act promptly and efficiently when you see the dead animal on the roadway. You must also remember to be very alert to other traffic on the road or you could share the same fate as the animal. Unfortunately, many states have laws that prohibit anyone from touching an animal that has been killed by a moving vehicle. Therefore please check your state laws before you pick up a dead animal because it may be illegal for you to do so in your state.

Meat Processors and Meat Storage Lockers: Many geographical areas have special cold storage facilities for storing and butchering deer, and similar wild game animals, for hunters. The typical fee is about $75 per deer. If you contact these businesses then they will probably be willing to sell you the hides they remove from the deer for a very reasonable cost. The reason is because the overwhelming majority of hunters only want the deer meat and they do not want the deer hide and therefore the deer hide is simply discarded unless someone else offers to buy it. Some of these businesses are well skilled at pulling the hide off the deer without damaging it. But other businesses may simply chop and slice the hide off the deer and ruin the hide with multiple knife cuts. Therefore it would be wise to inspect the hide before you buy it if that is possible, or only buy one hide from a location and then take it home and carefully inspect it. This will help you to strategically select the businesses you wish to give your repeat business to.

Trapping: If your area allows you to trap wild game animals then this is an excellent method of obtaining wild game for their hides and for their meat. If you use traps then you must have the time to walk your trap line twice a day: once in the morning and once in the evening. The most efficient trap for instantly and humanely killing a wild game animal by snapping its neck is a conibear trap. These traps come in a variety of sizes from small to medium to large and each size has been specifically designed to kill a specific size of wild game animal. On the other hand, a pan trap only captures the foot or paw of a wild game animal and the animal will usually still be alive when you check your trap line. This means you will need to dispatch the animal yourself in a safe and humane manner. Therefore most people will probably discover that a conibear trap is superior to a pan trap for providing meat and hides because a conibear trap kills the animal by breaking the animal's neck and the animal's meat and hide remains undamaged. Unfortunately, no animal trap can distinguish between a wild animal and a domestic animal so you will need to make sure that your traps are set where there is almost no chance of a family pet being terminated by one of your traps. Each state has its own trapping laws so you will need to verify and obey the laws in your area.

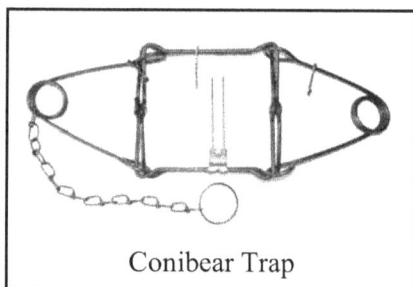
Conibear Trap

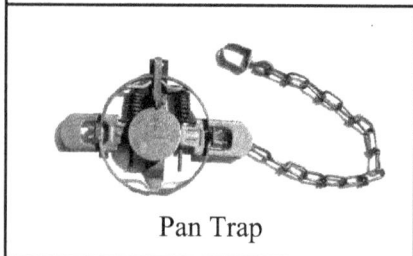
Pan Trap

Archery: If your area allows for bow hunting then this is another way to provide fresh meat and useable hides. The advantage of a bow and arrow is that it is almost silent and therefore you would not be making any loud noise that would attract the attention of predators to your kill site. When hunting with a bow the animal's heart and lung area is the most logical place to aim your arrow. The cost of a good hunting arrow is several dollars and it is not uncommon for an arrow to be damaged beyond repair when it does its job of bringing down one wild game animal. In addition, bow hunting is a time consuming activity and unless you have the time to invest in this sport then trapping would probably be a better choice for you.

Firearms: If your area allows for firearm hunting then it is almost always easier and more productive to hunt with a modern firearm than a bow and arrow. However, firearms do make a loud noise that will attract the attention of predatory animals and other hunters to your kill site. And depending on where you shoot the animal the hide may be in perfect condition or it may be riddled with bullet holes (buckshot from a shotgun). Depending on the direction in which the animal is facing in relation to where you are with your hunting rifle, you should try to shoot the animal in one of its eyes (animal is looking at you), or in the ear canal (animal is below you on a hill), or about one inch below the ear (animal is sideways to you and at about the same level as you), or in the back of the brain (animal is facing away from you). These types of shots will almost always result in an instant kill and the animal's hide will not be torn with a small bullet entrance hole and a large bullet exit hole in the body portion of the hide. Don't worry about damaging the animal's brains because you will be scooping the brains out a little at a time with a long handled metal spoon or ladle. Finally, hunting with a firearm is just as time consuming as hunting with a bow and arrow.

Starvation: If you are starving then food replenishment takes precedence over hide preservation. Shoot the animal with a semi-automatic rifle using three quick shots through the heart and the animal will drop where it is shot and not run off and be lost. Although you will have ruined a portion of the animal's hide, and some of the meat, you will have achieved your primary objective of replenishing your food supply so you do not starve to death. During hard times always use common sense and prioritize your actions based on your most immediate objectives.

Butchering: Transporting an animal that weighs more than 100 pounds is hard work. It is usually better to gut, skin, and butcher an animal where it was killed and then only transport the edible meat, fat, brains, and hide back to your homestead. Leave the guts, bones, feet or hooves, and everything else that you do not intend to use at the butchering site for other wild animals and birds to feast on. You may take the bones, hooves, and long sinews with you if you have a practical application for them.

It is true that the meat of a large game animal will improve in tenderness if it is left hanging in a cool area for several days before butchering it. But this may not be possible if the animal was killed too far from your homestead or your mode of transportation.

To process an animal you will need a good skinning knife and a backpack and several 2 gallon or larger clean plastic bags, or plastic totes, to transport the meat, brains, and hide back to your vehicle or homestead. If you wish you may scrape the bone marrow out of the larger bones and take that with you also. You will not need a bone saw because you will cut the edible meat away from the bones instead of trying to prepare nice looking steaks, or roasts, with part of the bone still in the steak or roast.

Backpack and Plastic Totes: To transport meat back to your vehicle or homestead you will need a backpack that is suitable for carrying meat. This is not the same type of backpack you would select for a hiking or camping expedition. The only purpose of this backpack will be to transport meat and it does not need pockets on the sides of the backpack or on the flap of the backpack. It does not need straps on the top or bottom of the backpack for attaching extra gear. However it should have an adjustable padded shoulder harness on each side and an adjustable chest strap between the two shoulder harnesses. It should have a single large compartment on the inside of the backpack instead of two or three separate compartments. Measure the inside rectangular bottom compartment of the backpack and the height of the inside compartment. Then carefully select some plastic tote containers with snap on locking lids that will fit inside the backpack with the bottom of the plastic tote on the bottom of the backpack and the lid facing the upper flap of the backpack. This will prevent any blood or other fluids from leaking out of the plastic tote while it is inside the backpack. Also consider the height of each tote so you can get the maximum number

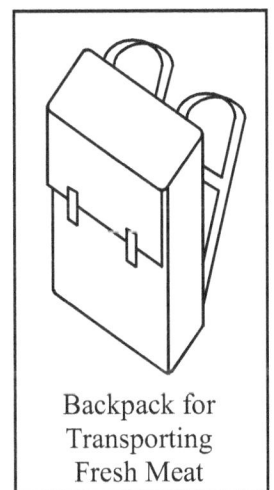

Backpack for Transporting Fresh Meat

of totes inside the backpack. This may require the purchase of totes that are of two or three different heights in order to fully utilize the inside of the backpack as completely as possible. You will also need two or three heavy-duty 3 mil or 4 mil large plastic bags that are larger than the inside compartment of the backpack. Place two or three of these bags inside one another and then inside the backpack. Then stack the empty tote containers inside the plastic bags. Take the backpack with all its empty containers with you when you are acquiring meat and hides. As you skin and butcher the animal you can put the hide in one tote, or one large heavy-duty plastic bag, and the meat into the other plastic totes and then snap the lid on each tote when it is full. Then return the full plastic totes of meat into the backpack and put the backpack on your back when you are finished. You are now ready to hike back to your vehicle or homestead. The meat inside the plastic totes will remain clean and you will not have the problem of nasty disgusting stains and smells on your backpack when you arrive at your destination.

Meat Processing

After you have the meat at your homestead you have several options as follows:

1. **Eat Some of It Now:** Although most of the meat from a medium size to a large size game animal will need to be preserved for future consumption, you will probably want to eat some of that meat immediately. The meat you chose to eat now can be consumed as a steak, or as cubed meat in a stew or other recipe, or as ground meat.

   a. **Steak:** One of the easiest ways to create the perfect steak is to sprinkle both sides of the steak with "Seasoned Meat Tenderizer" and allow the seasoning to absorb into the steak for at least thirty minutes. Then cook the steak the way you normally do. The "5th Season" brand of "Seasoned Meat Tenderizer" is available in a 5.5 ounce jar at most Walmarts for 50 cents per jar. Its major ingredients are salt, dextrose, onion, spice, paprika, and garlic. In my opinion it will convert any wild game meat into a truly delightful meal that everyone in your family will enjoy.

   b. **Cubed Meat:** Cut the meat into cubes or into long thin strips as specified in your recipe. Then follow your recipe directions to prepare the meal for your family.

   c. **Ground Meat:** After you grind the wild game meat it can be used in any recipe that requires ground meat. The easiest way to enhance the flavor of ground meat is to add a little seasoning to the meat when cooking it. For example, add taco seasoning when making tacos or burritos. Add chili seasoning when making chili. If money is not an issue then you could combine an entire package of seasoning mix with one pound of ground meat. However, if you are experiencing hard times then you do not need an entire package of seasoning to add flavor to your meals. I have successfully used between 1/4 to 1/3 of a package of a seasoning mix package to enhance the flavor of the ground meat and I have not heard any complaints from my family members at the dining table.

2. **Freeze It:** If you have access to a freezer or to a refrigerator/freezer then freezing the meat is a simple and easy option. Cut the meat into meal size portions that your family will be able to consume in a single meal. Later when you thaw the meat you will not have any leftovers at the end of the meal. The major shortcoming of freezing is that it is dependent on electricity. If there is a disruption in your electrical service for more than two or three days then all the food in your freezer will thaw out and it will have to be either eaten immediately or processed in some other way to keep it from going bad.

3. **Can It:** If you have a pressure cooker and glass canning jars and canning lids then you could dice the meat into cubes and pressure cook it inside canning jars following the instructions for canning meat that came with your pressure cooker.

4. **Smoke It:** Smoking the meat will extend its shelf life for approximately one year. It does not depend on electricity or the availability of canning jars and canning lids. Therefore it is a very logical option for preserving fresh meat. *Smoking meat into jerky can be done while the hide is soaking in a clean water bath.* Complete instructions for smoking meat are in Chapter 40 of this book.

Chapter Four

Skinning and Butchering a Wild Game Animal

Skinning Knife: A dead animal is easier to skin with a professional quality stainless steel fixed blade skinning knife that has a gut hook. The knife should also have a rubber or composite handle.

1. For all skinning tasks a 4 inch long blade is optimal.
2. For medium and large wild game animals a 1.5 inch wide blade works best.
3. For small game animals, such as squirrels and rabbits, a 1 inch wide blade is easier to use.
4. The fixed blade eliminates the possibility of the blade accidentally folding back onto your fingers. (A locking folding blade knife with a gut hook is also acceptable but a fixed blade is superior.)
5. The gut hook will allow you to open the underside of the animal with the smallest possible chance of rupturing, cutting, or tearing the internal organs of the animal and dumping some unpleasant body chemicals and smells onto the edible meat and onto the hide.
6. The composite handle will allow you to maintain a better grip on the knife during the entire skinning process, even after the vinyl glove on your hand becomes soaked with animal blood and body fluids.

Skinning Knife with Gut Hook

7. A sharp knife makes skinning easier, quicker, and safer. It will result in more of the meat and the fat being removed from the hide. This is important because it has two advantages:
    a. It provides more meat and fat for you to eat.
    b. It makes the hide scraping jobs that must be done later much easier.

The above skinning knife may be used to remove the internal organs and the meat from the animal but these two tasks can be done a little quicker with the following two special knives.

Folding Knife with Two Inch Locking Blade: A short sharp knife is useful for reaching up into the body cavity of an animal and cutting the internal organs free from the inner lining and muscle and tendons that are holding those organs to the inside of the animal. (Note: If your skinning knife does not have a gut hook then this smaller knife is easier to use to open the animal than the above skinning knife. Pinch the skin of the animal between your thumb and fingers and lift the skin away from the body of the animal. Then slip the point of your short sharp knife between the skin and the meat of the animal and make a short cut and stop. Reach further up on the skin and pinch and pull some more skin away from the animal and then continue the original cut a little further. Keep repeating this process of pinching and cutting, and pinching and cutting, and you will open the animal without puncturing its internal organs. This is a slow and labor intensive method of opening the animal. Therefore a knife with a gut hook is strongly recommended if you can acquire one. If your knife does not have a gut hook then this method will achieve the same end result.)

Butchering Knife: It is easier to remove large sections of meat from the bones of a medium size or large dead animal with a bread knife that has a serrated cutting edge and a one inch wide blade. Cut the meat close to the bones but do not try to cut through the bones with the knife.

Knife Sharpening: A standard Arkansas sharpening stone will sharpen a knife with a straight edge but it will not sharpen a knife with a serrated edge or a gut hook. On the other hand, a "Pocket Pal" sharpening tool will quickly and easily sharpen a knife with any type of edge including a serrated cutting edge or a gut hook. And a "Pocket Pal" sharpening tool is much easier to learn how to use correctly and it will put a professional quality edge on any knife (or pair of scissors). To sharpen a dull knife use moderate pressure to pull the knife blade 3 or 4 times through the carbide

Bread Knife

Pocket Pal

sharpening blades in the top center slot of the tool in the picture. To increase the sharpness of a blade on a sharp knife pull the knife blade through the ceramic sharpening blades on the top left side of the tool in the picture. The ceramic blades may also be used to sharpen a knife with a serrated edge. Or you can use the tapered diamond rod extending from the bottom of the tool to sharpen a serrated edge or a gut hook. The tapered rod folds into the bottom of the tool when it is not needed.

How to Skin a Dead Animal

The following instructions are for skinning a deer. Minor adjustments will need to be made in the following procedure as appropriate for other wild game animals, such as a beaver, groundhog, or raccoon.

1. **Timing:** Process the animal as soon as possible after it has been killed.

2. **Parasites:** Freshly killed animals almost always have ticks and bacteria on their hides. Therefore you must wear rubber, latex, nitrile, or vinyl gloves when handling dead animals, their meat, and their hides in order to protect your body from becoming infected.

3. **Bleeding the Animal:** Position the dead animal so its head is facing downhill. This will allow as much blood as possible to flow out of the animal when you cut the main artery in the neck of the animal. It is important to bleed the animal as soon as possible after it has been killed because the blood that remains inside the animal will become putrid and taint the meat of the animal.

4. **Recommended Neck Cut:** Begin the neck cut about one inch below the front chin area and cut in a slightly upwards curve towards the back of the neck at the base of the skull about two or three inches below the ear. This type of cut will yield the maximum amount of deer hide in the final buckskin.
   a. **Alternate Neck Cut:** Most of the hide tanning literature I have read recommends that you cut the deer hide near the bottom or base of its neck at the point where the back of the deer begins. Unfortunately this method does not salvage the deer hide around the neck of the deer and this is a significant useable piece of deer hide.
   b. **Face Hide:** Some skinners prefer to remove the hide from an animal with its face hide still attached. In other words, the hide around the entire skull is carefully removed and it remains attached to the rest of the hide. Extreme care is needed in the skull area to remove the hide without leaving multiple knife cuts in the hide around the eyes, nose, and mouth. This small piece of hide is of no practical use when making buckskin clothing so there is no good reason to leave it on unless you are selling the hide to someone who will pay more for the hide with the face still attached.
   c. **Head Removal:** If you wish to remove the head then cut through the neck at the base of the skull all the way to the bone completely around the neck. Then you can twist the head completely off where the skull and neck bones meet without using a bone saw. If the head will not twist off then cut the tendons around the joint where the skull and neck bones meet and then try twisting the head off again. It is not necessary to remove the head unless you have some reason for not wanting to remove the brains at the same time you skin and butcher the animal.

5. **Alternate Neck Cut for a Head Trophy:** If you are interested in removing the head for a trophy then you will need to cut the entire neck and head from the animal beginning at the back of its neck close to its back and continue cutting straight down through the front part of its chest. You will need a bone saw to cut through the neck or backbone. The head should be given to a taxidermist as soon as possible. You will now have a head trophy but you will have about 1/4 less hide for use as a buckskin. Or you could simply remove the antlers and mount them as a trophy instead of the head of the deer. It is relatively easy to mount antlers yourself on an antler wall trophy plaque, such as the European Mount. Antler mounts can be purchased in the hunting supplies section of many stores. If you only mount the antlers then you will still have a nice trophy, and the total cost of that trophy will be small (about $20) when compared to the expense of a taxidermist (about $375), and you will be able to convert about 20% to 25% more of the deer hide into a future buckskin.

6   **Small Animals:** If the animal is small and it does not weigh very much, and you are in an area where there are trees and some of the tree branches are about six feet off the ground, then you can tie each of the animal's hind legs to a low hanging tree branch so that you can skin the animal at a convenient height while standing upright. Or you can tie a rope around the animal's neck, just below its ears, and hang the animal upright by its neck.

7.   **Heavy Animals:** Heavy wild game animals will need to be completely processed while they are still lying on the ground. If possible rotate the animal so its underbelly is facing downhill.

8.   **Belly Cut:** Use the tip of your skinning knife to open the belly of the animal just below and in front of its urinary area. Then slip the gut hook of your skinning knife into the small opening you just made and pull the gut hook in a straight line from the rear of the animal towards the center of its neck to completely expose its internal organs. If you cut the animal's neck using the recommended procedure in Step Four above then you may continue using the gut hook to cut the hide in a straight line from the point between the animals front legs up through the front center of the animal's neck to the point directly below the center of the chin where you began your original neck cut. (Note: Instead of cutting from tail to neck, some skinners prefer to cut the animal from neck to tail and you may do it this way if you prefer.)   If the animal is a female then you can continue to use your gut hook to cut from the spot in front of the urinary area straight to the anus but do not cut into the anus. If the animal is a male then you should use your gut hook to cut around the genitals on both sides and then cut to the anus but do not cut into the anus. (Note: If you do not have a gut hook then you may open the animal following the instructions for using a **Folding Knife** at the beginning of this chapter.)

9.   **Removal of Internal Organs:** If you intend to butcher the animal where you killed it then you do not have to remove the animal's internal organs. But if you intend to transport the animal back to your homestead then you will need to remove its internal organs. On some animals it is easier to remove their internal organs if you cut, saw, or bust the animal's breastbone and then pull the breastbone apart to gain access to the entire inner body cavity of the animal. Or you can simply reach around the breastbone. Use your gloved hands to pull all the internal organs out of the animal and let them fall onto the ground. Proceed in a slow and steady manner and do not yank the guts out onto your legs or boots. You will occasionally need a knife to separate an internal organ from some muscle or tendon to which it is firmly attached.

10. **Heart and Liver:** If you wish to save the heart and liver then now is the time to separate these items from the other internal organs and put them into protective plastic bags or plastic totes.

11. **Continue to Process Now or Wait Until Later:** If the animal is not too heavy and you are able to transport the animal to your vehicle then you may place the gutted animal into a big heavy-duty plastic bag or plastic tote or clean 55 gallon garbage can and then take the animal to your homestead where you can work on the animal in a more comfortable atmosphere. Prop the body cavity of the animal open with several sticks so cool air can get inside the animal and this will help to cool the meat to slow down the speed at which it will spoil. If possible fill some plastic bags with ice or snow or cold creek water and place those bags inside the empty body cavity of the animal to help cool and preserve its meat while it is being transported.

12. **Tenderizing the Meat:** If you have access to a cold food storage compartment then it is usually better to allow a deer to hang in cold storage for a few days before you butcher the animal for its meat. The weight of the deer will stretch and relax its meat so its meat gradually becomes more tender for human consumption. However, you may continue to process the animal immediately if you need the meat for your family, or if you do not have access to a cold meat storage area, or if the animal is too heavy to transport to your vehicle or homestead.

13. **Small and Medium Size Animals:** Hang a small or a medium sized animal with its head up and its tail down. Later you can pull the hide off the animal from its head to its tail. However, some skinners prefer to hang an animal with its tail up and its head down. This allows the head to hang freely out of the way as

you skin the animal. The hide is then pulled from the animal from its tail towards its head. You may experiment with both methods and select the one that you personally prefer to use.

14. **Circular Leg Cuts:** Do not try to salvage the parts of the hide that cover the four legs. Cut the animal's hide in a circle all the way around each leg about six inches down each leg from its belly. Ignore the remainder of the hide that extends down each leg of the animal to its paw or hoof. These lower leg sections of the hide are extremely difficult to scrape properly, and they are too small to make something useful, and they will normally be much harder than the rest of the deerskin when you are finished. This means you will eventually cut off and discard these short leg pieces from the finished tanned hide because you will not be able to use them. Therefore the most logical procedure is to leave them on the deer and simply ignore them during the skinning process. This also means you will avoid the scent glands that are located on the lower part of the legs.

15. **Tail Cut and Hind Leg Cuts:** Now move the tip of your knife to a position just below the tail and just above the anal opening. Cut a half circle around the top of the anal opening, or cut about one-fourth of the way around the anal opening on each side until you can cut from that point straight down the middle of the rear of each of the two hind legs.

16. **Front Leg Cuts:** Plan your next two cuts from where the neck and belly of the animal meet. Cut straight from the belly down the inside middle of each front leg of the animal so that the hide will be as rectangular as possible when the hide is removed from the animal.

17. **A Rectangular Hide:** A hide that is approximately rectangular will yield more useable area for buckskin clothing than a hide that is in the traditional shape of a skinned animal as is commonly illustrated in most hide skinning books. The deer hide in the picture was removed using the procedure recommended in this chapter except the neck cut was about six inches below the chin of the deer. If I had cut the neck just below the chin then there would be a slightly longer neck area at the top center of the hide. The four leg cuts were done as recommended above. (Note: The hide in the picture was removed from a deer whose right rear leg was partially mutilated and that leg was removed during the skinning process. Therefore the hide in the picture is not as rectangular as it would have been if the right rear leg had not been damaged prior to skinning.)

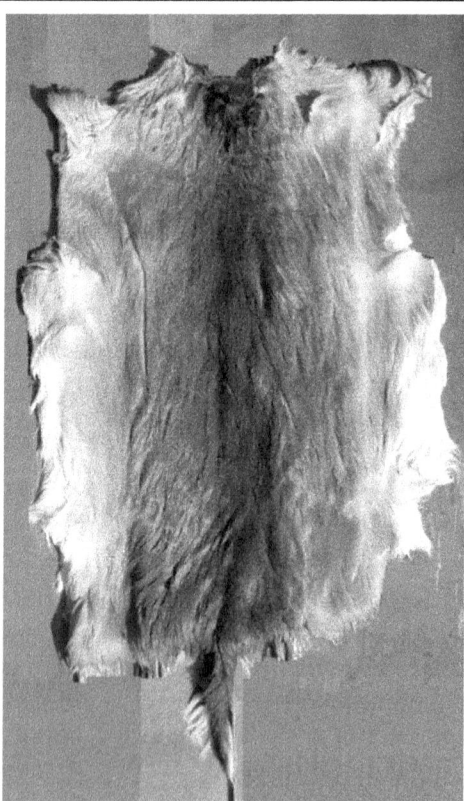

An Almost Rectangular Deer Hide
(Tail left on to illustrate rear of hide)

18. **Pull or Yank the Hide Off (also called "fisting" or "pelting"):** Although this process is called skinning the only time you should use a knife is to open the belly of the animal, and to cut around the neck, tail, and legs of the hide so the hide can be pulled off the animal. Use the skinning knife to separate the skin from the red meat so that only a very thin layer of white membrane, or connective tissue, is clinging to the skin. If you see some red meat clinging to the skin then you are cutting too deeply. Only cut the skin away from the meat for a distance of about two inches at the neck, tail, and each of the four legs. **Do not use a knife to skin the hide off the animal.** Now firmly grab the skin of the animal with both hands and pull or yank the hide off the animal to keep the hide in the best possible condition and to avoid knife cuts and holes in the hide. If the animal was freshly killed and it is still warm then the hide of the animal will usually pull off the animal with the least amount of effort. However, as time gradually passes after the animal has died then the fluids and the chemicals near the animal's upper layer of skin will gradually become drier and drier, similar to what happens to

glue as it dries, and more effort will be required to pull the hide off the animal. On most animals the hide will be easier to pull off the animal near its belly and it will gradually become more difficult to pull off near its backbone. Therefore you may need to use your knife occasionally to cut sinews and membranes that are clinging to the hide and which are too firmly attached to the hide to be pulled or yanked loose from the hide. You may also need to use your knife at the rump, or flanks, of the animal because the meat in these areas sometimes has a tendency to cling to the skin. When you are finished a very thin layer of membrane and fat will still be attached to the inside surface of the hide and this is normal. This thin layer of membrane and fat will be scraped off the hide later on a scraping beam.

19. **Sinew Removal:** Sinew is just another name for tendon. Tendons connect muscles to bones. Tendons enable the muscles to exert precise pressure on the bones and this makes movement possible. Each tendon is composed of multiple fibers and each fiber is extremely strong. Tendons, or sinews, have a multitude of practical uses that are listed in detail in Chapter 24. However, in order to use sinews later they must be removed from the animal now. On both sides of the backbone there is a long flat strip of sinew, or tendon, between one to two inches wide and as long as the backbone. These two strips are sometimes called backstrap tendons or sinews because they are attached to the strip of meat referred to as the backstrap or sirloin. To expose these two sinews you will need to make two very shallow cuts with each cut being close to each side of the spine from the shoulder to the tail of the animal. A thin layer of membrane will usually be covering each strip of sinew and you will need to use your knife to remove that thin layer of body tissue so you can see each of the two strips of sinew, one on each side of the backbone. Each sinew will look like a thin strap of shiny white wet threads attached to the top of a strip of meat directly below each sinew. That long strip of meat is called a backstrap, sirloin, or tenderloin. Remove and save both strips of sinew. The sinew near the neck of the animal will normally be easy to pull free from the meat strip to which it is attached. Therefore use a knife to separate the end of the sinew from the meat near the neck end of the spine. Then set your knife aside and pull the sinew away from the strip of meat. As you continue to pull the sinew away from the meat along the backbone you will notice that the sinew gradually becomes more and more difficult to pull free from the meat to which it is attached as you gradually approach the rear of the animal. At some point you will need to use your knife to cut the sinew free from the rear of the animal. Then use the edge of your knife to scrape off, not cut off, any meat still attached to each of the two strips of sinew. Place both sinew strips inside a plastic bag for processing at some future time. On a deer you can also find shorter sinews on the back of each hind leg. There is no usable meat on the lower part of the legs and therefore these tendons are usually easier to locate. The sinews will pull free from the upper part of the leg but they are firmly attached near the hooves and you will need to use your knife to cut them free at the hoof where the sinew splits into a "Y" shape near the "dewclaw bone" a little above the foot bone. Since these leg sinews are shorter than the sinews on the spine you will need to decide whether or not you want them. Place the sinews in a clean plastic bag and later when you get home lay the sinews out straight on a flat surface so they can dry out. After it has dried sinew will keep indefinitely unless it is attacked by insects. Each sinew strip will consist of many individual threads of sinew. Those threads may be separated from one another and the resulting sinew thread may be used as a bowstring, or twisted together to make a rope, or each thread may be used as a sewing thread to lace buckskins together to make clothing or moccasins, or the sinew threads may be used to tie almost anything together such as to tie a stone arrowhead onto the tip of an arrow or to tie split tail feathers on the rear of an arrow. Detailed instructions for processing sinew are in Chapter 24.

20. **Butchering Small and Medium Size Animals:** On small and medium size animals now is the time to remove the edible meat and fat from the animal with your butchering knife. Put the meat and fat into some sterile heavy-duty plastic bags as you remove it from the animal but do not close the tops of the bags. Allow the bags to remain open so the air can circulate inside the bag. This will allow the meat to continue to cool without trapping excess moisture and heat inside the bags that could begin to spoil the meat. When you get to your vehicle you should place the bags of meat inside an ordinary food cooler, or plastic tote, with some ice or snow or cold creek water around the outside of the bags to help preserve the meat on your trip home. If possible you should still not seal the bags unless you have more meat than will

fit on the bottom of your cooler and you must stack the bags on top of one another before you add the ice, snow, or cold creek water.

21. **Heavy animals:** If the animal is still lying on the ground then you will need to pull the hide from its underbelly and two legs towards the middle of its back. Then use your butchering knife to remove the edible meat that you can access on the side of the animal that has been exposed. When you have the edible meat removed and safely stored inside sterile heavy-duty plastic bags or plastic totes, then you should roll the animal over on the ground so you can pull the hide off the animal from its other two legs and belly towards the center of its back. You can then usually pull the hide completely off the animal and store it temporarily in a heavy-duty plastic bag but leave the top of the bag open so heat and moisture can still escape from the bag. Then you can remove the edible meat from the side of the animal that you now have access to and put that meat into some sterile plastic bags or plastic totes.

22. **Brain Removal:** To remove the brains from an animal you should first remove the hide from the top part of its skull. Although you can cut the skull with a saw it is easier and quicker to simply smash the skull with a hammer, or the blunt edge of a hatchet, or a large rock. (Note: If you have a good quality hatchet then you can chop through the skull with the sharp edge of the hatchet. But if you have an inexpensive hatchet this will damage the cutting edge of the hatchet and leave nicks or chips in the cutting edge.) Carefully pull the broken skull apart but use caution so you do not cut yourself on any sharp bone splinters that are still clinging to the busted skull. Scoop the brains out of the skull with a long-handled metal spoon or metal ladle into a heavy-duty one quart zipper freezer bag. Do not be concerned if a few very, very tiny bone splinters are mixed in with the brain. But you should remove and discard any large skull fragments. As soon as possible place the plastic freezer bag of brains into a freezer or process the brains using one of the methods described in Chapter 17 on Hide Tanning.

23. **Examine the Hide:** When you have finished butchering the animal you may take the time to more carefully examine the hide. If the hide only has one or two small knife cuts then you have done a very good job. As you gain experience you will frequently be able to remove a hide with no knife cuts in the hide. However, even experienced skinners occasionally misjudge the pressure required and a small knife cut in the hide will be the result.

24. **Render the Fat (suet or tallow):** It is critical that you render (melt) the fat on any wild game animal as soon as possible after its has been killed in order to safely preserve that fat for future human consumption, or for use in a variety of other practical applications. Some wild game animals have a lot of fat, such as a bear or a wild boar or a raccoon, but other wild game animals have no fat, or almost no fat, such as a deer. However, the tail of an animal will frequently contain some fat so remember to split the tail and remove the fat before you discard the tail (assuming you are not going to preserve the tail with the rest of the hide). Or you can save the rest of the tail and use the tail hair to make hand tied fishing flies.

Note: **Animal glue** can be made from short strips of animal sinew. However, animal glue is water soluble and it will separate if it gets wet. Therefore animal glue is not useful in most practical applications because it is extremely difficult to prevent an item from occasionally getting wet.

Temporary Hide Storage

1. If you have a garden hose, or if you are near a creek or stream or lake, then rinse the blood and other residue off the inside and the outside of the hide.

2. If a fresh hide has an insect infestation problem then soak the hide for 24 hours in a plastic bucket completely submerged under some cool water that has had some Sevin dust (or Sevin liquid) added to the water. If you don't have Sevin dust or liquid then you can spray some flea insecticide, such as the Raid brand, inside a large 55 gallon garbage bag and then put the hide inside the bag and secure the top of the bag with a twist tie. Do not breathe the insecticide when you put the hide inside the bag. Leave the hide in the bag for 24 hours and then remove the hide and discard the plastic bag.

3. Do not soak a hide in a salt and water bath and do not sprinkle salt on the hide. Do not use salt at anytime during the entire hide tanning process, except for the long-term storage of unprocessed hides as described next.

4. **Storage of Unprocessed Hides:** If you intend to store a freshly acquired hide for an "extended period of time" before you begin processing it then you will need to store the hide in a cool dry area after you have used one of the following three methods to preserve the hide. The following methods are listed in the order in which they are preferred with the least recommended method at the end of the list:

   a. **Freezing:**
      1. **Food freezer:** Place the hide inside a large plastic bag, press the bag to expel as much air as possible, and then tie off the end of the bag. Then place a second plastic bag around the first bag and seal it the same way. Then place a third plastic bag around the first two bags and seal it. Now you can place the triple sealed hide into a food freezer with other foods and the smell from the hide should not migrate to the other foods in the freezer. The triple bagging will also help to reduce the impact of "freezer burn" on the hide.
      2. **Outdoor Shed:** If you live in an area where it is below freezing outdoors during the day and at night then you can freeze the hide inside a plastic bag in an outdoor shed or barn where the temperature remains below freezing. If you do not protect the hide by placing it inside some type of storage building or container then there is a very good chance your hide will be dragged off by wild animals or dogs who will be able to smell the hide through the plastic bag.

   b. **Salting:** Use pure salt and not iodized salt. Sprinkle about one pound of salt over the entire flesh side of the hide in order to help protect it and to slow down the rotting process and to help the hide remain somewhat flexible. A thin layer of salt should be visible across the entire flesh side of the hide. Do not put any salt on the hair side of the hide. Hang the hide across a rope so both sides of the hide can air dry completely. Do not hang a salted hide on a metal wire because the salt will attack the metal if some of its gets onto the metal wire. The salting process will need to be repeated again two days later. After the second salting some tanners prefer to fold a "slightly moist" hide in half with the flesh side on the inside and the hair side on the outside and then store the hide in that condition, occasionally with several hides stacked on one another. Other tanners prefer to completely air dry the hide after the second

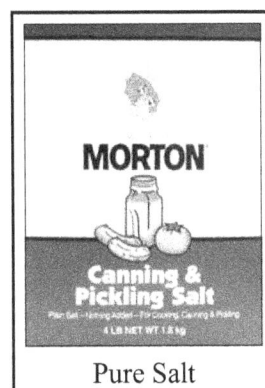

MORTON

Canning &
Pickling Salt

Plain Salt - No Iodine Added - For Canning, Pickling & Making

4 LB NET WT 1.8 kg

Pure Salt

salting and then fold the dry hide in half with the flesh side on the inside and then stack the dry hides together. The only advantage of salt is that it will help to break down some of the proteins in the hide so that the hide will more readily accept the tanning solution near the end of the hide tanning process. However, before the hide can begin to be processed all the salt will need to be completely rinsed off the hide. The salt rinsing process will need to be done dozens of times to get all the salt off the hide. The salt must be rinsed off in an area where the salt will not eventually kill desirable plants or trees. Any salt residue that is left on the hide will attract moisture when the rest of the hide is dry and this will cause the hide to deteriorate in those spots. In addition, any salt left on the hide will create hard spots on the hide and it will be more difficult to properly scrape those spots later. Therefore, instead of salting, it is better to process hides immediately for two reasons: (a) you will not be wasting precious salt that could be better used some other way, and (b) you will not be creating a significant amount of extra work later when have to remove and discard all the salt from the hide.

   c. **Drying:** A hide may be dried without salt if the flesh side of the hide is first completely scraped as described in Chapter 8 and all the flesh and meat is completely and totally removed from the flesh side of the hide. Then the hair side of the hide can be staked flat against the ground with the flesh side of the hide facing the sun until the hide is completely dry. Or a hide may be nailed, or tacked, onto an exterior barn or shed wall so the flesh side of the hide faces the sun. Staking, or nailing, helps to prevent the hide from shrinking and it helps to prevent the outside edges of the hide from curling up.

The drying can usually can be completed in less than one day if the sun is shining and the air is not cold or full of moisture. A dry hide can then be rolled into a cylinder with the hair side out (similar to the way a rug is rolled up when a rug is moved from one location to another) and the hide can be safely stored. The **disadvantages** of drying a hide are:
- while the hide is drying insects will sometimes lay their tiny eggs on the flesh side of the hide,
- while the hide is in storage small holes will sometimes be eaten through the dry hide by tiny insects after they have hatched out of their tiny eggs,
- later the hide will be more difficult to soften in a water bath and it will emit a more unpleasant odor,
- the hair side of the hide will be more difficult to scrape on the scraping beam, and
- the hide will require more time and effort on the stretching frame to make it soft enough and flexible enough to be used to make buckskin clothing.

5. **Grease Burns:** A "grease burn" on a hide is a spot where some fat was allowed to remain on the flesh side of the hide and that fat gradually melted and soaked into the hide. The grease burn will usually not become visible until near the end of the tanning process when you notice that the hide is unusually weak in that spot and it will not stretch and soften without coming apart at that spot.

6. Never stack "fresh" hides together, one on top of the other. This will cause bacteria to grow and the hides will rot.

7. Never store "fresh" hides inside plastic bags for any length of time because this will speed up the rotting process. However, it is okay to place a hide inside a large plastic bag for transport between locations but you should remove the hide from the bag as soon as your reach your destination.

8. Hang a fresh hide across a synthetic rope (nylon or polypropylene) with the hair side of the hide against the rope and the inside of the hide facing out.

9. One good place to hang a fresh hide is inside a cold smokehouse where the hide will eventually be smoked. However, if the hide is infested with parasites then you should resolve the parasite problem using the method in Step Two above before you hang the hide in a cold smoke house.

10. As soon as possible begin soaking the hide in some clean water following the instructions in Chapter 6.

Chapter Five

Introduction to Scraping

This chapter will briefly compare the two different methods for scraping a hide: Dry Scraping and Wet Scraping. This chapter will also answer the question of which side of the hide should be scraped first: the flesh side or the hair side? A discussion of scraping tools and detailed instructions for doing each type of scraping are in Chapters Seven, Eight, and Ten.

Should You Dry Scrape or Wet Scrape a Hide?

The reason this introductory chapter on scraping is included here is because dry scraping does not require that the hide be soaked in water (next chapter) before scraping. But wet scraping does require that the hide be soaked overnight in some water before it is scraped.

Therefore if you decide to experiment with dry scraping then you should skip the next chapter and go directly to the following chapter on scraping. But if you decide to experiment with wet scraping then you will need to follow the instructions in the next chapter before you begin scraping the hide.

Scraping is the most labor intensive step in the creation of buckskins. Scraping will require more physical work than all the other steps combined. Therefore the decisions you make about your scraping method will have a significant impact on the total amount of work you invest in the creation of a finished buckskin. Poor choices will result in a huge investment in physical labor and this means it will take you longer to create a finished buckskin. On the other hand, good choices will allow you to achieve the same final result with significantly less effort and fatigue on your part.

There are two basic ways to scrape a hide as follows:

1. **Dry Scraping:** Dry scraping is popular in regions that have limited water resources and in regions that are extremely cold (below freezing) for most of the year. The animal hide is not soaked in a water bath. The hide is scraped as soon as possible after the hide has been removed from the animal but after the hide has been allowed to dry a little. If the hide of a freshly killed animal is allowed to completely dry out then it will harden and it will not be possible to properly scrape the hide. Therefore the hide will need to be slightly moist and flexible in order for the hide to be dry scraped. Dry scraping requires a sharper scraping tool and this usually results in more cuts in the hide. Flesh and fat are scraped from the flesh side of the hide. Hair and membrane are scraped from the hair side of the hide. During dry scraping the flesh and the hair will require more work and careful concentration to remove them from the hide when compared to wet scraping. Theoretically dry scraping removes about 1/32 of an inch more membrane from the hair side of a hide than wet scraping. However, since each hide is of a slightly different original thickness, it is not possible to verify this statement because 1/32 of an inch is too small a measurement to make a noticeable difference in a finished hide. Tanners who recommend dry scraping also suggest that the hide be soaked in a water bath for a short period of time in order to soften the hide if the hide gradually becomes too dry to scrape properly. When you stop and think about this it becomes obvious that a tanner who prefers to dry scrape a hide will still occasionally get the hide wet in order to make the scraping task easier and to minimize the chance of accidentally damaging the hide while scraping. Finally, the hide must be thoroughly soaked in water and completely saturated with water before the final thin layer of membrane can be scraped off the flesh side of the hide. Therefore the final membrane scraping step always requires that the hide be wet scraped. In summary, dry scraping means:
   a. the hide is relatively dry but the hide is still a tiny bit moist and flexible when the scraping process begins, and
   b. the hide will need to be soaked in water if it gradually becomes too dry before the initial scraping process can be completed, and
   c. the hide must be thoroughly soaked in water before the final thin layer of membrane can be scraped off the hide.

2. **Wet Scraping:** The hide is soaked overnight in clean water. The hide is scraped immediately after it is removed from the water bath. The damp flesh and the damp hair are easier to remove from the hide compared to dry scraping and the wet scraping process requires less mental concentration because is it fairly mechanical. A wet scraping tool does not need to be as sharp as a dry scraping tool and this means the chance of damaging the hide by scraping the hide too vigorously is reduced.

A simple comparison between dry scraping and wet scraping can be made to the normal process of shaving the hair off your face if you are a man, or perhaps shaving the hair off your legs if you are a woman. It is possible to shave with the skin completely dry but this usually results in more abrasion on the surface of the skin, more nicks and cuts in the skin, and it also feels rather uncomfortable. However, if you apply some water to the skin, and some shaving lotion, then the razor glides across the skin and removes the hair with the least amount of resistance and abrasion, and the fewest number of accidental cuts in the skin, and the greatest overall degree of comfort. And the task can be completed in the least amount of time without having to focus continuously on how the razor is making contact with the skin. Although dry shaving is an option very few people select this option for the reasons just mentioned. This shaving concept can be compared to scraping an animal hide. If the hide is lubricated with water and the flesh and the hair have been softened with water, then the hide can be scraped using the least amount of effort and with the least amount of damage to the hide.

For all the above reasons I recommend that hides be wet scraped and not dry scraped.

If you wish to experiment with wet scraping then you should follow the instructions in the next chapter on how to soak a hide in water before you scrape the hide. But if you wish to experiment with dry scraping then you should skip the next chapter and go directly to Chapter 7.

Which Should Be Scraped First: The Flesh Side or the Hair Side of the Hide?

Some tanners prefer to scrape the flesh side of the hide first and then scrape the hair side of the hide. Other tanners prefer to scrape the hair side of the hide first and then scrape the flesh side of the hide. Both tasks need to be done but the order in which they are done can have an impact on the quality of the finished buckskin.

The reasons the flesh side should be scraped first are as follows:

1. The hair side of the hide is relatively uniform and when it is lying against the scraping beam it provides a relatively smooth level support surface so that the flesh side of the hide can be easily scraped. On the other hand, the flesh side can be a little bumpy in some areas due to small pieces of flesh or fat that are clinging to the flesh side of the hide. If this uneven surface is placed against the scraping beam then it can cause problems when scraping the hair side of the hide.

2. Any imperfections in the hide, such as holes and cuts, can be easily seen from the flesh side of the hide and these areas can receive the special scraping care they require. On the other hand, holes and cuts are sometimes invisible from the hair side of the hide because they may be covered by some hair. If the hair side is scraped first then this could result in some additional damage to the hide wherever there is a hole or a cut. But if the flesh side is scraped first then a small quantity of hair can be trimmed off the hair side of the hide wherever there is an imperfection on the flesh side. This makes it easy to see these imperfections when scraping the hair side so that these imperfections can receive the special scraping care they require.

Therefore I recommend that the flesh side of the hide be scraped first and that the hair side of the hide be scraped second.

Chapter Six

First Water Soak Before Scraping the Flesh Side of the Hide

If you wish to dry scrape a hide then you should skip this chapter and go directly to the next chapter on how to scrape a hide.

If you wish to wet scrape a hide then it is possible to omit the first water bath that is described in this chapter and immediately scrape the flesh side of the hide if the animal was recently killed and the flesh side of the hide is still relatively moist and flexible from the animal's natural body fluids. If you still have the strength and the hide is still moist after you have scraped the flesh side of the hide then you can skip the second water bath and immediately scrape the hair side of the hide. However, to do either or both steps immediately is extremely rare because the following situations are relatively common:

1. You arrive home late in the evening and there is not enough time before sunset to properly scrape the hide.
2. You arrive home and you are too tired to do all the work that is required to properly scrape the hide.

In either of the above two situations, or if the hide has become partially dry, then you will need to soak the hide in a bath of clean water until you have the time to properly scrape the flesh side of the hide.

If the hide of a freshly killed animal is allowed to completely dry out then it will harden. If the hide remains slightly moist for an extended period of time then it will begin to rot. Neither of these two extreme conditions is acceptable and a compromise must be achieved.

To prevent both hardening and rotting a fresh hide should be soaked in a clean water bath. A water bath has the following four major benefits:

1. **Parasites**: Any ticks, fleas, or other parasites on the hide will drown or they will have to leave the hide and go somewhere else. Deer ticks can be as small as a speck of ground black pepper and they can be extremely difficult to see.
2. **Time:** It will reduce the total amount of time required to scrape the hide.
3. **Effort:** It will reduce the total amount of work required and it will make the hair removal process less fatiguing.
4. **Quality:** It will result in a hide with a more consistent final thickness across the entire surface of the hide.

Tick < 1/4" Long

Flea < 1/8" Long

Do not add salt or any other chemicals to the first water bath.

Never use hot water to soak an animal hide. Water that feels warm to your touch is the best choice. But if the water feels so hot that you cannot comfortably leave your hand submerged in the water then the water is much too hot for soaking a hide. If you do not have warm water then cool or cold water will work fine but the hide will need to spend more time soaking in cool water when compared to warm water.

When a hide is soaking in clean water the undesirable chemicals and glues in the hide will gradually leech out into the water until the water becomes saturated with them. In other words, the chemicals still remaining in the hide will reach an equilibrium with the chemicals that have already leeched out of the hide and are now in the water. At this point the contaminated water needs to be discarded and replaced with clean water. The hide will then be able to continue releasing its undesirable chemicals into the clean water until that water also becomes saturated. This is the reason that you must discard the dirty water and replace it with clean water once every day during the soaking process. The purpose of the water bath is to remove the undesirable chemicals from the hide and not to simply saturate the hide with water. The hide will swell and become saturated while it is the water bath but this is a side effect and it is not the primary purpose of the water bath.

When the water bath process has been successfully completed the hide will be less swollen because the undesirable chemicals will have been removed from the hide and the hide will feel smooth and not sticky. If you capture an air bubble on the flesh side of the hide and then submerge the hide below the surface of the water and then squeeze the hide, the air should be able to penetrate the hide from the flesh side through the hair side, and the air should bubble to the top surface of the water.

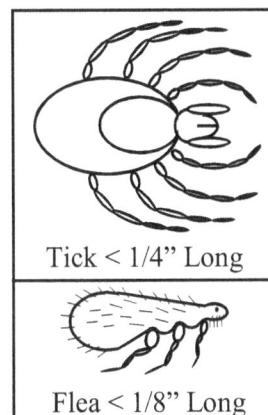

When you remove the hide from the water bath you should twist and squeeze the hide to remove as much extra water as you possible can so that the hide is just slightly damp or moist to the touch.

Water Bath Options

There are two different ways to soak a hide in a water bath:

1. **Creek or Lake:** Some tanners prefer to soak their hides in creek water or lake water. If you wish to use this method then you may occasionally discover that your hide is gone when you return to collect it. This could be due to the method you used to weigh the hide down and the hide just drifted away. Or it could be due to a wild animal that discovered your hide and dragged it off. Finally it could be due to a person who found your hide and decided to take it. This person could be an adult who wanted the hide or it could be a child who thinks he is simply playing a practical joke on you. If you decide to submerge your hide in a creek or lake then you should consider placing the hide inside a rustproof metal cage that is weighted down with rocks to keep the cage and hide below water. Then tie a waterproof rope to the cage so you can lower and raise the cage out of the water. If you use this method then you will not have to change the water every day because the creek or lake will leech the glue and chemicals out of and away from the hide.

2. **Plastic Bucket or Trash Can:** You may use a 5 or 6 gallon plastic bucket or a 13 gallon kitchen trash can as the container for your water bath. Put the container in a safe area where it will not be disturbed by wild animals, neighborhood pets, or other people. You have several choices for the water you use. The following list is arranged in order from the most desired type of water to the least desired type of water.

   a. **Rainwater:** The best water to use is rainwater. Rainwater is pure water.
   b. **Well water:** Well water is the next best choice. Well water will normally contain a few natural minerals that can be beneficial to the hide soaking process.
   c. **Ground Water:** Creek, river, or lake water may also be used if it is relatively clear and not muddy. If your source of ground water is cloudy or muddy then allow the water to remain undisturbed inside a large barrel for a few days until most of the sediment has had a chance to sink to the bottom of the barrel. Then scoop or ladle the water out of the top of the barrel without disturbing the sediment in the bottom of the barrel.
   d. **City Water:** Most municipalities add chlorine, and sometimes fluoride, to the water that they pipe into your home. These chemicals react unfavorably with a hide and this type of water should be avoided if possible. You should consider collecting rainwater if you only have access to city water. However, if it doesn't rain very often where you live then your only source of water may be city water. In this situation allow your city water to sit for several days in an open shallow pan so that most of the chlorine will have a chance to evaporate out of the water into the air.

Water Bath One

Safety Precautions: Always wear rubber or vinyl or latex gloves when handling an animal hide. The bacteria and germs on an animal hide will contaminate the water in which the hide is soaking. Therefore the water will need to be thrown away after the hide has finished soaking and that water cannot be used for any other purpose. Do not handle a hide or the bath water without wearing your protective rubber or vinyl gloves.

First Water Bath in Clean Water for One Day: The first water bath will kill parasites and it will make the flesh side of the hide easier to scrape. Put enough water in your container to completely cover the hide with water. Dip the hide into the water and remove the hide several times to give the water an opportunity to make complete contact with both sides of the hide. Then completely submerge the hide below the surface of the water and put one or more large heavy rocks on the hide to keep the hide completely under the water. Check the hide every few hours to make sure the rocks are still on top of the hide and that the rocks are not on the bottom of the bucket. An animal hide has a natural tendency to float to the surface of the water and it will do so unless the rocks are placed on the hide so the rocks cannot slip off the hide and fall into the bottom of the bucket. After approximately 24 hours pour out and discard the water and then scrape the flesh side of the hide as described in the next chapter.

Procedure For a Hide That Was Allowed To Dry Out

If the hide was allowed to dry out then you will need to remove the hide from the water bath after it has soaked for four hours and you will need to pull and stretch the hide by hand to make it more flexible so the water can properly penetrate into the hide. If you don't pull and stretch the hide then the hide may begin to rot in any spot where the water cannot adequately penetrate. After pulling and stretching the hide by hand you should put the hide back into the water bath for another four hours. After four hours remove the hide from the water bath and pull and stretch it, and then put the hide back into the water bath. Repeat this process every four hours until 24 hours have passed. However, you do not need to get out of bed during the night to stretch the hide every four hours.

Chapter Seven

Scraping Techniques and Equipment

Scraping is sometimes called "fleshing" and scraping is sometimes called "membraning." The flesh that is scraped off the inside of a hide is called "hypodermis" by biologists but it is called "membrane" by tanners. In this book the word scraping will be used to describe the process of removing the flesh and the hair from an animal hide.

Scraping is the most labor intensive step in the creation of buckskins. Scraping will require more physical effort than all the other steps combined. Therefore the decisions you make about your scraping equipment and your scraping method will have a significant impact on the total amount of work you invest in the creation of a finished buckskin. Poor choices will result in a huge investment in physical labor and this means it will take you longer to create a finished buckskin. On the other hand, good choices will allow you to achieve the same final result with significantly less effort and fatigue on your part.

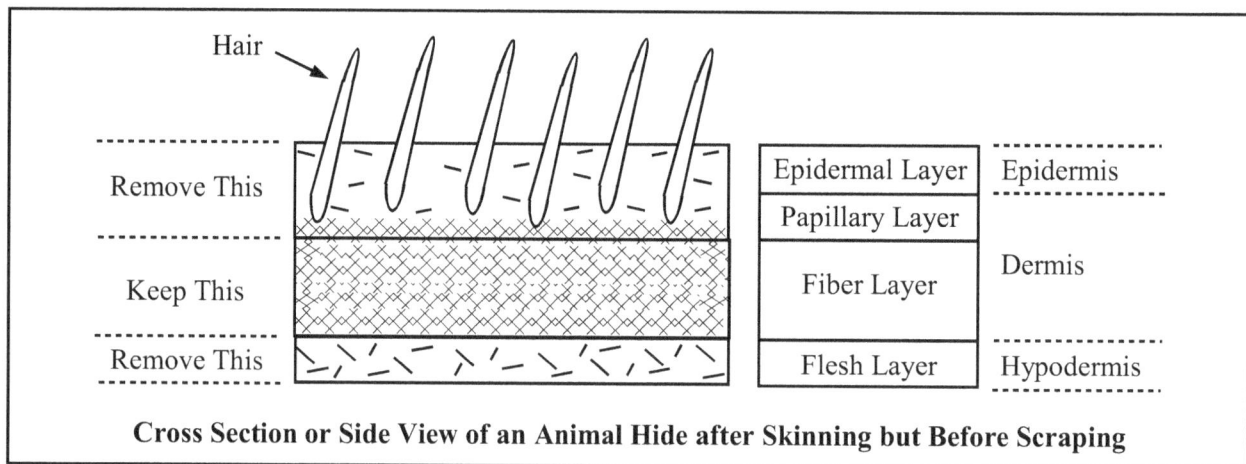

Cross Section or Side View of an Animal Hide after Skinning but Before Scraping

An animal hide is usually scraped three times as follows:

1. **First Scrape - Flesh Layer:** The flesh and fat that adheres to the inside of the hide is scraped off. This flesh and fat is called the hypodermis or the membrane. The flesh side is usually easier to scrape from side to side instead of from neck to tail.

2. **Second Scrape - Hair Layer:** The hair and the epidermal layer and the papillary layer is scraped off the outside of the hide. The hair side is usually easier to scrape from the neck towards the tail.

3. **Third Scrape - Flesh Layer:** Any residual flesh or membrane that still remains on the inside of the hide is scraped off.

Scraping Accessories

Plastic Apron: To protect your clothing you should wear a plastic apron around your waist. Or you can tie a large plastic trash bag around your chest and allow the trash bag to hang down below your knees.

Plastic Tarp: Place a tarp or a large sheet of painter's plastic below your scraping beam. The tarp will catch the material you scrape off a hide and this will make the cleanup job relatively easy when you are finished.

Optional Nose Plug and Breathing Mask: Some people are not able to tolerate the smell of an animal hide while it is being scraped. The simple solution is to wear some ordinary nose plugs of the type that a person might wear when swimming. If you wear nose plugs then you should also wear a doctor's face mask or a painter's face mask over your nose and mouth to filter the air you breath into your lungs. However, this option is not necessary unless you are seriously nauseated by the smell of an animal hide.

The reason a hide is scraped is to remove all the flesh from the inside of the hide and all the hair from the outside of the hide. Hide scraping is done on a **scraping beam** using a **scraping tool**.

A Scraping Beam

A scraping beam should be about five or six feet long and it can be made from either of the following two materials:

1. **A Wood Log:** An aged log is better than a freshly cut log, if you have one. A freshly cut log will usually develop cracks as it gradually ages and those cracks will cause problems when scraping a hide. The log should be approximately five or six inches in diameter and as round and smooth as possible. It should not have any cracks, bumps, or imperfections. It should resist swelling when it gets wet. The advantage of a log is that an animal hide will not slide excessively on a wood log and this makes it a little easier to scrape a hide. The disadvantage of a log is that your scraping tool will occasionally slide off the end of the hide onto the log and sometimes this will result in a nick or slice being removed from the log. These nicks and slices will need to be smoothed out when you finish a hide scraping session. In addition, the wood will gradually absorb moisture from the wet hides and then dry and this action of wetting, scraping, and drying will gradually wear down and soften the outside surface of the log and the log will need to be occasionally shaved down to the solid wood underneath.

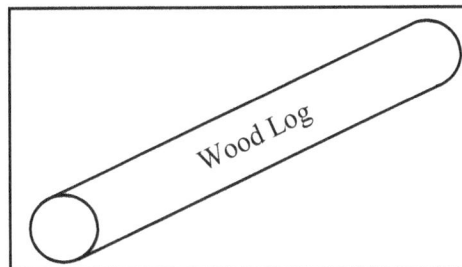

2. **A Plastic Pipe:** Instead of a wood log you may use a six inch diameter plastic water pipe. A plastic pipe will be strong, round, smooth, it will shed moisture easily, it will not gradually warp, splinter, split, or develop cracks, and it will consistently provide a smooth round surface for scraping a hide. Some metal C-clamps or vise-grip pliers may be used to hold or anchor a hide to the open end of a plastic pipe. The advantage of a plastic pipe is that your scraping tool will not accidentally remove pieces from the pipe and the pipe will last a very, very long time. The disadvantage of a plastic pipe is that an animal hide will shift and slide a little bit on the pipe as you scrape the hide.

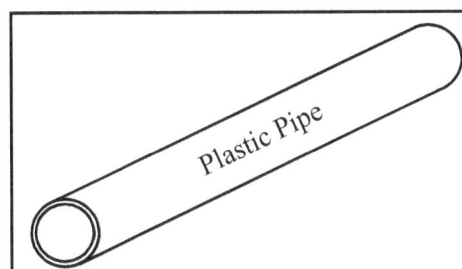

The scraping beam (either wood or plastic) must be anchored so it will remain stationary and it will not slide, slip, rotate, or move sideways while it is supporting a hide for scraping. The scraping beam may be positioned in any one of the following three ways:

1. **Almost Upright:** The scraping beam may be leaned against a tree or a wall so that it is nearly vertical and the top of the beam is somewhere between eye level to shoulder level. A hide is then positioned between the top end of the beam and the surface against which the beam is leaning. This will hold the hide stationary while the hide is being scraped. The hide is scraped at chest level while you are standing upright by pulling the scraping tool down the hide to remove flesh and hair. Normally one end of the hide is scraped from the center of the hide towards its outside end, and then the hide is rotated on the beam so the opposite end of the hide can be scraped in the same manner at chest level. The advantage of the upright position is that you can stand directly in front of the beam with one foot on the ground on each side of the beam. This will position the hide on the beam directly in front of your chest and this makes it easier to reach the hide and to scrape the hide. An upright beam puts the least possible strain on your back and it will minimize the possibility of a future back problem that results from bending over to scrape hides. However,

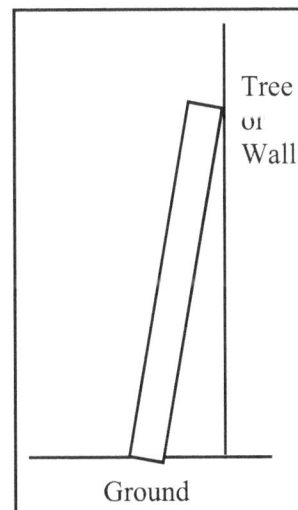

Tree or Wall

Ground

an upright beam requires that the majority of the work be done with your arms and shoulders instead of the weight of your body and this can become fatiguing more quickly. In addition, when the hide simply hangs down an upright beam it will usually have a crease or wrinkle in it that must be smoothed out in order to properly scrape that section of the hide. A hide also tends to shift a little more to the right and left on an upright beam while it is being scraped when compared to a horizontal beam or a slanted beam. Finally, to reposition the part of the hide that is trapped between the beam and the surface against which the beam is leaning you will need to lift the beam away from the surface and hold it with one hand while you adjust the position of the hide with your other hand. Then you will need to lower the beam so it makes contact with the hide in the right spot so you can continue to scrape a new section of the hide. This work of constantly shifting and repositioning the hide can gradually become both challenging and fatiguing. One advantage of the upright beam is that permits the use of a drawknife as a scraping tool. The slight downward curve in the handles of a drawknife are designed to minimize fatigue and wrist discomfort when the drawknife is pulled towards you and therefore a drawknife works well when it is used as a scraping tool on an upright beam.

2. **Horizontal:** The scraping beam may be supported horizontally with both ends off the ground so the top of the beam is about level with your navel or with your elbows. This is a comfortable height to reach while standing upright and you will not have to bend over at the waist to scrape the hide. One advantage of the horizontal beam is that you may either pull or push the scraping tool depending on whichever motion is the most comfortable for you. Therefore a drawknife can be used effectively with a horizontal beam. The disadvantage of the horizontal position is that you will need to stand on one side of the beam and then lean over the beam sideways with your upper body at a slight angle in order to scrape a hide.

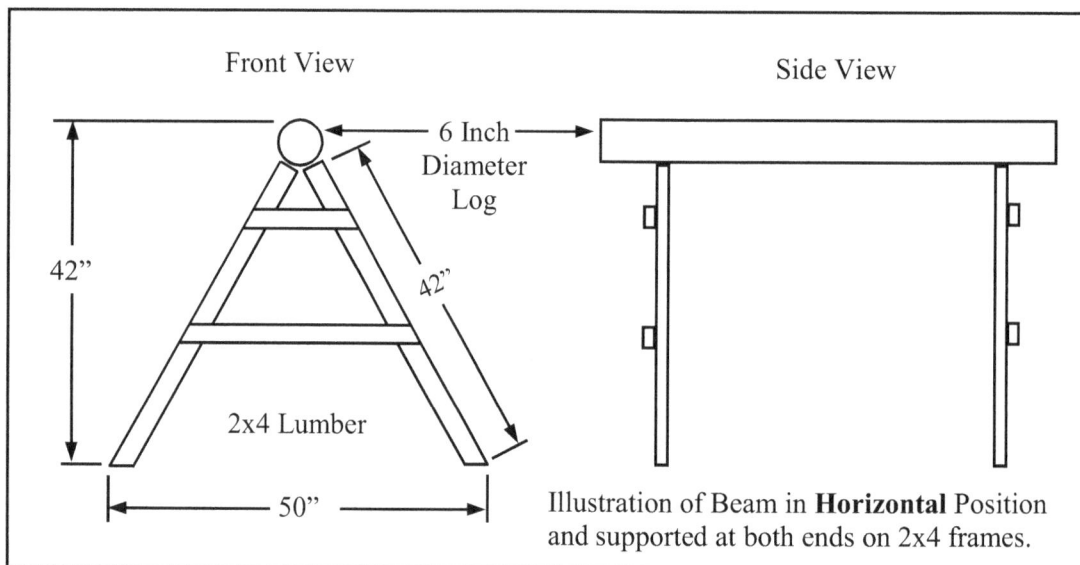

Front View   Side View

6 Inch Diameter Log

42"   42"

2x4 Lumber

50"

Illustration of Beam in **Horizontal** Position and supported at both ends on 2x4 frames.

3. **Slanted** (see illustration on next page): Place one end of the beam on a 2x4 bipod frame, similar to a narrow sawhorse, and the other end of the beam partially buried in the ground or pressed against the trunk of a tree, or a tree stump, or the bottom of a building in order to prevent that end of the beam from sliding when you put pressure on the beam. The top end of the beam should extend off the top of the 2x4 frame approximately 18 inches but no more than 1/3 of the length of the beam. The top of the extended beam should be about level with your navel or your elbows. The top end of the beam should be cut so that it is at a 90 degree angle to the ground. Then place one end of a hide over the top end of the beam and lean against the hide using the weight of your body to press the hide against the top end of the beam. This will allow you to scrape the hide while standing straight up in front of the top end of the beam with your body pressing against the hide that is draped over the beam. You can then scrape down the hide from the top of the beam as far as you can comfortably reach. You will be scrapping from near the center of the hide

towards the outside end of the hide. Then you shift the position of the hide on the beam and scrape some more. The advantage of a slanted beam is that you can add the weight of your body to the strength of your arms as you scrape a hide. The disadvantage of a slanted beam is that you must bend over at the waist in order to reach and scrape the section of a hide that is a little lower on the slanted beam. This method also does not allow you to use a drawknife as a scraping tool because the handles of a drawknife are curved slightly downwards away from the blade and this makes a drawknife fatiguing to use in a pushing motion away from your body.

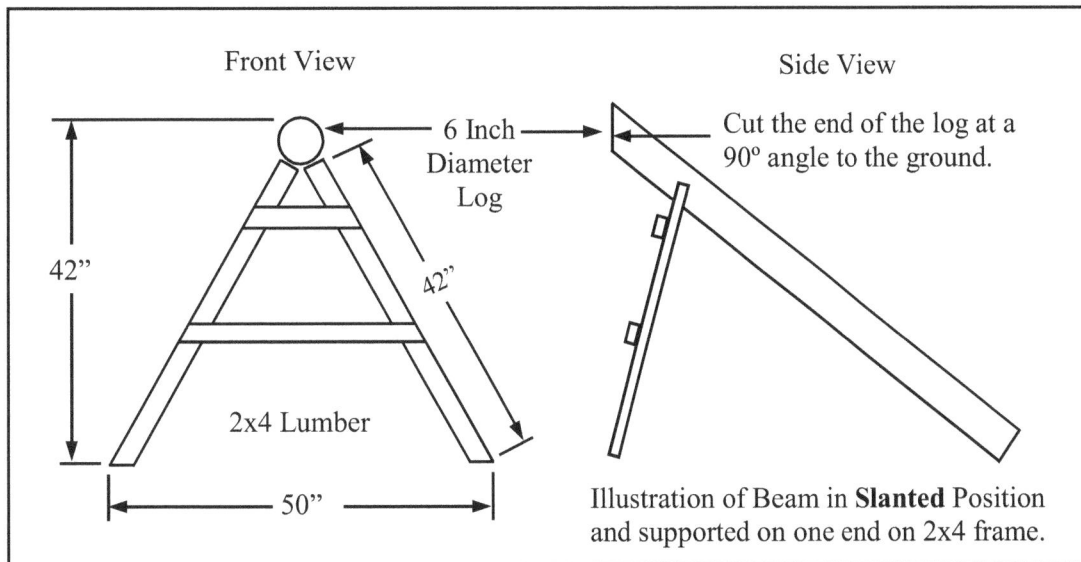

Front View — Side View

6 Inch Diameter Log

Cut the end of the log at a 90º angle to the ground.

42"

42"

2x4 Lumber

50"

Illustration of Beam in **Slanted** Position and supported on one end on 2x4 frame.

A Scraping Tool

A wide variety of different tools may be used scrape the flesh (membrane) and hair off an animal hide. A few tanners prefer a scraping tool that has a square flat edge but most tanners prefer a tool that has a tapered edge.

1. **Square Edge:** A tool with a square edge should be held at a 45 degree angle to the hide when scraping the hide. A square edge is less likely to damage the hide. However a square edge requires a significant amount of extra effort to push the membrane off the hide. The membrane bunches up in front of the tool and this requires a lot more force (effort) to remove the membrane from the hide.

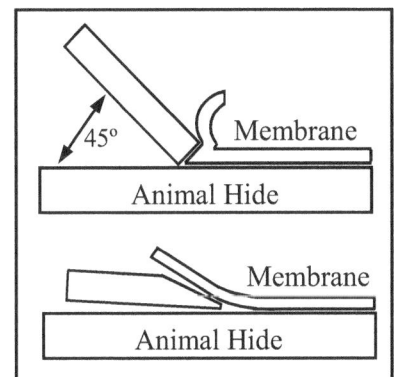

45º — Membrane

Animal Hide

Membrane

Animal Hide

2. **Tapered Edge:** A tool with a tapered edge allows the tool to be held almost flat against the animal hide and the tapered edge of the tool more easily slides under the membrane (or the hair) and lifts it up off the hide. The membrane slides up the tapered edge of the tool and then the membrane gradually curls over on top of itself in front of the tool. I recommend the tapered edge but you may experiment with a square edge if you wish.

All of the following items will do a good job of scraping the flesh (membrane) and the hair from an animal hide.

1. **Hard Rock:** Any hard rock that is comfortable to hold in your hand and that has a dull knife edge may be used as a scrapping tool. A hard rock requires more manual effort than any of the following tools. However, if a hard rock is all you have then it will get the job done.

2. **Steel Knife:** The sharp edge of a knife may be held at a 90 degree angle to the hide and used as a scraping tool. There are two major problems with a knife: (a) it is used with one hand and that one hand will quickly become tired, and (b) if the blade tips a little bit off a 90 degree angle then you can quickly cut right through the hide. However, if you are patient and careful then a steel knife will successfully remove all the flesh and hair from an animal hide.

3. **Lawnmower Blade:** An old lawnmower blade may be converted into a scraping tool if it does not have any rust, and it is about 2.25 inches wide, and it is relatively flat for at least 12 inches in the center of the blade between the two outside cutting edges of the blade that curve downwards. The two outside sharp edges of the blade will need to be cut off and then the center piece of the blade can be used to make an handmade scraping tool by following the instructions that appear next.

4. **Handmade Tool:** A handmade scraping tool can be made from any piece of straight flat steel about 16 inches long, between 1 to 2 inches wide, and between 1/8 to 1/4 inch thick. This type of steel may be purchased at a hardware store but it is also common in automobile junkyards as leaf springs. Some leaf springs are flat and some are gently curved. The gently curved springs are a better match for a curved scraping beam. The leaf springs may be cut to the correct length using a cutting torch (quick) or a hacksaw (requires a lot of work). The cut ends of the leaf spring should be smoothed with a grinding wheel or with a metal file.

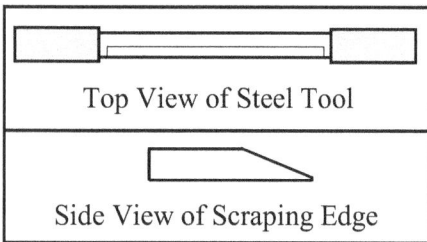

Top View of Steel Tool

Side View of Scraping Edge

The ends of a handmade steel scraping tool may be wrapped with:
   a. leather or tape, or
   b. a worn out automobile rubber heater hose, or
   c. rubber handlebar bicycle grips that are available for sale at any store that sells bicycles.

The wrapped handles at both ends of the tool should be approximately round so your hands can grip them comfortably. A simple way to create a round hand grip on a flat surface is to split a wood dowel in half that is the same width as the tool. The put each half of the round dowel on each end of the flat tool and tape each end securely to the tool. The tool should have a dull knife edge in the center of the tool that is created using an electric bench grinder or a stone grinding wheel. The edge should be straight and it should not contain any nicks or rough spots. If you put too sharp an edge on the tool then it will cut through the hide. If you have too dull an edge on the tool then it will not remove the flesh or the hair. Though trial-and-error you will gradually learn the correct tradeoff between sharp and dull that is just right for you and the amount of strength you normally use to scrape an animal hide. A weaker person will need a sharper tool. A stronger person will need a slightly duller tool to prevent damage to the hide. You can use a metal file to sharpen (or dull) the edge of the tool to meet your specific needs. It is better to start with a tool that is a little duller than you think you will need, and try it out, and then gradually sharpen it a little bit at a time, until you achieve the scraping edge that is just right for you.

5. **Drawknife:** This is the same tool I used in 1975 when I was scraping the bark off pine trees to build a rustic log cabin. This bark removal tool also works exceptionally well for scraping the hair and the flesh off an animal hide. First, however, let me explain how to use a drawknife to remove the bark from a pine log. The reason I wish to explain this procedure is because you may decide to create your own log scraping beam from a pine tree and a drawknife will allow you to remove the bark from the tree with the least amount of effort. Begin by sawing the log to the proper length which will usually be about six feet long. Support one end of the log on a tree stump and allow the other end of the log to rest on the ground. Then you can straddle the log and sit on the log and begin scraping the end of the log that is elevated. Continue to scrape about halfway down the log by gradually shifting your sitting position further down the log. Then rotate the log on top of the stump and scrap some more. Rotate

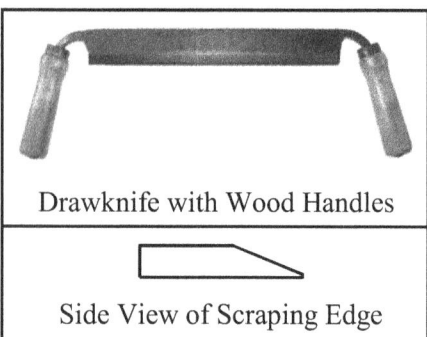

Drawknife with Wood Handles

Side View of Scraping Edge

and scrape again. Continue rotating the log on the tree stump until all the bark is off one end of the log. Then put the other end of the log on the tree stump and repeat the process. This method allows you to sit comfortably on the log with your feet on the ground, one on each side of the log, and you are able to reach the log without having to bend too far forward. This allows you to complete the task with the least amount of effort and the least amount of fatigue. A drawknife is used in the same way to scrape an animal hide except you do not sit on the log. The scraping beam will either be vertical or horizontal and you will be standing upright as you scrape the animal hide. The drawknife if the picture has wood handles that are at a slight angle to the scrapping blade. This design is better if you have the scrapping beam at waist level on a horizontal level. Another model of drawknife has the wood handles at approximately a 90 degree angle to the blade. This design is better if you have the scrapping beam at chest level in an upright position.

6. **A Curved Scraping Tool that is Thick and Narrow:** This type of professional quality scraping tool is designed for scraping hides. Therefore it requires the least amount of effort to use it. It can be purchased from some of the same stores that sell hide tanning supplies.

Although most of the above tools have a tapered scraping edge that is between 6 to 13 inches long, only the center 2 or 3 inches of the scraping edge will make contact with the hide on the curved scraping beam. That is why the center of a lawnmower blade can be used to make a good scraping tool.

The bottom surface of the scraping tool must be flat. The top surface of the scraping tool will need to be beveled at an angle towards the bottom surface of the tool as shown in the previous sketches of the side views of the scraping edge. Do not put any type of angle or bevel on the bottom surface of the tool. The bottom surface of the scraping tool must slide straight across the surface of the hide and lift the unwanted flesh and hair off the hide onto the beveled surface of the tool.

Tool Sharpness: One mistake new tanners sometimes make is using a scraping tool that is too sharp or too dull. The scraping edge of the tool needs to be a little dull but not too dull. If the scraping edge can be used to easily whittle wood then it is too sharp. If the scraping edge will just barely scrape a very thin layer of wood from a log if you use moderate pressure then it has the correct sharpness (or dullness). If the scraping edge will slide across a piece of wood while applying moderate pressure without removing any wood then it is too dull. If the tool is too sharp then use an Arkansas sharpening stone and hold the stone at a 90 degree angle to the blade and move the stone along the edge to gradually dull the scraping tool just a little bit. In other words, instead of using the stone to put a sharp edge on the tool use the stone to take the sharp edge off the scraping tool. If the scraping tool is too dull then an ordinary metal file may be used to gradually enhance the sharpness of the edge of the scraping tool.

Scraping Basics

Always wear rubber, vinyl, or latex gloves when handling an animal hide.

Scraping needs to be outdoors because the flesh and the hair needs to fall on a tarp on the ground below the scraping beam.

Do not scrape a hide in the sun. Always scrape in a shaded area unless it is really cold outdoors.

There are two basic ways to scrap a hide: **Dry Scraping** and **Wet Scraping**. The advantages and disadvantages of these two methods were discussed in Chapter 5.

The procedure used to dry scrape a hide is basically the same procedure that is used to wet scrape a hide. The primary difference between dry scraping and wet scraping is the amount of moisture in the hide. When a hide is dry scraped there is usually just barely enough residual moisture in the hide for the hide to be flexible so that it can be scraped without damaging the hide. When a hide is wet scraped the hide is saturated with water and the hide is extremely flexible and there is a much smaller chance that the hide will be damaged as it is being scraped.

Do not allow the scraping tool to slide or slip sideways while scraping because the tool could quickly cut all the way through the hide. Always scrape in a straight motion down the hide and be careful to not let the tool begin to slip to the right or left during a scraping motion.

Scraping Motion: Scrape in short motions between six to twelve inches in length depending on what feels comfortable to you. When scraping either the flesh side or the hair side of a hide each scraping motion should begin with the scraping edge firmly in position at the top of the area to be scraped, and then you should apply as much pressure as you can to the scraping tool and either push or pull the tool across the hide between six to twelve inches in a straight line and then come to a complete and abrupt stop with the scraping edge of the tool still beneath the flesh or hair that is being scraped. The scraping tool is then backed out of its groove and repositioned a little to the right of the strip that was just scraped and about even with the original starting position on the previous scrape or just a little above the previous starting position to make sure you have good overlap at the top as well as on the side. The next strip that will be scraped should overlap the strip that was just scraped by approximately one inch. This is similar to the way you would use a lawnmower to mow a yard. The wheels on one side of the lawnmower are inside the strip that was just mowed so the mowing blade overlaps the previous strip of mowed grass by a little bit. This overlapping process completely removes all the grass without leaving a thin strip of grass sticking straight up between two adjacent mowed areas. This same procedure is used when scraping a hide so that thin layers of flesh or hair are not left on the hide between each strip. Always overlap each new strip so that you scrape a small portion of the previous strip a second time and then stop the scrape at approximately the same position between six to twelve inches down the hide beside the last place you stopped. Continue this process until you have reached the outside edge of the hide and then shift the hide on the scraping beam and begin the scraping process again. Repeat until the entire surface of the hide has been scraped. Always scrape with the hide surface flat against the beam so there are no folds or creases in the area you intend to scrape.

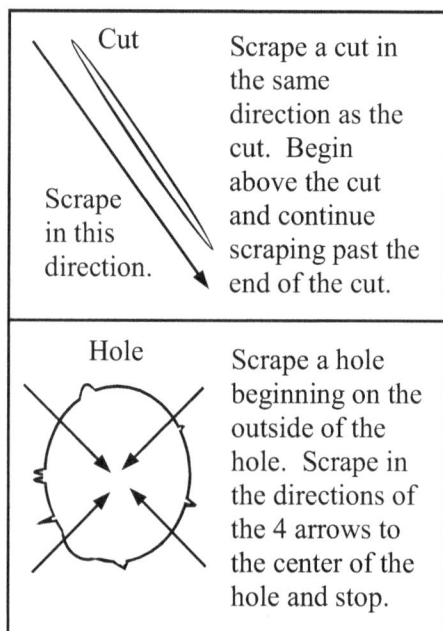

Cut

Scrape in this direction.

Scrape a cut in the same direction as the cut. Begin above the cut and continue scraping past the end of the cut.

Hole

Scrape a hole beginning on the outside of the hole. Scrape in the directions of the 4 arrows to the center of the hole and stop.

Holes, Cuts, and Scars: The exception to scraping is a straight line is when you encounter a hole, cut, or scar in the animal hide. Always scrape in the direction of the imperfection instead of against it. In other words, if there is a cut from left to right across the hide and you are scraping from neck to tail then just before you get to the cut you should stop scraping, lift up your scraping tool, and then scrape the cut area of the hide from right to left in the same direction as the cut. On holes you should scrape gently from the outside of the hole towards the center of the hole by lifting your scraping tool up and continuously moving it around the outside edge of the hole so each short gentle scrape is towards the center of the hole. The objective is to not make the cut, scar, or hole area any bigger or worse than it already is.

Blood Stain Spots: Depending on how the animal met its death there may or may not be blood stain spots on the hide. If there are blood stains then you should scrape them as hard as you can to remove as much of the blood stain from the hide as possible. It is normally not possible to completely scrape off a blood stain but it is possible to make a blood stain lighter in color on the hide.

Waste Material: As you scrape a hide the top edge of the scraping tool will gradually accumulate some fat, flesh, or hair on its surface. This waste material should be periodically removed so the scraping edge can make good contact with the next area that needs to be scraped. This waste material is usually damp and it will cling to the tool and it is very difficult to shake off. The easiest way to clean the edge of the tool is to pull it across the underside of the scraping beam so the waste material is pushed off the end of the scraping tool onto the tarp that is on the ground below the scraping beam. However, if you are scraping off fat then it is easier to clean the top surface of the tool by pulling it across the top edge of a cook pot so the fat falls into the cook pot.

Chapter Eight

Scraping the Flesh Side of an Animal Hide

Lay the hide across the beam with the hair side against the beam and the flesh side facing you. Some tanners recommend scraping the hair side first but I recommend scraping the flesh side first.

The flesh side of the hide is easier to scrape from side to side instead of from neck to tail (or from tail to neck). Scrape from the center of the hide towards the outside edge of the hide. Unless the hide is relatively small you will not be able to scrape from the center of the hide to the edge of the hide in one motion. You will probably need to reposition the hide on the scraping beam at least once or twice before you reach the outside edge of the hide. When you reach the outside edge of the hide then shift the position of the hide on the scraping beam and start your next scraping motion near the center of the hide beside the area you just scraped. Repeat this process until you have removed all the flesh and membrane from one-half of the hide (either the right half or the left half of the hide). Then rotate the hide on the beam and do the other half of the hide.

Scrape the flesh and the fat off the hide using your scrapping tool in a smooth motion. Only scrape off as much flesh and fat as you can comfortably remove in one smooth motion.

On animals that have a lot of fatty tissue, such as raccoons and opossums, you will need to be a little more careful when scraping the flesh side of the hide because of the amount of soft fat tissue that is present. If you use too much pressure then you can cut down through the hide.

If the weather is near or below freezing then the hide can be laid flat on the scraping beam for a short period of time in the cold weather and the entire hide can be allowed to partially freeze a little bit. The flesh and the thin layer of membrane are usually easier to scrape off a partially frozen hide.

Amount of Pressure: All hides are similar in some ways and all hides are unique in other ways. Therefore it is important to determine the correct amount of pressure that should be used on each hide when you first begin to scrape that hide so you will only need to scrape each area one time. After you make that first scrape down a small section of a hide you should stop and carefully examine the area you just scrapped.

1. **Not Enough Pressure:** If you can still see membrane or flesh then you need to scrape that same area a second time using a little more pressure. That also means each future scrape should be with a little more pressure so you only need to scrape each area one time.
2. **Too Much Pressure:** If it looks like you have scraped too deeply and you have removed some of the inner fiber network that should have been left on the hide then you are using too much pressure. You need to use less pressure when you scrape the area that is adjacent to the area you just scrapped. Then examine that new area to see if you are now using the correct amount of pressure.
3. **Correct Pressure:** If you can just see the inner fiber layer and you do not see any membrane or flesh remaining then you are using the correct amount of pressure for that particular hide.

Animal Fat or Fell: The white layer of body tissue that adheres to the inside of an animal's hide has a variety of different names but it is basically just the animal's thin layer of fat. As you slowly and gradually scrape the fat off the inside of a hide you should put that fat into a cold cook pot. Pull the edge of the scraping tool across the top edge of a cook pot so the fat falls off the tool into the cook pot. After you have scrapped all the fat off the inside of the hide you will need to examine the fat carefully and remove any lean pieces of pink or red flesh that might still be clinging to the fat. Also remove any foreign particles or dirt that might be present by rinsing the fat with some clean water if necessary. Then render (melt) the fat so it can be safely used at a later date in a variety of different ways. Rendered deer fat can be used to lightly oil your footwear, or to oil a homemade bow, or to make soap or candles. Deer fat has a higher melting point than beef or pork fat and therefore it can be used to make good soap and good candles.

Thoroughly rinse the hide in clean water after you have scraped the flesh side of the hide. You may rinse the hide in a moving stream or with a garden hose. The objective is to remove any small particles of flesh that have been scraped off the hide but are still clinging to the hide. Then proceed to the next chapter on soaking.

Chapter Nine

Second Water Soak Before Scraping the Hair Side of an Animal Hide

If you do **not** wish to remove the hair from a hide, such as a bear hide, then skip this chapter and the next two chapters. Instead go directly to Chapter 12 on how to soak a hide in a solution of water and vinegar.

Objective: The purpose of the second water bath is to loosen the hair on the outside of the hide so that the hair can be scrapped off the hide using only a moderate amount of effort. The glues and other chemicals in the hide will gradually leech out of the hide into the water. This means the hair will gradually become looser and you will eventually notice that a small amount of the hair can be pulled out of the hide using your fingers. This is similar to the hair shedding process that many animals go through when the weather turns warm in the spring of the year.

Caution: Acids will cause the hair layer to tighten. Therefore acids will help the hide to retain its hair or its fur. Therefore never add anything that is acidic to the second water bath.

Time Required: The soaking process takes an average of three days. But it is possible that it could be completed in only two days or it could take as long as ten days.

Bucking: Many native American Indian tribes used a water and wood ash solution to help loosen the hair on their animal hides. Soaking an item in water that contains wood ashes is called **bucking.** Wood ashes are alkaline so the water and ash solution is also alkaline.

When the wood ashes are stirred in some water a weak lye solution is created. Lye is caustic so you must wear some rubber, latex, or vinyl gloves when handling the lye water and when you are handling the hide after the hide has been saturated with the lye water.

Do not use an aluminum container for the lye solution of water and wood ashes. The lye will adversely react with the aluminum and the aluminum will contaminate the lye solution and the animal hide.

A weak solution of lye made from water and wood ashes will yield all the following benefits:

1. Wood ashes contain some of the same chemicals as wood smoke. While soaking in the water and ash solution the hide will absorb the solution and begin to swell and some of the glue and other chemicals will more easily leech out of the hide. This makes it easier to scrape the hair layer off the hide. However, the lye will not dissolve the hair nor will it make the hair just fall off the hide.

2. The chemicals in the wood ash will enhance the tanning process that will be done later. The tanning chemicals will more easily and completely penetrate the hide when it is time to tan the hide using brains, or eggs, or oil and soap, or acorns.

3. It will make the hide easier to soften and stretch into a comfortable buckskin.

Quantity of Wood Ashes: You will need approximately one gallon of wood ashes for a medium size hide and about two gallons of wood ashes for a large hide. You will need about 1/4 less ash from a hardwood fire, such as oak. You will need about 1/4 more ash from a softwood fire, such as pine. Do not change the water during the first 24 hours. Allow the wood ash solution to penetrate the hide as completely as possible.

When to Add Wood Ashes: Wood ashes are only mixed into the water the first day. After the first day the water and ash solution is discarded and clean water is then used to complete the soaking process.

Soaking Without Wood Ashes: Most tanners do not add wood ashes to the water in which they soak their animal hides. Therefore if you do not have access to the ashes from a wood fire then you may use clean water without any ashes added.

Soaking Container: Put the hide in the bottom of a large plastic garbage can or container, such as a 5 to 13 gallon can or bucket. Do not use an aluminum container if you are using wood ashes. Pour enough water into the container to completely cover the hide. After you have covered the hide with water, lift the hide out of the water, shake out any folds, and push the hide back below the surface of the water. Then remove the hide a second time, shake out any folds, and push it back under the water again. The objective is to make sure both sides of the hide are soaked with water and that there are not any dry spots in any areas where the hide is folded over onto itself. Place one large heavy rock, or several medium size heavy rocks, on top of the hide inside the container to keep the hide completely submerged under the water while it is soaking.

Check the hide every few hours during the day to make sure the hide has not slipped out from beneath the rocks and the hide is floating on top of the water. If the hide is floating on top of the water then the hide will be making contact with the air and it will begin to rot. Therefore it is important to check the hide every few hours during the day when it is in the water bath to make sure it is still under the water to avoid potential rotting problems. When you check the hide you should also stir the hide inside the water bath to help the wood ash solution penetrate more thoroughly into the hide.

Changing the Water: Once per day, remove the hide from the container and pour out the old water. Return the hide to the container and cover it with fresh water. Each day make sure that both sides of the hide are soaked with water before you place the rock, or rocks, back on top of the hide.

If you are using a water and wood ash solution then do not change the water for 24 hours. However, beginning the second day it is better to change the water twice each day, once in the morning and once in the evening. This will decrease the total amount of time the hide needs to soak because the chemical reaction of the hide with the water will begin with a fresh start each time the hide comes in contact with clean water. As the water gradually becomes full of chemicals the rate at which the chemicals can leech out of the hide decreases.

Test Scrape the Hide: Each time you change the water in the bucket check the hide to see if the hair is a little loose on the outside of the hide. If the hair will scrape off the hide using moderate effort then the hide has finished its water bath. However, if it very difficult to scrape the hair off the hide then the hide needs to continue in its water bath for at least one more day.

How to Scrape: Read Chapter 10 on how to scrape the hair side of an animal hide. Each day you should attempt to scrape the hair off the hide following the instructions in Chapter 10. The hair will not just fall off the hide and it will not be easy to scrape the hair off the hide. However, after each day of soaking you should notice that the hair becomes a little easier to scrape off the hide. When you can scrape the hair off the hide using a moderate amount of effort then the hide is ready to be scraped.

Time Estimates: The total time the hide needs to spend in the water bath depends primarily on the thickness of the hide. Thicker hides need more soaking time. But the soaking time also depends on the type of hide (elk or deer), when the animal was killed (summer months or winter months), where the animal was killed (cold climate or warm climate), and the temperature of the water bath. The following time estimates may be used as a general guide but there are too many variables to yield a consistent time that will be appropriate for all hides in all situations:

a. Temperature 70°F or higher (or 21°C or higher): When the air temperature, and the water temperature, is in the 70s or higher then two or three days of soaking will usually loosen the hair.

b. Temperature 50° to 69°F (or 10° to 20°C): When the air temperature, and the water temperature, is between 50 to 69 degrees, then three to six days of soaking will usually loosen the hair.

c. Temperature 33° to 49F° (or 1° to 9°C): When the air temperature, and the water temperature, is between 33 to 49 degrees, then six to ten days of soaking will usually loosen the hair.

	°C	°F
A higher temperature will require less soaking time.	38	100
	32	90
	27	80
	21	70
	16	60
	10	50
A lower temperature will require more soaking time.	4	40
	-1	30
	-7	20
	-12	10
	-18	0

Maximum Soaking Time: Do not soak a hide for more than ten days. It is okay to leave the hide in the water for ten days even in warm weather but more than ten days in any type of weather will usually destroy the hide.

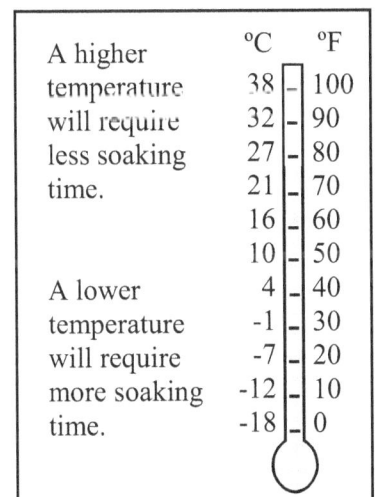

The longer a hide soaks in a water bath the more the hide will begin to smell. Each day in the water bath will increase the bad smell of the hide. Therefore it is better to scrape the hair side of the hide a little too soon instead of waiting too long. Scraping a little too soon will only result in a little more effort on your part. However, waiting too long will result in a rotten hide that will have to be buried because it will have become infectious.

Therefore a shorter time in the water bath is better than more time in the water bath. If you can keep your room temperature, and the water bath temperature, at 50°F (or 10°C) or higher, then the water bath time can be minimized. The longer the hide remains in the water bath the greater the chance the hide may begin to rot in different spots on the hide. You will be able to see the bad spot on the hide and you will also be able to smell it. If the hide has several spots that have begun to rot then the entire hide will need to be thrown away. However, if the area that has begun to rot is very small and it is near the outside edge of the hide then you may be able to cut it off and discard the small rotted piece of the hide and salvage the rest of the hide.

Chapter Ten

Scraping the Hair Side of an Animal Hide

After soaking the hide in a water bath you are now ready to scrape the hair side of the hide. Scraping the hair side of an animal hide is called "graining."

Before you begin scraping the hair side of the hide you should carefully inspect the flesh side of the hide to find any holes or cuts in the hide. When you find a hole or a cut or a scar on the flesh side of the hide then turn the hide over and trim the hair away from that area on the hair side so it will be easy to see when you are scraping the hair side of the hide. You may trim the hair with some scissors or a knife. You do not need to shave the hair off. You only need to cut the hair short around each area that contains a hole or a cut or a scar. Later when you are scraping the hair side of the hide you will be able to easily see the short hair and you can scrape each of those areas in the manner that is appropriate for the type of imperfection that is in the hide.

If you scrape level with the roots of the hair and you leave the flesh (grain) just below the roots on the hide then you will be creating leather instead of buckskin. When it dries leather is stiff and hard. If you need shoe leather then do not scrape the grain off the hide but stop scraping approximately level to the bottom of the roots of the hair.

If you scrape the flesh (grain) a little below the roots of the hair then you will be creating buckskin instead of leather. When it dries buckskin is soft and flexible and it can be used to make clothing. In most of the very old hide tanning literature the removal of the grain was called "frizing."

When you scrape the hair side you will need to remove the hair and the thin layer of skin directly below the roots of the hair. This thin layer of skin is called the "scarf skin." It must be scraped off the hide with the hair because any scarf skin that is left on the hide will result in a rough spot on the final finished buckskin and this is undesirable.

How will you know if you have scraped the hair side deep enough?

1. **Deep Enough:** If the area you have just scraped does not contain any hair roots (stubble) then you have scrapped deep enough.

2. **Not Deep Enough:** If you can see some of the hair roots still attached to the hide then you have not scraped deep enough and you need to scrape that area again. Or if the hide feels rough or stubbly when you run your hand across the area you just scraped then you did not scrape deep enough.

If you do not scrape off the flesh (grain) below the hair then that area will appear white on the buckskin. It will not properly absorb the brain tanning solution, and it will not absorb the wood smoke, and the area will be hard and stiff on the finished buckskin. This is extremely undesirable so it is important to remove all the grain and not just most of it.

However, when you are first learning how to remove the grain it is better to make the mistake of leaving a little too much grain on the hide than to scrape too deeply into the hide. If you scrape too deeply then the hide will be too thin and it will have a shorter life expectancy. But if you leave a little too much grain on the hide then that excess grain can be removed later by sanding it when the hide is stretched and softened. Although this will create some extra work later it is better than producing a low quality buckskin that you will not be happy with.

Graining is the most labor intensive step in the production of buckskins. An average size hide will usually require between three to six hours of hard labor to properly remove the grain. If you become exhausted before you have finished graining then put the partially scraped hide back into a water bath until you regain your strength and then you can complete the scraping process the next day.

A hide is ready to be scraped of hair and grain if the hair side of the hide feels a little spongy or mushy.

The most difficult area to scrape is the neck and down the center of the back about halfway to the tail. Therefore it is usually better to start scraping on either the left side or the right side of the hide and then gradually work your way over to the other side of the hide. After the neck and the top half of the middle of the back has been scraped some tanners will turn the hide at a 90 degree angle on the beam and scrape those difficult areas again in a crosswise direction.

You will also notice that the hair and skin requires more effort (pressure) to remove at the neck and down the center of the back. As you gradually work away from these areas it will take less pressure to completely remove the skin and the hair from the hide.

Place the hide on the beam with the flesh side against the beam and the hair side facing you. The hair side is easier to scrape from the neck to the tail or from the center of the hide to its left and right sides. This is the direction in which the hair is growing and the hair will be lying against the hide in these directions. If you scrape in these directions then you can get beneath the root of the hair and you will be able to scrape off the entire length of each hair. But if you scrape against the way the hair is lying on the hide then you will frequently shave the hair off above its root and the root of the hair will remain in the hide to cause problems later.

The most challenging part of scraping the hair side of a hide is to get a good start. If you simply try to scrape the hair off then your scraping tool will slide across the hair and you will not be able to force the edge of the scraping tool under the layer of hair. To overcome this problem you will need to create a starting spot on the hide using some scissors or your skinning knife. Trim the hair close to the hide in a rectangular area that measures about two inches wide and about four inches long at the spot where you wish to begin scraping. Do not shave the hair smooth to the hide. Instead simply trim off most of the hair so the edge of your scraping tool can make contact with the skin portion on the hair side of the hide instead of the hair itself. Now use your skinning knife to make a two inch long straight but very shallow cut across the top of the rectangle area you just trimmed to a depth just below the roots of the hair. Do not cut through the hide. Do not cut through the hide. Do not cut through the hide. Only cut a starting position for your scraping tool that is a tiny bit below the roots of the hair. Now put your skinning knife aside because you will not be needing it again.

Place the scraping edge of your scraping tool into the shallow cut you just made and use a much strength as you possibly can to scrape the hair side of the hide the entire length of the four inch long rectangle that is in front of the scraping tool. Then abruptly stop scraping with the scraping edge of the tool pressed hard against the hide below the skin and the hair. Now relax the pressure on the tool and withdraw the scraping tool from the hide. Closely examine the short rectangle you just scrapped. The skin and hair should be piled up at the end of the rectangle and you should be able to see a white streak down the center of the rectangle you just scraped. That white streak is the hide. On each side of the white steak you will see a slightly darker streak that runs the entire length of the area you just scraped. These two slightly darker areas will be a little higher than the white streak because they both still contain some water and a very thin layer of skin that needs to be scraped. You will now know exactly what you are trying to accomplish and what the entire hair side of the hide will look like when you have finished scraping all the hair and grain off the hide. If you do not see a white streak between two slightly darker raised streaks then you did not put enough pressure on the scraping tool the first time. If this is the situation then scrape that same exact area a second time using as much strength and pressure as you possibly can beginning at the top of the original rectangle and continuing to the bottom of the four inch long rectangle. If you used enough pressure the second time then this second scrape of the same area should reveal a white streak in the middle and two slightly darker raised streaks on each side of the white center streak.

Put the edge of your scraping tool onto the hide in the same position from where you just removed it but about 1/2 inch above the roll of body tissue in front of the scraping blade so you can apply pressure to the tool to get it back under the roll of body tissue that you just scraped. Now apply as much pressure as you possibly can and continue to scrape in a straight line for whatever distance you can comfortably reach and then stop with your scraping tool buried beneath the hair and the grain. Withdraw your scraping tool and transfer the scraping tool to a position beside the beginning of the original two inch by four inch area that you trimmed of hair. As you look down at the area you just scraped you should see a white streak in the middle of the scrapped area and a slightly darker raised area on each side of the white streak. You now need to scrape that slightly darker area on either the right side or the left side of your original scrape. If you decide to continue on the right side then you should work the entire right side of the hide until you reach the outside edge of the hide. When you reach the outside edge of the hide then you can return to the other side of your original first scrape and scrape that other side of the hide beginning at the slightly darker raised area on the left side of the area that you first scraped.

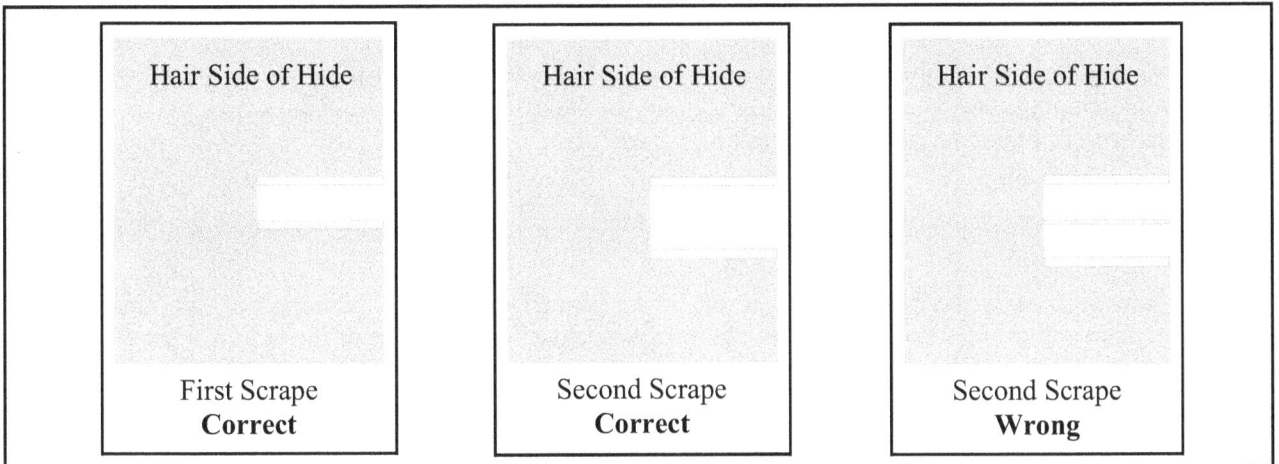

Hair Side of Hide	Hair Side of Hide	Hair Side of Hide
First Scrape **Correct**	Second Scrape **Correct**	Second Scrape **Wrong**

The slightly darker raised area that you can see contains water and body tissue that still needs to be removed. In order to completely remove the slightly darker raised area you will need to overlap each of your scraping strokes about 1/2 inch onto the white raised area that has already been scraped clean. This is similar to the way a person would mow a lawn of grass. Most people will mow a straight line for a specific distance using a lawnmower. Then another straight line is mowed immediately beside the first straight line in the opposite direction but the wheels of the lawnmower are allowed to overlap the first strip that was cut by an inch or two in order to avoid a long strip of grass that stands straight up between the two strips of mowed lawn. This is the same principle as scraping a hide and you should place your scraping tool at the start of each new scrape so that the new scrape overlaps the previous scrape by approximately 1/2 inch. Each new scrape should completely eliminate the slightly darker raised area that was left behind by the previous scrape. If you will overlap each new stroke onto the previous stroke then when you finish you will have a really nice hide that is clean and smooth over the entire hair side of the hide.

Do not experiment with the hide and scrape a different section of the hide to determine how difficult that section will be and what the hide will look like in that area. If you keep moving around on the hide then the slightly darker raised area that is beside a nice clean white streak will gradually dry out and it will no longer appear darker than the white strip that has just been properly scraped. Later when you return to an area that you haven't scraped for awhile then you will not be able to easily see what needs to be scraped. And when you finish scraping a new strip you will not be able to just look at it and verify that you have not left a very thin narrow layer of skin on the hide because the entire strip that you just scraped will be white. But if you always immediately scrape a new strip beside the strip that you just scraped then you can easily see if you have removed all the skin from that area or if your scraping blade slipped just a little bit to one side and you missed a very narrow 1/16 inch wide darker strip between two white strips of hide. When you can easily see those very narrow darker strips that you will occasionally miss then it is very easy to immediately clean them off by scraping that small area again before you begin a new strip that still has hair on it.

Continue to adjust the hide on the scraping beam so you can scrape an adjoining section of the hide until you have completely scraped to the outside edge of the hide. Then shift the hide on the scraping beam so you can continue scraping the hair off the adjoining section of hide. Continue this process of gradually shifting the hide on the scraping beam until you eventually finish the entire hide. Remember it is easier to scrape in the direction that the hair lies down flat against the hide from neck to tail, or from the backbone towards the belly.

It is not unusual for the hair scraping process to take between three to six hours. During this time the hide will gradually begin to dry out. When you notice that the hide is become too dry and it is becoming more difficult to see the slightly darker raised areas beside a white streak that has been scraped clean, then submerge the entire hide under some clean water in a big bucket for about 15 minutes and take a short break while the hide reabsorbs some necessary moisture.

Be careful when scraping holes or cuts or scars in the hide.

Holes: Scrape the hide from the outside of a hole towards the center of the hole. In other words, keep shifting your scraping tool around the outside edge of the hole so that you are always making short scrapes towards the center of the hole (see the illustration on page 30).

Cuts and Scars: Scrape a cut and a scar in the same direction as the cut or scar. Do not scrape sideways across a cut because your scraping blade could catch in the cut and make the cut worse (see the illustration on page 30).

After the entire hide has been scraped it should be soaked in clean water for about two hours. Then remove the hide and examine the hair side of the hide very closely. Any areas of the hide that are darker than the adjacent areas will still contain flesh (grain) that needs to be scraped off. Scrape those areas again to remove the flesh so the finished buckskin will be of a uniform thickness and flexibility across its entire surface.

Summary

The more hair and flesh that you remove at this step will make the hide easier to soften and stretch. However, it is better to leave a very thin layer of flesh on the hide than to scrap so deeply that you cut through the hide or that you make the hide too thin in one area.

When you are finished scraping both sides of the hide you should have a hide that appears to have a smooth surface on both sides of the hide.

You will need to properly dispose of the hair and skin that you remove from the hide or it will begin to rot and attract flies and other pests and create a health hazard. Do not add the waste material to a compost pile because it contains meat that may contain pathogens that can be fatal to humans. Instead bury the waste at least six inches below ground.

Chapter Eleven

Aging an Animal Hide

If the hide was put into storage and it was allowed to dry for several months before you began processing the hide then it does not need to be dried again at this time. But if you began processing the hide soon after it was acquired then drying at this time is highly desirable.

After scraping the hair and the grain off the hide the hide should be allowed to thoroughly dry in the air by hanging it across a rope. Do not hang a hide on anything that is made of metal because rust will begin to attack the hide and ruin it. Be sure to hang the hide in a safe place where dogs and wild animals will not be able to get to the hide.

Aging or drying the hide has the following advantages:

1. All the water trapped inside the pores of the hide will evaporate.
2. The natural animal glues and the other undesirable compounds inside the hide will gradually break down.
3. It will be easier to remove the last bit of membrane from the flesh side of the hide.
4. The hide will more completely absorb the brain tanning solution.
5. It will be easier to stretch and soften the hide.
6. The hide will more completely absorb the wood smoke.

Aging a hide will result in a superior quality, softer, more flexible buckskin that can be used to make high quality buckskin clothing. About three months is the minimum drying time and twelve months is the maximum drying time. If you can allow the hide to air dry for twelve months then you will produce the highest quality buckskin. However, if you need the hide immediately to make buckskin clothing then you can air dry the hide for about one week and then move on to the next step in the hide tanning process.

Chapter Twelve

Third Water Soak in Clean Water
or in a Solution of Ammonium Sulfate Fertilizer and Water
or in a Solution of Vinegar and Water

Always wear rubber, vinyl, or latex gloves when handling an animal hide.

The hide needs to be completely submerged in a water bath again. Use the same type of clean water you used previously and the same rocks to keep the hide submerged below the surface of the water.

The amount of soaking water required will vary depending on the size of the hide (or hides) that you wish to process. For a small deer hide about three gallons of warm water will completely cover the hide. For an average size deer hide about four gallons of warm water will completely cover the hide. For a large deer hide about five gallons of warm water will completely cover the hide. The water should feel warm to your touch but not hot. **Never** use hot water to soak an animal hide.

A six gallon plastic bucket may be used as the soaking container unless you are processing a large hide and then a ten gallon or larger plastic container may be used.

The hide may be soaked using any of the following three methods:

1. Clean water with **nothing** added. The total soaking time will be somewhere between three to seven days.
2. Clean water with 1/16 cup of pure **ammonium sulfate fertilizer** added per gallon of water required. The total soaking time is about 12 hours.
3. Clean water with 1/8 cup of **vinegar** added per gallon of water required. The total soaking time is about 15 minutes.

The only two chemicals that should be added to the water bath are vinegar or pure ammonium sulfate fertilizer. Do not add both chemicals to the same water bath. However, if you wish you may soak the hide in a water and vinegar solution first, and then soak the same hide in a water and ammonium sulfate solution next.

Hides that are allowed to soak in a water and chemical solution are noticeably softer than hides that are soaked in water without any chemicals added. Therefore you should add one of the two chemicals to the water bath if you have the correct chemicals available. However, if you do not have either of the two recommended chemicals then you can still create good buckskin clothing but that clothing will not feel as soft as clothing made from buckskins that were soaked in a water and chemical solution.

There is a significant difference between the three soaking methods so each method will now be described in detail.

1. **Clean Water with Nothing Added:** The hide will need to soak for between three to seven days. Do not add anything to the water bath. Do not add any special chemicals or fabric softeners or soap or salt or anything else. Use clean water, such as rainwater, that does not contain any chemicals of any kind. The first day you may see blood, glue, and whatever else that was still inside the hide floating on top of the water or mixed in with the water. It is better to change the water twice each day, once in the morning and once in the evening. This will decrease the total amount of time the hide needs to soak because the chemical reaction of the hide with the water will begin with a fresh start each time the hide comes in contact with clean water. As the water gradually becomes full of chemicals the rate at which the chemicals can leech out of the hide decreases. Always remove the hide from the water container, pour out the nasty water, replace the hide, and cover it with clean water and one or more heavy rocks to keep the hide completely submerged below the surface of the water. This process will need to be continued for somewhere between three to seven days until the water does not contain a significant amount of discoloration when it is time to change the water. This is important because the water bath will remove almost all the remaining natural glue and other body chemicals that are still inside the hide and this will make the hide easier to process at the next step and it will result in a higher quality finished product.

When you remove the hide from the water bath for the last time you should immediately scrape the final residual membrane from the flesh side of the hide as described in the next chapter.

2. **Clean Water with Ammonium Sulfate Added:** Add 1/16 cup of pure ammonium sulfate fertilizer for each gallon of warm clean water that is required to completely submerge the hide. Use pure ammonium sulfate and do not use fertilizer with other ingredients included. Stir the ammonium sulfate so it completely dissolves in the warm water. Then put the hide in the solution, stir the hide, and then place a large rock on the hide to keep the hide completely below the top surface of the water. Three hours later remove the hide, rotate the hide, and drop the opposite end of the hide into the solution first, stir, and then weigh the hide down with the rock. Three hours later remove the hide, rotate the hide, and drop a different edge of the hide into the solution first, stir, and then weigh the hide down with the rock. Three hours later remove the hide, rotate the hide, and drop the final edge of the hide into the solution first, stir, and then weigh down the hide with the rock. After three more hours (or a total of twelve hours) remove the hide from the solution and discard the solution. When you remove the hide from the water and ammonium sulfate solution for the last time you should immediately scrape the final residual membrane from the flesh side of the hide as described in the next chapter.

3. **Clean Water with Vinegar Added:** The hide will need to soak for a total of about 15 minutes. Vinegar is acidic. This is the opposite of the alkaline in wood ashes. Vinegar should be added to the warm water before you submerge the hide. Any type of vinegar may be used, such as apple cider vinegar or distilled white vinegar. Use 1/8 of a cup of vinegar for each gallon of clean warm water that is needed to completely submerge the hide. Stir the vinegar until it is completely mixed with the water. Then immediately submerge the entire hide in the warm water and vinegar solution. Stir the hide around in the solution for about ten seconds and then lift the hide out of the bucket. Rotate the hide and drop the opposite end of the hide into the solution first. Stir the hide around in the solution for about ten seconds. Then put a heavy rock, or several heavy rocks, on top of the hide to keep the entire hide submerged below the top of the water and vinegar solution. After five minutes remove the rock, remove the hide from the solution, and drop a different edge of the hide into the solution first. Stir the hide in the solution for about 10 seconds and then place the rock back on top of the hide to keep the entire hide below the surface of the solution. After five more minutes remove the rock, remove the hide from the solution, and drop the last edge of the hide into the solution first. Stir the hide in the solution for about 10 seconds and then place the rock back on top of the hide to keep the entire hide below the surface of the solution. After five more minutes (or a total time of 15 minutes) remove the hide from the solution and discard the water and vinegar solution. However, if you have another hide to process then you may use this same solution again immediately. But if you are finished then pour out the solution. When you remove the hide from the water and vinegar solution for the last time you should immediately scrape the final residual membrane from the flesh side of the hide as described in the next chapter.

Chapter Thirteen

Scraping the Residual Membrane from the Flesh Side of an Animal Hide

This final scrape is to remove the last amount of membrane (fat) that might still be clinging to the flesh side of the hide. Hide tanners call this step "membraning."

Membrane is a thin layer of fatty tissue that clings to the flesh side of the hide. Because it consists of fatty tissue this thin layer of membrane should be scraped off the hide and rendered (melted) as soon as possible after you have finished scraping the hide so the fat can be used for a variety of practical purposes.

If you miss some membrane then that spot will crust over like plastic when the hide is put on the stretching frame and that portion of the hide will not stretch properly. It will also cause problems if the hide is rubbed across a softening cable. Finally, it will gradually collect into tiny itchy balls on the inside of the buckskin when it is made into clothing. Therefore it is important to take the time now to completely remove any residual membrane that is still clinging to the inside surface of the hide.

The hide should be soaking wet. Place the wet hide on the scraping beam. As you scrape the inside surface of the hide remember to overlap each scrape onto the previous scrape so that no part of the hide is missed. Scrape carefully and methodically so that every spot on the inside of the hide is scraped.

Some areas you scrape will have no membrane. But a different area may yield some membrane on the top surface of your scraping tool. This is fatty tissue and it should be wiped off the tool against the top inside edge of a steel cook pot so the fat can be melted and saved after you are finished scraping the hide.

There may be some dark spots on the hide from blood stains or from the wood ash solution and these spots cannot be completely scraped off. Therefore do not waste time scraping and scraping and scraping and scraping an area simply because it is a slightly different color than the rest of the hide.

When you are finished you should have a hide that has a smooth surface on both sides of the hide.

Chapter Fourteen

Dyeing a Hide a Different Color (Optional)

If you wish to change the color of a hide then the hide should be dyed before it is tanned and smoked. The tanning and smoking steps will help to set the color in the hide and the color will remain in the hide longer. However, after the buckskin clothing has been worn and washed many times, the color will gradually begin to fade from the buckskin clothing the same way that color gradually begins to fade from ordinary clothing.

If you dye a hide after it has been tanned and smoked then the color will wash out of the hide a lot quicker when compared to hides that were dyed prior to being tanned and smoked.

Chapter 17 explains some of the color shades you can expect when using different tanning agents, such as brains, eggs, and acorns. The information below is for other materials that can be used for dyeing.

1. **Orange or red:** Alder tree bark from young alder trees. (Do not remove too much bark or you may kill the tree.)
2. **Pink or slightly red:** Oak tree bark. (Do not remove the bark in a complete circle around the tree or you will kill the tree.)
3. **Yellow or tan:** Acorn caps or crowns.
4. **Light brown to dark brown:** Exterior hulls of black walnuts (not the shells).

Shred the material into short thin pieces. More material yields a darker shade than less material. Simmer the shredded material in some rainwater in a stainless steel pot for about two hours. Allow the dye water to cool. Strain the material out of the dye water. Add enough clean rainwater to cover the hide and stir the dye water. Then completely submerge the hide below the dye bath and stir the hide for five minutes. While wearing vinyl gloves, remove the hide, wring some of the dye water out of the hide back into the pot, and inspect the color of the hide. If you want a darker shade then put the hide back into the dye bath until you get the shade you desire. If the hide becomes too dark then there is no quick easy way to remove the extra color.

Do not boil the water in a cast iron pot because the cast iron may react with the material and it may add a very dark shade to the hide or turn the hide almost black. If you want the color black then put some steel wool pads in some vinegar and wait three weeks. Strain, add water, and dip the hide in the iron and vinegar bath.

Chapter Fifteen

Wringing Most of the Water Out of an Animal Hide

Now is the time to wring most of the water out of the hide. If the hide is too wet in some areas then the brain tanning solution will not penetrate those areas and a stiff spot will appear on the hide in each place that was too wet.

Wringing the water out of a hide does two things:

1. **Drying:** A hide that has been properly wrung will contain less moisture and the hide can be softened using less effort more quickly.

2. **Stretching:** As the hide is being wrung it is also being stretched and this helps the fibers to separate so the hide remains more flexible.

Wringing can be done twice as follows:

1. **Before brain tanning:** If the hide is wrung before brain tanning then more of the brain tanning solution is able to penetrate the hide. Wringing will also help to separate the fibers and open the pores in the hide so it is easier for the brain tanning solution to penetrate into the hide.

2. **After brain tanning:** If the hide is wrung after brain tanning then most of the moisture will be extracted from the hide and therefore the hide can be stretched on a stretching frame, or across a rope or cable, using less effort and the stretching and softening process can be completed quicker.

There are a multitude of different ways to wring the moisture out of a hide. However, the water in the hide will pass more easily from the flesh side of the hide to the hair side of the hide so it is better to roll the hide into a tube with the flesh side on the inside and the hair side on the outside of the roll.

The hide will need to be rolled into a tight double cylinder as follows:

1. **First Roll:** The hide should be rolled from the left side to the center of the hide. Then the right side of the hide should be rolled to the center of the hide as shown in the illustration. After the hide has been rolled into a tight double cylinder then the hide may be wrung using either (or both) of the following two methods:

   A Rolled Hide

   a. **Hand Twist:** Place the center of the hide over a fence rail, or tree branch, or any stationary strong thin cylindrical object. Then grasp the two loose ends of the hide with both hands. The hide should then be twisted from left to right into a tight spiral to squeeze as much water as possible out of the hide. As you twist the hide pull outwards on the hide to stretch it as you twist it. If you pull hard on the hide while you are twisting it then you can put more spirals in the hide before the hide folds over onto itself into a huge knot. After the hide has been twisted into a huge knot hold the hide in this position for about three minutes to allow as much water as possible to make its way out of the hide while it is under pressure. Then untwist the hide. Twist the hide a second time but this time twist from right to left in the opposite direction to form another spiral to squeeze as much water as possible out of the hide.

   b. **Pole Twist:** Place the center of the hide over a fence rail or similar stationary object. Then loop the two loose ends of the hide around a strong pole or a stick or a shovel handle. Then rotate the pole in a circle several times to twist the hide into a tight spiral. Pull hard on the pole as you are rotating the pole in order to add more spirals to the hide before it forms into a huge knot. After the hide has been twisted into a huge knot hold the hide in this position for about three minutes to allow as much water as possible to make its way out of the hide while it is under pressure. Then untwist the hide and rotate the pole in a circle in the opposite direction several times to twist the hide into a tight spiral. Hold the hide in this position for about three minutes. Then untwist the hide and remove the pole.

2. **Second Roll:** The hide should be unrolled. Pull the hide from every direction to help restore the hide to its original shape. The hide should then be rolled a second time from the neck to the middle of the hide and from the tail to the middle of the hide. Then repeat either or both of the above twisting procedures.

3. **Third Roll:** The hide should be unrolled. Pull the hide from every direction to help restore the hide to its original shape. The hide should then be rolled a third time from the front left leg toward the rear right leg but stop the roll in the middle of the hide. The opposite end of the hide should then be rolled from the rear right leg towards the front left leg until the hide meets the other side of the rolled hide in the middle of the hide. Then repeat either or both of the above twisting procedures.

The hide should now be unrolled. At this time you must pull the hide from every direction to help restore the hide to its original shape and to remove all the creases and wrinkles in the hide. This is easier to do if someone will grasp the opposite end of the hide and the two of you work together to stretch the hide between you with as much force and weight as you can put on the hide while still maintaining your grasp on the hide. You must switch your hand holds and move your hands along the outside edge of the hide and then stretch the hide from a different direction. Keeping switching your hand holds around the outside edge of the hide and stretching the hide from different directions until the hide looks like it did before you wrung the water out of the hide.

After the hide has been returned to its original smooth shape without any wrinkles or creases then you may use an old ragged clean dry towel to remove any water spots from the hide by patting the hide with the towel. When you are finished you may wash the old ragged towel with soap and water by itself. Do not put the old towel in with your other laundry because the old towel may have some germs or bacteria on it.

Now drape the smooth unwrinkled hide over a rope or other object in the shade for one day to allow the hide to continue to dry in the air. You must dry the hide in a place that it is protected from dogs and wild animals or the hide will not be there when you return. Do **not** dry the hide in the sun. The objective is **not** to expel 100% of the water from the hide. The objective is to expel most of the water from the hide while leaving the hide feeling a little bit damp or slightly moist to the touch, but not spongy.

Chapter Sixteen

Repairing a Hide Before Tanning and Smoking

Any holes or cuts in the hide will need to be repaired before the hide is tanned and smoked.

Some tanners prefer to repair a hide when it is totally dry. Other tanners prefer to repair a hide when it is very wet. The best option is a compromise between these two extremes. A hide should be repaired after most of the water has been wrung out of it but before the hide has completely dried out. The reasons are as follows:

1. Hides are easier to sew when they are a little wet. The sewing needle will more easily pass through a moist hide and leave a smaller needle hole than the same size needle when it is used on a dry hide.

2. If a hide is a little moist then the edges of holes and the edges of cuts will be easier to flatten out before they are sewn together. However, if a hide is too dry then the edges of holes and the edges of cuts will curl up and they will be very difficult to sew together.

3. If a hide is just a little moist then the imperfections in the hide will be reasonably close to their true size when the hide is dry. But if the hide is too wet then the imperfections in the hide will be swollen with water and it will be more difficult to visualize what the imperfections will look like when the hide is dry. This makes it more difficult to determine the best way to repair each imperfection.

4. If a hide is a little moist then the hide will shrink just a little bit as it dries. This will put a little pressure on the stitches and this will cause the edges of each repaired area to draw a little closer together and this will help to make each of the imperfections more difficult to see in the finished hide.

If possible sew holes, cuts, and score marks together using an ordinary handheld sewing needle and a good quality thread, such as buttonhole thread or quilting thread. Or you may use backstrap sinew and it will also do an excellent job of holding the holes, cuts, and score marks together.

In my opinion there is no manmade primitive tool that can compare to a steel sewing needle. There is also no manmade primitive substitute for a steel knife. Although many survival manuals and back-to-nature manuals suggest primitive substitutes for both of these two items, those substitutes are inferior in so many ways that I will not even mention them in this book. If you do not have a few good sewing needles and at least two good steel knives in your emergency backpack (or suitcase) then you will regret it later in life when you discover how often you need both of these simple basic tools on a regular basis.

When choosing a thread color you should consider the finished color of your buckskin and not the color of the hide before tanning and smoking. Almost all hides are white, or off-white, before they are tanned and smoked. After tanning and smoking most hides will be somewhere between a dark beige color and a light brown color. A hide will gradually take on a darker color the longer the hide is smoked. Some hides may also have a slight yellow tint and some may have a slight orange tint depending on the type of wood used during the smoking process. Therefore do not select white as your thread color for making repairs. If this is your first hide then select a thread color about halfway between beige and light brown. On the other hand, if this is not your first hide and you have some finished buckskins available then you can match your thread color as closely as possible to your average buckskin color based on your previous work. However, if there is some noticeable variability in your previous buckskin colors then a thread color about halfway between beige and light brown may be your best choice.

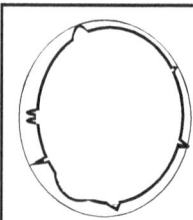

This hole has an irregular shape. Cut along the thin line drawn around the outside edges of the imperfections. This will make the hole a little bigger and more round and it will be much easier to sew closed.

If a hole has rough or jagged edges then the hole should be trimmed a little to make the outside edge around the hole relatively smooth and even.

If a score mark is more than 1/3 of the way through the hide then it should also be sewn at this time to prevent it from tearing apart later.

All repairs should be done on the flesh side of the hide so that the repair work is almost invisible from the hair side, which will be the outside of the buckskin when it is made into clothing.

If a hole or cut is within two inches of the outside edge of the hide then you will probably be able to arrange your pattern pieces on the hide in such a way that the hole or cut is not inside one of your pattern pieces. Therefore it will be cut off and removed when you cut your buckskin to make your clothes. Therefore most tanners do not bother to repair holes or cuts that are relatively close to the outside edge of the hide.

If a hole or cut is anywhere inside the large center area of the hide then it should be repaired at this time.

In order to minimize the amount of repair work, and to avoid wasting your time, if you know the type of clothing you are going to make with the finished buckskin, and if you have the actual pattern pieces handy, then you should temporarily place them on the hide and try to accomplish both of the following objectives simultaneously:

1. **Holes and Cuts:** Move the pattern pieces around on the flesh side of the hide so that most of the holes and cuts are not inside a pattern piece. In other words, when the buckskin is eventually cut into pieces to make clothing those holes and cuts will be discarded as small scraps of buckskin.

2. **Hide Utilization:** Move the pattern pieces around to utilize as much of the hide as possible. In other words, try to position the pattern pieces so that very little of the buckskin will be discarded as scrap pieces. However, do not align pattern pieces in a diagonal line across the hide. Align all the pattern pieces from neck to tail, or align all the pattern pieces from the left side to the right side of the hide.

When you have the pattern pieces in their optimal positions to achieve both of the above two objectives then use some ordinary straight pins to mark any holes or cuts or score marks that are on the outside of the pattern pieces. Make a rough sketch of how you have the pattern pieces arranged on the hide. Then remove the pattern pieces and sew up any holes, cuts, and score marks that don't have a pin beside them. Although the hide will stretch a little bit on the cable or stretching frame, you should still be able to align your pattern pieces in the same approximate locations on the finished buckskin after tanning and smoking.

You will need a piece of sewing thread or backstrap sinew that is about four times the length of the area you need to repair plus ten inches. The additional ten inches if for your first knot (four inches) and for your final three stitches (six inches) so that you have enough thread to push the needle through the hide and make your final knots.

Threading the Needle: Push one end of the thread through the eye of the handheld sewing needle. A handheld sewing needle has the point at one end of the needle and the thread hole (eye) at the opposite end of the needle. The easiest and quickest way to thread a needle is to use a needle threader or a thread guide (discussed in Chapter 26).

Pull the thread though the needle eye until the middle of the thread is in the eye hole and the two ends of the thread are hanging down at equal lengths from the eye hole. Then tie the two loose ends of thread together using a double knot.

First Stitch: Push the needle through the hide about 1/8 of an inch **before** the beginning of the cut or hole and pull most of the thread through the hole (see illustration on right). Now push the needle between the two pieces of thread just a little below the knot that you tied in the ends of the thread. Then gently pull the stitch tight so the knot is against the hide and there is no slack in the thread. Make your next stitch and pull it tight. Now stop and trim off the two short loose ends of the thread just a little above the knot. Do not cut too close to the knot or the knot may become unraveled.

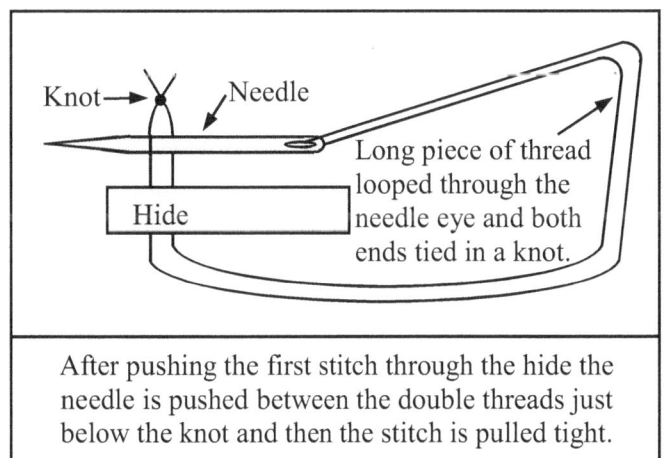

After pushing the first stitch through the hide the needle is pushed between the double threads just below the knot and then the stitch is pulled tight.

End of double thread from the previous stitch.

Long piece of double thread looped through the needle eye.

Hide

Needle →

After pushing the needle halfway through the hide, wrap the thread around the end of the needle two times and then pull the stitch tight.

Side View of Single Running Stitch Completed

Top View of Single Running Stitch Completed

Side View of Double Running Stitch in Progress

Top View of Double Running Stitch in Progress

Side View of Whip Stitch

Top View of Whip Stitch

Continue

Start

Top View of Buttonhole Stitch

Enlarged View of One Stitch

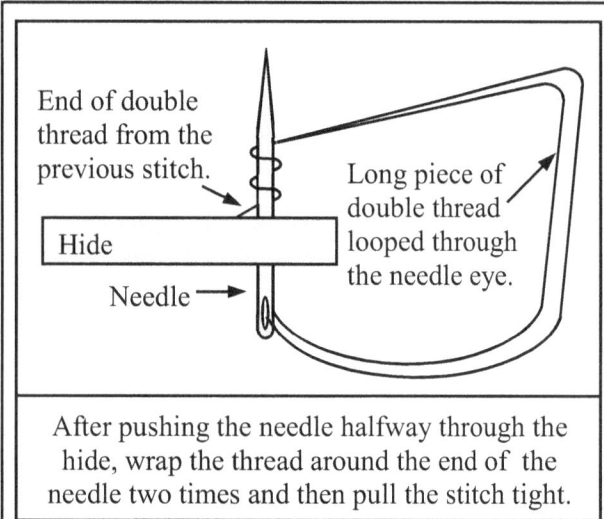

Last Three Stitches (see illustration): Push the needle halfway through the hide and stop. Now grasp the double thread that is still extending from the top of the previous stitch and wrap the double thread around the pointed end of the needle two times. Grasp the pointed end of the needle above the thread that was just double wrapped around the needle and pull the needle through the hide so the thread is now inside the two loops you just formed around the needle. Gradually pull the thread tight and it will form a knot on the top of the hide. Repeat this same exact sequence two more times so that when you are finished you have the double thread knotted on top of the hide in the last three stitches. Now cut the double thread about 1/4 inch above the last stitch in the hide.

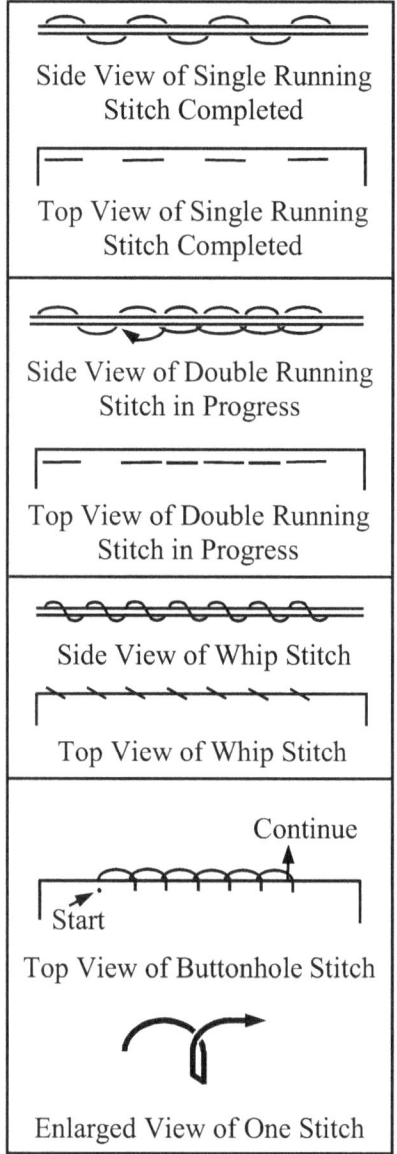

There are three basic stitching techniques as follows:

1. **Running Stitch or Top Stitch** (see illustration): The stitch alternates from one side of the hide to the other side of the hide. For example, push the needle from the top to the bottom of the area that needs to be repaired and pull the thread tight. Then move the needle a short distance to the right (about 1/4 inch) and push the needle from the bottom to the top of the area that needs to be repaired and pull the thread tight. Move the needle to the right and push it through from top to bottom and pull tight. Move the needle to the right and push it through from bottom to top and pull tight. In other words, each new stitch begins on the same side that the last stitch ended. The running stitch is preferred on seams where the edge of the seam will frequently be rubbed against other objects because the stitches do not overlap the edge of the seam and the stitches are therefore protected from abrasion. The strength of the running stitch can be enhanced when you reach the end of the seam by sewing back in the opposite direction to the beginning of the seam. This puts two sets of stitches in the same seam at the same spot. The illustration shows a double running stitch in progress.

2. **Whip Stitch or Overcast Stitch** (see illustration): The stitch always begins on the same side of the hide and the stitch always ends on the opposite side of the hide. For example, push the needle from the bottom to the top of the area that needs to be repaired and pull the thread tight. Then move the needle around the edge of the hide and a short distance to the right (about 1/4 inch) and push the needle from the bottom to the top again. Each new stitch will always start on the bottom and it will end on the top of the area that is being repaired. Holes, cuts, and score mark repairs should be done using the whip stitch. The whip stitch is a good choice on seams and hems that are on the inside of a garment and that are not be subject to a lot of abrasion.

3. **Buttonhole Stitch or Blanket Stitch** (see illustration): The stitch is similar to the whip stitch but the thread is passed under the previous stitch before the previous stitch is pulled tight against the edge of the material.

Repairing Cuts and Holes

To repair cuts or holes try to match the two sides of the cut or hole together as smoothly as possible. If necessary trim a little off the edges of the cut or hole so they mate together smoothly.

1. **Cuts:** A cut can only be sewn together in one logical direction.

2. **Ovals:** If the hole looks like an oval then pull the hole closed along its long diameter. While the oval shaped hole is folded in half and pulled at both ends, stitch the hole closed using a whip stitch.

3. **Round Holes:** If the hole is almost round then experiment with the hide by pulling the hole closed from the neck to the tail, and then from the right side to the left side, and then from the right foreleg to the left hind leg, and finally from the left foreleg to the right hind leg. Each time you pull the hole closed examine it to determine if the outside edges of the hole align smoothly together. When you pull the hole from one direction the outside

1. Top View of Oval Shaped Hole	2. Side View of Oval Shaped Hole Folded in Half
3. Oval Shaped Hole Pulled at Ends	4. Oval Shaped Hole Sewn Closed using a Whip Stitch

edges of the hole may curl and they may not mate together nicely. But when you pull the hole from a different direction the outside edges of the hole may align smoothly and evenly along the entire width across the hole. This is the direction that the hole should be held closed while it is being sewn.

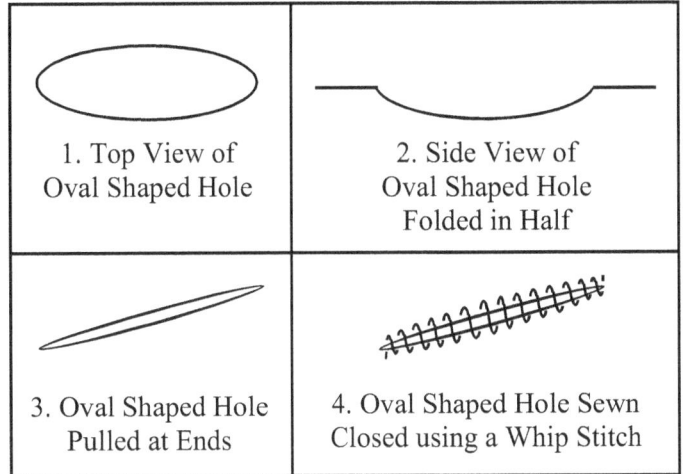

Chapter Seventeen

Tanning a Hide Using Brains, or Eggs, or Oil and Soap, or Acorns

Which Should Be Done First: Brain Tanning or Smoking?

One of the most controversial issues in making buckskins is what should be done first: brain tanning or smoking? Most tanners, including the majority of the hide tanning literature, firmly agree that brain tanning should be done before smoking. But a few tanners recommend that smoking be done before brain tanning.

Most of the societies around the world, including the North American Indians, have a history of doing it both ways. But the majority of the tanners in each society historically have preferred tanning before smoking. Consequently there is no simple quick answer to which should be done first: brain tanning or smoking?

The answer probably depends on a variety of different variables, such as the type of animal hide being processed (moose hides should be smoked and then brain tanned), the age of the animal when it was killed, the thickness of the hide, and whether or not the hair or fur will be left on the hide.

It is entirely possible that it really doesn't change the final buckskin in one way or the other as long as both tanning and smoking are done. Or it could be that for a specific combination of the above mentioned variables that a better buckskin results when tanning is done before smoking, but with a different combination of variables then a better buckskin results when smoking is done before tanning.

Some native American Indians, including my Cherokee Indian ancestors, would brain tan their hides before they smoked them. This process was developed over many centuries of trial-and-error and it was done this way because it produced the highest quality buckskins for the Indians to wear. The resulting buckskins were more comfortable, more flexible, and they had a longer life expectancy. However, other native American Indian tribes created their buckskins by smoking before tanning and those Indians were extremely happy with their results. It is possible that each tribe eventually settled on the technique that produced the most durable buckskin clothing for their specific climate and geographical region when taking temperature, humidity, and natural obstructions such as forests or prairies or deserts, into consideration.

One valid reason for smoking before tanning is that brain enzymes (and their substitutes) help to dissolve the natural animal glue that is still trapped inside a hide and this makes it easier to rinse that glue away using ordinary water. Wood smoke enhances the natural brain enzymes and the smoke helps those brain enzymes to accomplish their task more efficiently. However, it is entirely probable that it doesn't matter if the hide is smoked before or after brain tanning because the smoking process will activate the brain enzymes equally well using either method.

The chemicals in the wood smoke will combine with the chemicals that are still inside the hide and any remaining glues in the hide will be permanently neutralized. This makes the hide flexible. When the hide gets wet, from rain or sweat or normal washing with soap and water, the hide will remain soft and flexible and the glues in the hide will never be reactivated. The smoking process also increases the temperature at which the hide will remain stable and this will help to prevent the hide from mildewing or rotting.

If you wish you may experiment with these two steps and determine if you achieve better results if one step is always done before the other step. The only suggestion I can offer is that you remain objective and open minded and that you honestly compare two different buckskins that have been processed in each of the two different ways. If you form an opinion one way or the other before you have experimented with both procedures then your mind will reinforce your original opinion as you look at your two finished buckskins and your final conclusion will exactly match your original opinion on this issue. This is not unusual because it is simply the way the human mind works.

In the southeastern United States the majority of tanners will brain tan their hides and then smoke their hides. This is also the sequence that I personally recommend.

Moose Hides: Although I lived deep in the backwoods of the state of Maine for six months I never saw a moose. Therefore I have never eaten moose meat and I have never tanned a moose hide. However, I am aware of the differences between moose hides and deer hides. Moose hides are frequently smoked before they are brain tanned because the smoking process allows the brains to more easily penetrate and soften the thick tough moose hide. Therefore if you are working with a moose hide then you should follow the instructions in the smoking chapter before you follow the instructions in this chapter.

Safety Precaution: Always wear rubber, vinyl, or latex gloves when handling an animal hide or the brains of an animal.

Introduction to Tanning

Tanning is the process where some type of "tannin" or some type of oily fatty substance is applied to the hide of an animal. The primary purpose of tanning is to lubricate the tiny fibers inside a hide so they will stretch and slide and realign themselves so the hide feels softer to your touch. Tanning does not "tan" a hide the way the sun tans your skin. The color of a hide after tanning may be the same as before tanning or the hide may absorb some of the color of the tanning solution. However, this color change is a by-product of tanning and it is not the reason a hide is tanned.

Tanning a hide in a solution of brains, or similar substances, is called "fat-liquoring." Tanning does all the following:

1. Saturates the fibers of the hide and makes the hide softer.
2. Makes the hide more comfortable to wear.
3. Makes the hide feel less abrasive to the skin.
4. Helps the hide feel cooler in the summer because it allows your skin to breathe and it absorbs the moisture from your body and evaporates it into the surrounding air.
5. Helps the hide feel warmer in the winter.
6. Makes the hide stronger so that it will last longer.
7. Helps preserve the hide and helps to prevent the hide from decaying and rotting.
8. Adds a very small degree of waterproofing to the hide.
9. Helps the hair or fur remain attached to the hide, if the hair or fur was not removed from the hide.

The brain of each animal is just the right size to completely and properly tan its hide. Animal brains have been used for thousands of years to tan hides because some type of animal brains were usually available when an animal hide was ready to be tanned. But in most cases the brain that was used was not from the same animal whose hide was being tanned. The reason is because animal brains begin to rot very quickly but animal hides are usually not ready to be tanned for several weeks.

Since the animal's brain will not be needed until several days (or weeks) after the animal has been killed, the animal's brain must be protected from rotting, or you will need to the brains from a different animal to tan the hide you are currently working on, or you will need to use something besides brains to tan the hide.

How to Avoid Rotten Brains:

1. **Freezing:** Freeze the animal's brain as soon as possible after the animal has been killed. When you need the brain in the tanning process you can thaw the brain and use it at that time.
2. **Drying:** You may dry the brains in an oven the same way you would dry meat for meat jerky or pemmican. Do not cook the brains. Do not add any salt. Later when you need the dry brains you can simply add water to the dry brains to return them to a usable form.
3. **Canning:** You may can the brains in a glass canning jar using the same procedure you would use if you were canning fresh meat. This will cook the brains as well as preserve the brains. However, do not add any salt or other chemicals to the canned brains.
4. **Substitutions:** You may use the brain from any animal to tan the hide of a different animal.
   a. **Large game animals:** The brain from a large animal will be adequate to tan the hide of another large animal of the same size, or two medium size hides, or six to eight small hides.

b. **Medium game animals:** The brain from a medium size animal will tan the hide of another medium size animal or two to four smaller hides. But you will need the brains from two medium size animals to tan the hide of a large animal.

c. **Small game animals**: The brain from a small animal may be used to tan the hide of another small animal. But you will need the brains from three or four small animals to tan one medium size hide. You will need the brains from six to eight small animals to tan one large hide.

5. **Fresh Cow Brains:** You can order fresh cow brains from your local grocery store by the pound. The brains will normally arrive in a one pound plastic bag and the brains will either be fresh or frozen. If you do not need one pound of brains for the hide, or hides, that you are currently tanning then you can freeze the brains you don't need and use them later.

If you purchase fresh cow brains then you should buy from a reputable source in order to avoid the potential problem of being sold the brains from diseased animals that might have had "Mad Cow Disease."

Whenever you are handling brains of any type always wear vinyl, latex, or plastic gloves and practice good personal hygiene about touching yourself or other objects while working with the brains.

A medium size hide, such as a deer hide, will require about one-half pound (eight ounces) of animal brains to completely and thoroughly saturate the entire hide.

After you acquire some animal brains you have several options for creating a brain tanning solution. A brain tanning solution is simply finely crushed brains in some clean warm water. Use the same type of water that you used for the first water bath. In other words, if you have fresh clean rainwater then use it. The water should feel comfortably warm to your touch but not hot.

1. **Smashing:** Add a little warm water and smash the brains with your gloved hands or with a potato masher until there are no large pieces and the consistency looks like mashed potatoes with just a little too much water in them.

2. **Meshing:** Add a little warm water and push the brains with your gloved hands through a fine wire mesh screen several times until you have a mushy mess of brains that contain no large pieces.

3. **Blending:** Put the brains in an ordinary food blender (electric), or use a hand cranked mixer with two rotating intermeshing blades (the old fashioned rotary mixer type). Gradually add just enough warm water to create a mixture that looks like a thick strawberry milkshake. Thoroughly and completely clean the inside of the blender and the metal blender blades when you are finished. This is the recommended method if you have access to an electric food blender or a hand cranked mixer. But you must take the time to clean and sterilize the blender or the mixer in scalding hot water after you use it.

Substitutes for Animal Brains

If you use animal brains to tan a hide then the hide may have a very, very light pink color after tanning. If you don't have access to any fresh animal brains then you can substitute any of the following in place of the brains and achieve very similar final results. However, professional tanners will usually go out of their way to obtain brains instead of using any of the following substitutes because they believe they are able to detect subtle differences in a hide that has been brain tanned as opposed to being tanned with one of the following substitutes.

1. **Eggs:** Twelve chicken eggs may be substituted for one-half pound (eight ounces) of brains. Separate the eggs from their shells and discard the shells. Only the yokes of the eggs contain the chemicals required in the hide tanning process. However, most tanners use the yokes and the whites because the whites of the egg contain a slippery substance that helps to lubricate the fibers inside a hide. Mix the eggs together as if you were making an omelet and then use the eggs instead of brains. If you use eggs then the hide will have a very slight yellow tint after tanning. However, when the hide is smoked the yellow tint will become more of a smoke color. Later when the finished hide is washed with soap and water a lot of the original yellow tint will gradually be washed away. (Note: If you wish you may separate the yokes from the whites and then use the whites of the eggs in a recipe that requires egg whites.)

2. **Oil and Soap:** There are two different types of oil that may be used as follows:

   a. **Neatsfoot Oil:** Use 1/4 cup of Neatsfoot Oil plus 1/4 bar of grated Ivory soap as a substitute for one-half pound of brains. Shred the soap into fine shavings using an ordinary food grater or cheese grater and then dissolve the soap shavings in some boiling water. Wait for the soapy water to cool and then add the oil and mix them together. Then proceed as if you were using brains. If you use Neatsfoot Oil then the hide will be a slightly darker color after tanning. (Note: The word "neat" is an old synonym for cattle. One of the primary ingredients in the original Neatsfoot Oil was an extract from the lower leg bones of cattle. Some of the current versions of Neatsfoot Oil may include lard or a mixture of non-animal oils. Some of these other ingredients have been known to oxidize and leave behind a rough crust and this is very undesirable on buckskin clothing. Therefore the Neatsfoot Oil that is currently available may not yield the same hide tanning results as the original version of this oil that was popular many years ago.)

   b. **Murphy's Oil Soap:** Use 1/2 cup of Murphy's Oil Soap as a substitute for one-half pound of brains.

3. **Acorns:** Oak tree acorns contain tannin and that tannin must be removed from the acorns or you will get sick if you eat them. Instructions for processing acorns for human consumption are in my book **"Grandpappy's Recipes for Hard Times."** All acorns contain tannin but red oak acorns contain a lot more tannin than white oak acorns and therefore you will only need about one-third as many red oak acorns as white oak acorns to yield the same amount of tannin. The easy way to distinguish a red oak acorn from a white oak acorn is to break open one of the acorn exterior shells. The inside lining of a red oak acorn shell is hairy but the inside lining of a white oak acorn shell is smooth. If you just want the tannic acid from the acorns for tanning hides then you should collect several pounds of acorns from the ground shortly after they fall off the oak tree in the fall. Let the acorns dry and turn brown and then store the acorns inside their shells in a paper bag until you need them. But inspect them once a week to make sure they do not start to mold. Any acorns that have mold on them should be discarded. The nutmeat inside the acorn shell will gradually shrivel and dry out but this will not affect its tannin content. When you need some tannic acid, remove about six pounds of white oak acorn nutmeats from their shells and discard the shells (or use two pounds of red oak acorn nutmeats). Collect enough rainwater to completely cover the acorns and bring the water to a boil. Then drop the acorn nutmeats into the boiling water. Immediately reduce the heat and allow the acorns to simmer in the water for about two hours. Stir the acorns inside the water every ten minutes while they are simmering. Then strain the brown water away from the acorn nutmeats. The brown water will contain tannin and some of the natural nut oil from inside the acorn nutmeats. Substitute the brown acorn water for one-half pound of brains. If you use brown acorn water then it will darken the hide somewhere between the original color of the hide and the color of the brown acorn water.

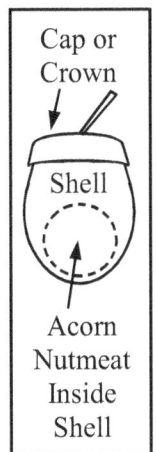

   Note 1: Acorns are nuts and acorns contain nut oil just like other nuts. Therefore when you simmer the tannin out of the acorn nutmeats you will also be releasing some of the natural nut oil from inside the nutmeats into the water. This nut oil is very beneficial to the hide tanning process.

   Note 2: The bark off an oak tree may be boiled instead of acorn nutmeats. However, removing the bark from an oak tree will usually kill the tree. In addition, oak tree bark does not contain the natural oil that is inside an acorn nutmeat. Therefore I do not recommend using oak tree bark instead of acorns.

4. **Combinations:** You may use any combination of brains, eggs, oil and soap, or acorns that you wish because they all contain the chemicals needed in the tanning process. The chemicals in brains, eggs, oil and soap, and acorns lubricate the hide and this allows the hide to be softened and stretched. These lubricants allow the fibers inside the hide to slide and stretch without damaging the hide. As an example, if you need eight ounces of brains but you only have four ounces of brains then you may thoroughly mix those four ounces of brains with six eggs and then use the resulting mixture in the hide tanning process described next.

How to Tan an Animal Hide

Always wear rubber, vinyl, or latex gloves when handling an animal hide or the brains of an animal.

If you are leaving the hair or fur on the hide then only rub the tanning solution into the flesh side of the hide and do not submerge the entire hide below water. If the hair or fur is still on the hide then skip to the instructions at the end of this chapter.

If possible use more brains or brain substitutes if you have them available. A few extra ounces of brains, or brain substitutes, in your tanning solution is far superior to not having enough brains in your tanning solution.

After the brains have been converted into a brain tanning solution the brains will remain active for between 24 to 36 hours before they begin to rot. When the brains begin to rot they will smell like rotten meat and at that time they should be safely disposed of. Never add brains to a compost pile.

Place the hide in a plastic garbage can or a plastic tote that is bigger than the hide so you can stir the hide in the solution without splashing the solution out of the container. Add just barely enough clean warm water to completely cover the hide. The water should feel warm to your touch but not hot. Immediately remove the hide and pour the brain solution into the warm water in the plastic container. Stir the solution inside the plastic container until it appears to be of a uniform consistency. An old broom handle or a clean stick works well for this task. Place the wet hide back into the plastic container and submerge it below the brain tanning solution. Use the broom handle or stick to stir the hide around inside the plastic container to help every part of the hide come into contact with the brain tanning solution.

Cover the container with some type of lid so flies and other insects cannot get into the tanning bath.

Allow the hide to soak in the solution for one hour (first hour). Then stir the hide around in the solution. Allow the hide to soak in the solution for one more hour (second hour). Then stir the hide and allow it to soak for one more hour (third hour). Stir again and allow the hide to soak for one more hour (fourth hour).

Potential Problem - Residual Membrane: Remove the hide from the solution. If you discover some residual flesh or membrane on either side of the hide then you will need to scrape the hide again on the scraping beam using your scraping tool to remove the residual flesh or membrane that you just discovered. Then soak the hide in the tanning solution for an additional hour.

Remove the hide from the solution and pull the hide across a metal cable or rope to help the tanning solution penetrate deeper into the pores of the hide. Pull the flesh side across the cable or rope. If the hair was removed from the hide then also pull the hair side of the hide across the cable or rope. Pull both sides several times. The pulling procedure across a rope or cable is described in detail in the next chapter on softening and stretching.

If possible reheat the tanning solution until it feels warm to the touch but not hot.

Put the hide back in the tanning solution and stir the hide in the solution. Then allow the hide to soak in the solution for about twelve more hours. Place some heavy rocks on the hide to keep the hide under the solution. Stir the hide in the solution every two or three hours.

Remove the hide from the solution. Put a lid on the container that contains the tanning mixture but do not discard the solution until you are certain that you will not need it again for this same hide.

Stretch and dry the hide following the instructions in the next chapter. You should notice that the entire surface of the hide becomes soft and flexible, with the exception of the very edges around the outside of the hide. The edges of a hide will almost always be stiffer than the rest of the hide but these rough edges will be removed at the final processing step so they can be ignored.

Potential Problem - Stiff Spots on the Hide: Except for the outside edges of the hide, if you notice some stiff spots anywhere else on the hide when you stretch it then you should thoroughly coat the stiff areas of the hide with the tanning solution. The most likely areas that will need special treatment are the neck, down the upper backbone area, and on both side of the rump. Then submerge the entire hide in the hide tanning solution for an additional six hours. Then remove the hide and begin the hide stretching process in the next chapter once again. This may not happen very often but when it does happen the remedy to this problem is simply a few more hours of soaking the hide in the bucket that contains the hide tanning solution.

Maximum Time Constraint: Brains, and brain tanning solution, will begin to rot and smell really, really bad in approximately 24 to 36 hours. Therefore you need to complete the hide tanning process while the brains are relatively "fresh" in the brain tanning solution.

Thick Hides: If you are tanning a thick hide, such as a beaver hide, then a thick hide needs to be brain tanned and thoroughly stretched the first time following the instructions in the next chapter, and then brain tanned and stretched a second time. The second brain tanning allows the brain tanning mixture to more fully saturate a thicker hide and make it softer. However, the brain tanning solution will begin to rot before the second tanning session and you will need to prepare a fresh tanning solution using fresh brains.

Hand Application of the Tanning Solution

You will need to apply the tanning solution by hand in the following two situations:

1. **Hair or Fur Still on the Hide:** If the hair or the fur was intentionally left on the animal hide then you will not be able to submerge the hide in a tanning solution. Smear the tanning solution onto the flesh side of the hide by hand while wearing protective gloves. You must press the tanning solution deep into the flesh side of the hide using as much pressure as you can. Do not miss any areas. Fold the hide in half with the flesh side of the hide on the inside and the hair side of the hide on the outside of the fold. Allow the tanning solution to penetrate the hide for eight hours. Unfold the hide and pull the flesh side of the hide across a rope or cable to help the tanning solution penetrate deeper into the hide. Do not pull the hair side of the hide across the rope or cable. Then fold the hide in half once again. Allow the solution to penetrate into the hide for another twelve hours. Then unfold the hide and follow the instructions in the next chapter.

2. **No Container Available:** If you do not have access to a bucket or other container then you will need to apply the tanning solution to the hide by hand. Smear the tanning solution onto both sides of the hide by hand while wearing protective gloves. You will need to press the solution into the hide to help it penetrate the hide. This is not as effective as soaking the hide in the tanning solution but it will yield acceptable final results if you diligently press the tanning solution into the hide consistently over both surfaces of the hide without missing any areas. Roll the hide into a cylinder, similar to a rug for transport, and allow the tanning solution to more fully penetrate into the hide for about four hours. Unroll the hide and pull both sides of the hide across a rope or cable to help the solution more fully penetrate deeper into the hide. Then roll the hide into a cylinder again. Allow the solution to penetrate into the hide for another twelve hours. Then unroll the hide and follow the instructions in the next chapter.

Chapter Eighteen

Softening, Stretching, and Sanding - Part 1: How to Use a Rope or Cable

One of the differences between a soft buckskin and a hard piece of rawhide is the softening and stretching step. Buckskins are softened and rawhide is not. Softening and stretching is the second most labor intensive step in making a buckskin. The most labor intensive step is scraping.

Softening and stretching is the step during which a damp, smelly, slippery hide is transformed into a dry, soft, velvety smooth, luxurious buckskin. Therefore this is an extremely important step in the production of any buckskin that will be used to make clothing.

Professional tanners may refer to this step using a variety of different words such as: softening, stretching, finishing, breaking, buffing, or fluffing. Although different tanners may use different words, they are all describing the same basic process.

The objective of softening and stretching is to separate the hide fibers so smoke can enter the pores of the hide and the smoke can completely penetrate the hide when the hide is placed inside a smokehouse. You are not trying to stretch the hide to make it bigger. Softening and stretching also helps to prevent any glue that is still inside the hide from hardening. Stretching prevents these glues from achieving their natural purpose and the final result will be a soft pliable buckskin instead of a stiff piece of leather.

There are two different ways to soften and stretch a hide:

1. **Rope or Cable:** The hide is pulled across a braided rope or across a steel cable many, many times to soften and stretch the hide. This method requires the minimum investment in equipment but it does require **more manual labor** to achieve the same final results. This method is the best method to use if your hide has several holes or damaged spots because the hide will be stretched by hand and there will be no unusual pressure applied to any weak spots that may be present in the hide. This method will also help to force a little more of the tanning solution deeper into the hide as the hide gradually stretches and dries. The rope or cable technique is described in detail in this chapter.

2. **Stretching Frame:** The hide is tied inside a stretching frame and a stretching tool is used to apply pressure to the hide to soften and stretch the hide. This method requires some additional equipment but it requires **less manual labor** to achieve the same final results. In addition, a hide that is stretched using a stretching frame will end up a little bigger and a little thinner than a hide of the same size that is stretched using a rope or cable. Some of the stretch in the hide will also be lost. The stretching frame technique is described in detail in the next chapter.

Regardless of which of the above two methods is selected, the hide will also need to be sanded with ordinary sandpaper or a piece of porous rock while the hide is being softened and stretched. The sanding process is described in Chapter 20.

Rope or Cable Method

Softening and stretching needs to be done on a moist hide and not a dry hide. The hide should be softened and stretched until the hide is relatively dry. This will usually take several hours. On a warm day a thin hide can be finished in about one hour and a thicker hide in about two hours. On a cool day these times will be tripled. Sandpaper or a pumice stone will also be used with this method. The best strategy is to pull the hide for a few minutes and then let the hide rest for a few minutes. While the hide is resting you can also rest but while the hide is resting it will contract a little in any area in which it was overstretched and the hide will return to a more uniform thickness and shape.

Flesh Side: Only pull the flesh side over the rope or cable and do not pull the hair side over the cable. Instead use a piece of sandpaper or a pumice stone to correct any problems on the hair side.

Note: If you are in the middle of the brain tanning process as described in the previous chapter then it is okay to pull the hair side of the hide across the rope or cable to force the tanning solution deeper into the hide. But if you have completed the brain tanning process then the hair side of the hide should not be pulled across the rope or cable again.

As the hide gradually dries a thin glaze or crust will begin to form on the hide. This glace or crust will not be present on a wet hide and it will only gradually appear at random spots on the hide as the hide begins to dry. This glaze or crust is what you will wipe off the *flesh* side of the hide using the cable as you also stretch the hide. The glaze or crust will be sanded off the *hair* side of the hide using sandpaper or a pumice stone.

Always alternate your stretching efforts from head to tail, and then diagonally, and then from side to side. Do not keep stretching the hide in the same direction all the time or you will pull the hide out of its natural shape. Shake the hide out in the same manner as a rug each time you change directions to allow the fibers in the hide to realign themselves into their original natural shape.

Any area of the hide that contains a healed scar will dry a little harder than the rest of the hide and this is normal and nothing can be done about it.

You will need five or six feet of either one of the following:

1. **Braided Rope:** A 1/4 inch diameter braided rope.
   A twisted rope will not work because the rope will gradually become untwisted as a hide is worked continuously back and forth along the surface of the rope. The disadvantage of rope is that the hide will put friction on the rope and that friction will sometimes heat the rope and cause it to gradually come apart if it is made of cotton, or it may melt the rope if it is made of nylon or polypropylene.

2. **Wire Cable:** A 1/4 inch diameter wire cable, either galvanized or steel.
   If you use a wire cable then curve the end of the cable back onto itself to form a short loop and lash the loop closed using a separate piece of very thin wire the same way you would lash the cut end of a rope to keep it from unraveling, except with the wire you will be lashing two pieces of cable together. Or you can purchase a cable clamp and clamp the loop end to keep the loop from shortening or extending. Or you can purchase a six feet long weatherproof vinyl coated steel cable for approximately $4.77 at Walmart in their hardware department. This steel cable already has both ends looped and secured and it is ready to be used as a hide finishing cable. However, the steel cable at Walmart has a thin plastic sleeve around the entire length of the cable. The hide needs to make abrasive contact with the steel cable and the thin plastic sleeve will prevent this from happening. Therefore the thin plastic sleeve will need to be cut off the cable and discarded.

Six Feet Long
Steel Cable

If you use any type of steel cable then you will probably notice that a gray residue or a gray powder will gradually begin to accumulate on the cable. This is part of the factory coating that was applied to the cable and it will very gradually wear off the cable. When you notice that the cable appears to have a little gray residue or powder on the cable then use a clean damp cloth and wipe the entire cable from end to end to remove the gray powder. In the future when you notice a little gray powder on the cable just wipe it off with a clean damp cloth. If a little of the gray powder gets onto a hide then it will not hurt the hide. You can sand the gray residue off a hide with a piece of sandpaper. If you miss any of the gray residue on the hide then it will simply blend it with the rest of the hide when the hide is smoked and it will not cause any problems with the finished buckskin because it will gradually wash off the buckskin when the buckskin clothing is periodically washed with ordinary soap and water.

You do not need both of the above. You will only need a rope or a metal cable but not both. In my opinion a metal cable is the best choice. A metal cable can be stretched almost straight between two stationary objects and it will not stretch when you put pressure on it. The surface of a metal cable is harder than a rope and this is desirable because one of the objectives of softening is to scrape any rough or crusty spots off the hide and a metal cable does this better than a rope.

You will need to secure each end of the rope or cable between two trees, or between two buildings, or between a tree and a building, or between any two objects that are firmly planted in or on the ground. The rope or cable should be pulled as tight and a straight as possible between the two objects and the rope or cable should be level with the ground and at the same height above ground as your elbows. When you are finished using the rope or cable you may take it down, coil it up, and store it until the next time you need it to process an animal hide.

The hide is pulled or rubbed over the cable to stretch and soften and buff the hide.

How to Stretch a Hide Using a Rope or Cable

Safety Precaution: Always wear rubber, vinyl, or latex gloves when handling an animal hide.

Wring the Hide: Remove the hide from the tanning solution and wring as much of the tanning solution out of the hide that you can. You may press the hide, or twist the hide, or use any method available to you to extract as much moisture from the hide as possible. However, do not heat the hide and do not expose the hide to direct sunlight at this time. Wring the moisture out of the hide in the shade. This wringing process was described in detail in Chapter 15.

Equipment Setup: Stretch the rope or cable as tight as possible between two stationary objects as explained previously in this chapter. Do not roll the hide into a roll like a carpet. Instead pull the entire flesh side of the hide across the rope or cable to soften the hide and to remove hard spots from the hide.

Pulling the Flesh Side: Place the hide on the cable so the hide is lying flat against the cable. Hold one end of the hide in your left hand close to the cable and hold the other end of the hide in your right hand far away from the cable. Lean backwards and use the weight of your body and your shoulders with the strength in your arms to pull the hide across the rope or cable from your right hand towards your left hand so when you are finished your left hand is far away from the cable and your right hand is close to the cable. Repeat this process several times by pulling with your right hand and then your left hand so the hide is pulled across the cable for its entire length.

The pulling action on the hide across the rope or cable will create friction on the hide and this will help to dry the hide. The pulling action will also cause any crusty abrasive areas on the flesh side of the hide to be scraped off the hide as it is pulled hard against the rope or cable. This will also pull the hide fibers apart and stretch the hide and this will make the hide softer.

First Pull: Pull the hide across the rope or cable using gentle but firm pressure from neck to tail, and then from tail to neck, again and again, for about five minutes. After pulling the hide you should shake the hide the same way you would shake out a dirty rug. Then hang the hide across the rope or cable in the shade. Wait twenty minutes.

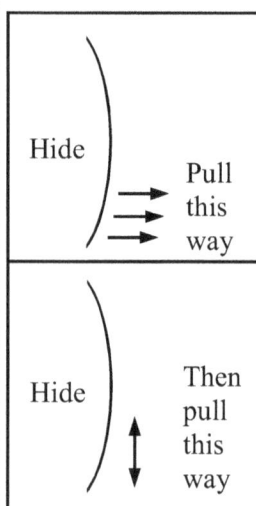

Hide — Pull this way

Hide — Then pull this way

Pull the Edges: The outside edges of the hide will usually dry faster than the center of the hide and the edges will have a tendency to shrink and form a rim around the edge of the hide instead of remaining flat with the rest of the hide. To prevent this from happening the edges must be pulled and stretched by hand as the center of the hide continues to dry. This edge stretching will need to be repeated between three to five times as the center of the hide slowly dries. To stretch the edge of a hide, first grab near the middle of the hide with one hand and grab the outside edge of the hide with the fingers of your other hand and then pull the edge of the hide away from the center of the hide. Now shift the fingers of your hand about two inches to the right on the outside edge of the hide and pull again. Shift your fingers two inches and pull again. You will now have pulled about six inches of the edge of the hide away from the center of the hide. Use one hand to grasp one end of the six inch section of the hide you just pulled and use the other hand to grasp the other end of the six inch section of hide that you just pulled and then firmly pull the outside edge of the hide between your two hands. Now repeat this entire process for the next six inches of hide that is adjacent to the area you just pulled. Gradually work your way around the entire outside edge of the hide six inches at a time.

Second Pull: Now pull the flesh side of the hide across the rope or cable but this time pull diagonally from the right front foreleg towards the left rear hind leg of the hide, back and forth many times for about five minutes. Shake the hide several times after you have finished pulling it. Hang the hide up again. Wait twenty minutes. Then pull the outside edge of the hide as described above.

Third Pull: Pull the flesh side of the hide across the rope or cable but this time pull from the right side of the hide to the left side of the hide, and then from the left to the right, back and forth many times for about five minutes. Shake the hide several times after you have finished pulling it. Hang the hide up again. Wait twenty minutes. Then pull the outside edge of the hide as described previously.

Fourth Pull: Pull the flesh side of the hide across the rope or cable but this time pull diagonally from the left front foreleg towards the right rear hind leg of the hide, back and forth many times for about five minutes. Shake the hide several times after you have finished pulling it. Hang the hide up again. Wait twenty minutes. Then pull the outside edge of the hide as described previously.

Sanding the Hair Side: While the hide is still damp you will need to use a piece of sandpaper or a pumice stone to sand or buff the hair side of the hide. Hang the hide on the rope or cable with some ordinary clothespins with the hair side facing you. Pull the outside edge of the hide and sand the hair side of the hide following the sanding instructions in Chapter 20. Do **not** put anything behind the hide while you are sanding it to increase the pressure of the sandpaper or pumice rock against the hide. The sanding should be done against the hair side of the hide without any support behind the hide so the hide is not forced against the sandpaper. After sanding you may need to pull the outside edge of the hide again if the outside edge is beginning to curl up.

Final Drying: Now you can hang the hide across a rope in the shade and wait for it to dry completely. Remember to protect the hide from dogs and wild animals or it will not be there when you return. During cold weather you will need to hang the hide indoors at room temperature.

Chapter Nineteen

Softening, Stretching, and Sanding - Part 2: How to Use a Stretching Frame

As explained in the previous chapter, a hide may be softened and stretched using a rope or cable, or a hide may be softened and stretched on a stretching frame. The previous chapter described the rope or cable method. This chapter will describe the stretching frame method. You do not need to soften and stretch a hide using both methods. You will need to select the method you prefer. In other words, you may use a rope or cable as described in the previous chapter, or you may use a stretching frame as described in this chapter. The choice is yours.

If the hair or fur is still on the hide then mount the hide in the stretching frame with the hair side of the hide facing the sun so the hair can dry as you push on the flesh side of the hide with your stretching tool. If the weather is below 50 degrees outdoors then you should consider stretching your hide in a heated shed or in a heated barn.

A hide needs to be stretched immediately after it is removed from the tanning solution while it is still wet.

The purpose of stretching is to help keep the hide soft and flexible and to help prevent the hide from hardening. Stretching will make a hide a little bigger but it does not make a hide significantly bigger. The two pieces of equipment that will be needed to stretch a hide are: a **stretching tool** and a **stretching frame**.

A Stretching Tool

Either one of the following tools may be used to "stretch" an animal hide: an ordinary baseball bat or a handmade stretching stick. Either tool will do a good job of "stretching" an animal hide.

1. **Baseball Bat:** An ordinary baseball bat will do an excellent job of stretching an animal hide. And when you don't need the bat for processing buckskins you can always use it to play baseball.

2. **Handmade Stretching Stick:** An ordinary round stick of wood that is approximately three feet long and that has a diameter of approximately two inches will work exceptionally well as a stretching tool.

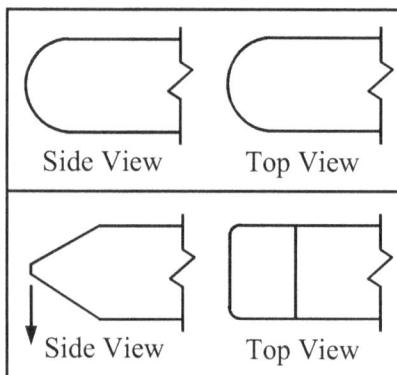

Side View   Top View

Side View   Top View

You may convert one end of the stick into a slightly rounded end similar to the hitting end of a baseball bat. This can be done by carving a little wood off the outside edge of the end of the stick using a sharp knife. Then use some medium or coarse sandpaper to smooth the end of the stick into a gradually rounded surface without any sharp edges. Or you may taper one end of the stick into a blunt end as shown in the illustration. The advantage of the round end is that it will slide across the buckskin and you can exert maximum pressure without worrying about pushing the tool through the buckskin. The advantage of the blunt tapered end is that it will help to scrape any residual membrane off the hide as you drag the end of the tool across the hide in the direction indicated by the arrow in the illustration.

Either of the above stretching tools may be used to stretch an animal hide after the hide has been secured into a stretching frame. Or you may use anything that is at least three feet long and that has at least one smooth end, such as the hand end of a canoe paddle.

A Stretching Frame

When a hide is placed inside a stretching frame it will exert significant pressure on that frame as the hide is stretched using the stretching tool. The frame is also used to dry a hide and as a hide dries it will shrink and put significant pressure on the frame. If the frame bends then the hide will wrinkle and cause problems later. Therefore the stretching frame needs to be constructed of sturdy materials and it must be securely fastened together at each of its four corners. If the frame has some movement after it is finished then you can improve its stability by placing cross braces at each of the four corners to increase the rigidity of the frame. Weight is also a factor because you will need to turn the frame upside down, and from back to front. This will allow you to comfortably reach the entire hide from neck to tail, and the flesh side and the hair side of the hide.

A standard size stretching frame may be constructed using either poles or lumber as follows:

1. **Wood Poles or Strong Sticks:** Four poles, or four strong wood sticks, about 3 inches in diameter, are lashed (tied) together near their ends to form a rectangle. The corners of the poles should be notched as shown in the center illustration so they will not slip when they are under pressure. The notches should be cut to a depth of between 1/4 to 1/3 of the way through the diameter of each pole. The two upright poles should be cut about six feet long. The two horizontal poles should be cut about five feet wide. Optional corner reinforcement sticks may be lashed where the dashed lines are shown in the illustration. An animal hide will be tied in the center of the frame between all four poles. Instead of lashing (tying) the frame together you can use nails. If you decide to use nails then you should drill a hole for each nail using a drill bit with a diameter that is a little smaller than the diameter of the nail. This will allow you to drive each nail through the poles without splitting the poles and each nail will be in the exact location that you desire and each nail will penetrate the poles in a straight line instead of bending as it is being hammered.

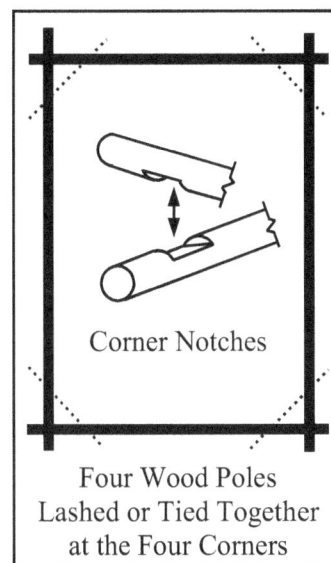

Corner Notches

Four Wood Poles
Lashed or Tied Together
at the Four Corners

2. **Wood Lumber** (illustration on next page): You may use 2x4 lumber or 2x6 lumber. I prefer 2x4 lumber because it is strong enough, it is less expensive, it weighs less, and therefore it requires less effort to turn the frame around when an animal hide is lashed inside it. Three pieces of lumber will be required. Two eight feet long pieces of lumber will each be cut to a length of approximately six feet long and these two pieces with form the upright left side and right side of the frame. One ten feet long piece of lumber will be cut in half into two five feet long pieces and these two pieces will form the horizontal top and bottom pieces of the frame.

Instead of the above standard size stretching frame you could build a frame that is more perfectly suited to your standing height and the type of hides you will be processing as follows:

Optimal Frame Height: The left and right sides of the frame should be cut to a length that you can comfortably reach while standing. For most people this will be about three inches taller than their height. For example, if you are 72 inches tall then cut the two side pieces of lumber 75 inches long. If you are 66 inches tall then cut each side piece 69 inches long. If you are 75 inches tall then cut each side piece 78 inches long. However, in addition to your standing height you will also need to consider the maximum length of hide that you will be stretching in your frame. The following table may help you with this decision:

Type of Hide	Average Length	Maximum Length	Average Width	Maximum Width
Moose (1/4 section)	40 Inches	50 Inches	38 Inches	48 Inches
Elk	56 Inches	61 Inches	52 Inches	55 Inches
Deer, White Tail	48 Inches	52 Inches	36 Inches	40 Inches
Pronghorn (Antelope)	36 Inches	40 Inches	31 Inches	34 Inches

Note 1: A moose hide is relatively square and it is a lot bigger than the hides of other animals. Therefore most tanners will cut a moose hide in half or in quarters and then scrape and tan the individual hide sections.

Note 2: Moose hides and elk hides are relatively square. Deer hides and pronghorn hides are more rectangular.

Note 3: Most buckskin clothing is made from cut pieces of buckskin that are no more than 48 inches long. Pants for a man will usually be 36 to 40 inches from waist to ankle. A woman's dress will usually be longer than a man's trousers. A dress may extend from a woman's shoulders down to her knees, or down to her

A Stretching Frame
Made From Four Pieces of 2x4 Lumber

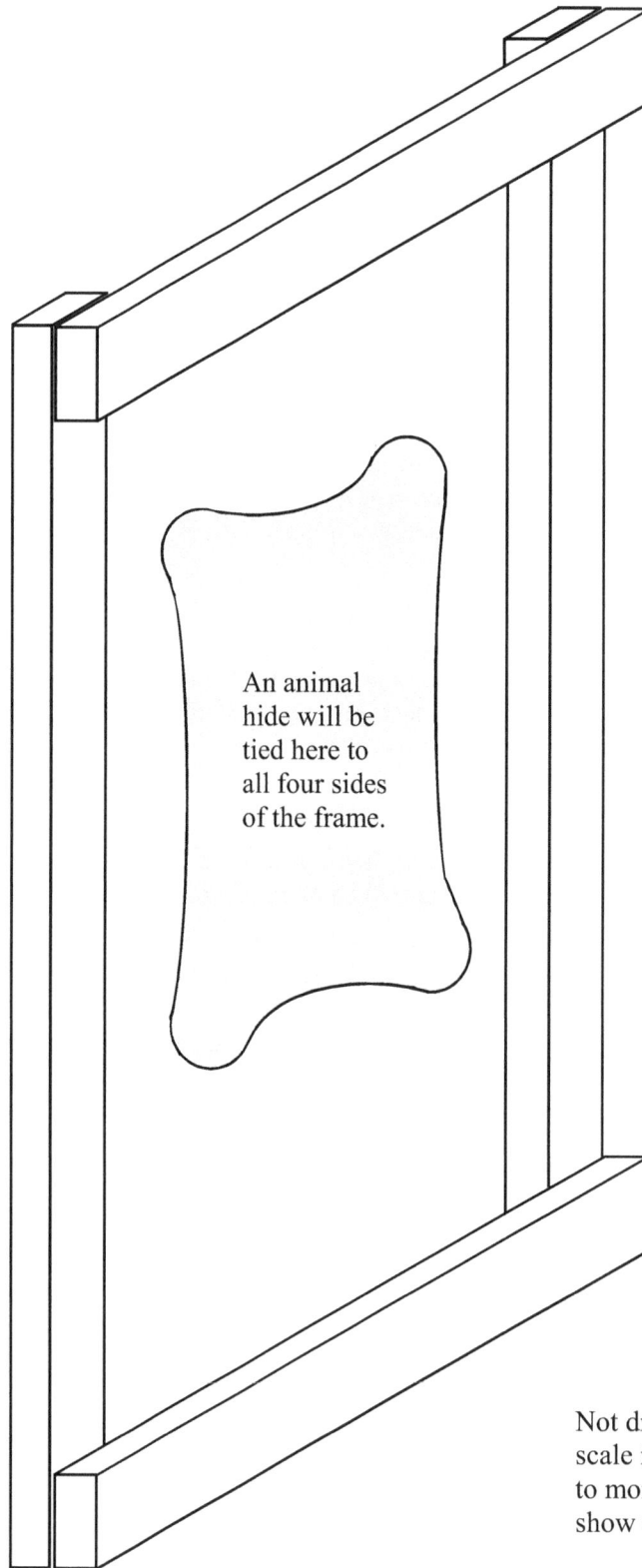

An animal
hide will be
tied here to
all four sides
of the frame.

Not drawn to
scale in order
to more clearly
show the details.

ankles, depending on a variety of factors, such as current fashions, modesty, average temperatures, and average wind speeds. In a tropical environment a knee length dress is usually preferred but in a cold environment an ankle length dress is usually preferred. Therefore if you have a hide that is too big to fit in your stretching frame then there is nothing wrong with cutting the hide into two pieces before you stretch and tan it, based on the size of the article of clothing that you intend to make from the buckskin.

Optimal Frame Width: The top and bottom pieces of the frame should be cut about twelve inches wider than the maximum width hide that you intend to process based on the dimensions in the previous table.

Some tanners use a fixed frame and some tanners use an adjustable frame. I do not know of any tanners who use a collapsible frame. However, all three types of frames will be described next:

1. **Fixed Frame:** A fixed frame is nailed together, or lashed together, at all four corners.

2. **Adjustable Frame:** An adjustable frame is nailed together at two corners and the other two corners are fastened together with removable bolts. The bolts allow the right side of the frame to be moved closer to the left side of the frame when a smaller hide needs to be stretched.

3. **Collapsible Frame:** A collapsible frame is made by bolting all four corners together. The bolts allow the frame to be assembled into the optimal size required to stretch the exact size hide that is currently being processed. This puts uniform consistent pressure on the hide and therefore it is easier to stretch and soften the hide. If the frame will not be used again for an extended period of time then it may be disassembled and the four pieces of wood stored in a very small area until it is needed again. I have not seen this type of frame recommended in any hide tanning literature nor have I seen it discussed anywhere on the internet. However, of the three different ways to construct a stretching frame I strongly recommend that you bolt all four corners together. This makes the frame easily adjustable so it will accommodate many different hide sizes, and it is easily portable, and it requires very little space to store the frame when it is disassembled.

How to Assemble a Stretching Frame

Place the cut lumber together to form a rectangle with the two 5 feet long pieces at the top and bottom of the rectangle between the two longer side pieces. Lay the lumber on the floor in a rectangle pattern with the wide side of the lumber against the floor and the thin side of the lumber pointing into the middle of the rectangle. Two inch wide lumber is actually 1.5 inches wide so the 1.5 inch wide edge of each piece of lumber should face into the center of the rectangle. This will allow the thick side of the lumber to provide the strength to support your hide while it is being stretched without the lumber bending in towards the center of the rectangle.

The two long side pieces of lumber should be resting flat on the floor. The two shorter pieces of lumber should be resting on top of the long side pieces at each end so that the four corners are flush. The two pieces of overlapping lumber will be three inches thick at each corner but 1.5 inches thick everywhere else.

You may now assemble the pieces together using nails, or nuts and bolts, or a combination of the two as follows:

Nails: Use 2.5 inch long nails to hold the frame together. The pointed end of a 2.5 inch long nail will not stick out past the opposite side of a corner. Use a hammer to drive one nail into each of the four corners to hold the frame together. Then use a tape measure and measure across the two diagonals on the inside of the rectangle. Since there is only one nail in each corner you can move the sides until you achieve a good rectangle with each of the two inside diagonals being almost the same exact length. Then add a second nail into each of the four corners diagonally across from the first nail. Now flip the frame over so the top and bottom of the frame is against the floor and the left and right sides are supported above the floor. Check the diagonals again and adjust as necessary to once again achieve a good rectangle. Drive a third nail into each corner and check the diagonals again and adjust as necessary.

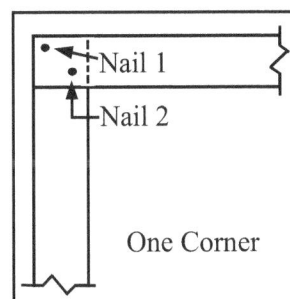

Drive a fourth nail into each corner and you should have a rectangle with center diagonals that are almost exactly the same length. Two nails will be holding each corner from one side of the frame and two nails will be holding each corner from the opposite side of the frame. This will help the frame remain stationary and reduce the chance that the frame will pull apart at the four corners.

Nuts and Bolts: Drive one 3 inch long nail in each corner but do not hammer the nail tight against the wood. Instead leave about 1/2 inch of the nail extending above the top surface of the wood so you can easily remove the nail later with the claw end of a hammer. Use a tape measure and measure across the two diagonals on the inside of the rectangle. Since there is only one nail in each corner you can move the sides until you achieve a good rectangle with each of the two inside diagonals being almost the same exact length. Then add a second 3 inch long nail into each of the four corners diagonally across from the first nail, leaving 1/2 inch of the nail exposed, and then check the diagonals again and adjust as necessary so the four boards form a good rectangle. Now drill one hole through both boards in each of the four corners. Carefully countersink the hole so the end of the bolt will be flush with the surface of the wood. Install a bolt and a nut in each of the four corners. Verify once again that the frame is still rectangular and adjust if necessary. Drill a second hole through both boards in each of the four corners, countersink the hole, and install a bolt and a nut. Verify the frame is still rectangular. Now use the claw end of the hammer to remove one of the nails from each corner and drill a hole where the nail was, countersink the hole, and install a bolt and nut. Verify the frame is still rectangular. Use the claw end of the hammer to remove the final nail from each corner and drill a hole where the nail was, countersink the hole, and install a bolt and a nut. Verify the frame is still rectangular.

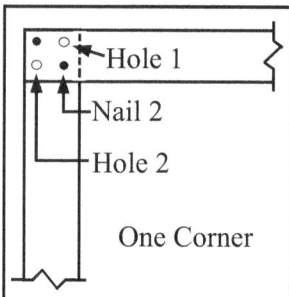

If you intend to have an **adjustable frame** or a **collapsible frame** then now is the time to drill additional holes in the stretching frame. Remove the eight bolts in the right side of the frame and set the right side of the frame aside. From the center of each of the four holes in the end of the top piece of the frame measure exactly 8 inches towards the opposite end of the frame and mark the position of four more holes where each new hole is exactly 8 inches from one of the original four holes. Now measure and mark four more hole positions exactly 16 inches from the original four holes. Finally measure and mark four final hole positions exactly 24 inches from the original four holes. The top board should now have the positions of twelve new holes marked on the board where the grouping of holes are now 8 inches apart. Drill the twelve new holes. Repeat this same procedure for the bottom piece of the frame. The right side of the frame may now be assembled to the top and bottom pieces to accommodate hides that are between 24 inches wide up to 48 inches wide (assuming a five feet wide original frame).

If you wish to have a **collapsible frame** then repeat this procedure for the left and right sides of the frame so that you add twelve new holes in the lower half of both the right and left sides of the frame. The bottom piece of the frame will then be adjustable up and down the left and right sides of the frame to accommodate hides that are as short as 36 inches or as tall as 60 inches (assuming a six feet tall original frame).

It is not necessary to build an adjustable frame. Any size hide that will fit inside a frame can be processed on the frame by using more or less rope to secure the hide to the four sides of the frame. The primary advantage of an adjustable frame is that it allows a hide to be stretched using a uniform amount of pressure from your arms on the stretching tool because the length of rope from the hide to the frame will always be about the same if you adjust the sides of the frame. But if you work small, medium, and large hides in the same size frame then you will need different lengths of rope for each hide. Shorter ropes will hold the bigger hides tighter to the frame so less pressure will be needed on the stretching tool. Longer ropes will hold the smaller hides tight in the frame but more pressure will be needed on the stretching tool because the longer ropes will allow the shorter hide more movement away the frame.

Optional Coating: If you wish you may coat the entire wooden frame with a waterproof weather seal or with a coat of paint.

Hardware or No Hardware

At this time you may install nails, or staples, or eye screws, or cup hooks, or you may leave the frame as it is without any additional hardware.

Holes or Slits: The following discussion assumes you will punch small holes or cut short slits around the entire outside edge of the hide with the holes or slits being approximately three inches apart and each hole or slit about 3/8 of inch from the outside edge of the hide.

1. **No Additional Hardware**: You can loop one long cord around the outside of the frame and then through a hole in the hide, and then over the frame and through the next hole in the hide, and so on, until you have the hide tied inside the frame. In other words, the cord goes over and around the wood frame instead of being threaded through a staple or an eye screw or a cup hook. Instead of one long cord another option is to tie many, many short pieces of cord to the frame at 6 inch intervals. The two loose ends of each individual short piece of cord can then each be tied to a different hole in the hide where the holes in the hide are at 3 inch intervals. This method requires you to tie both ends of each short cord to the hide when you put the hide into the frame. You will also need to untie and retie each end of each cord to the hide each time you need to adjust the hide in the frame to maintain consistent pressure on the hide. The only reason this method is mentioned in this book is because you may not have any long cords and the only cords you have available are all relatively short. This method will allow you to use those short cords but this method will require more of your time and labor.

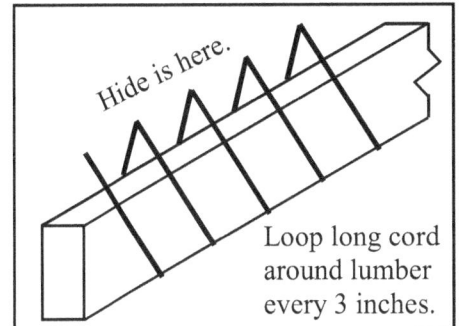

Loop long cord around lumber every 3 inches.

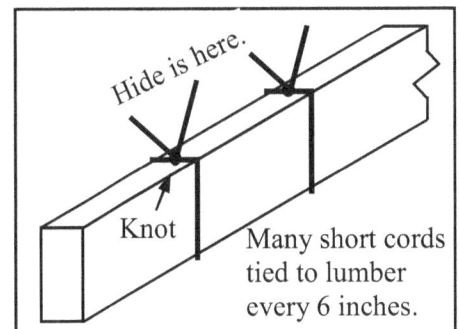

Many short cords tied to lumber every 6 inches.

2. **Nails:** You can drive some heavy-duty 1.5 inch long nails almost all the way into the side of the frame that is facing outwards. But leave the head of the nail protruding about 1/4 inch from the wood. Then you can loop the stretching cord around these nails each time you stretch a hide instead of looping the cord around the entire outside edge of the frame. The advantage of nails is that they keep the stretching cord off the ground on the bottom side of the frame. The disadvantage of nails is that you cannot build an adjustable frame or a collapsible frame because the nails will be in the way.

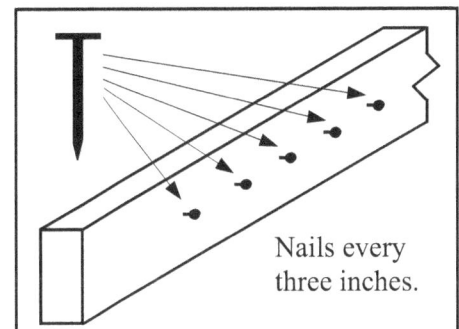

Nails every three inches.

3. **Staples:** You will need a box of fence staples and a hammer. The fence staples may be 1.5 or 2 or 2.5 inches long. Begin at any corner and hammer a fence staple into the center of the 1.5 inch wide piece of lumber approximately 5 inches from the corner, but do not drive the staple flush with the lumber. Allow approximately 1/4 inch of the top of the staple to remain extended so you can lace a 1/8 inch diameter cord below the staple and the cord should still be able to move freely. You will add the cord later but you need to allow for the thickness of the cord now. Continue to hammer a fence staple into the lumber around the entire inside of the rectangle so the fence staples are about 3

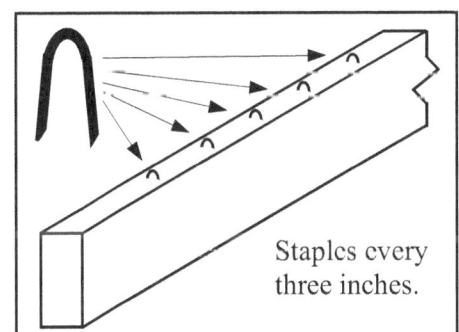

Staples every three inches.

inches apart. The staples must be on the inside of the frame facing the hide that will be stretched. The staples should be driven into the lumber so that the spaces at the top of all the staples are in a straight line and you could see through all the spaces at the same time if you look down the length of the lumber.

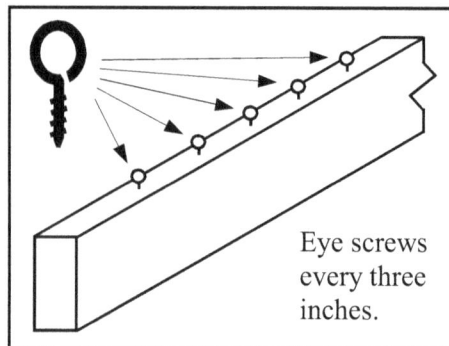

Eye screws every three inches.

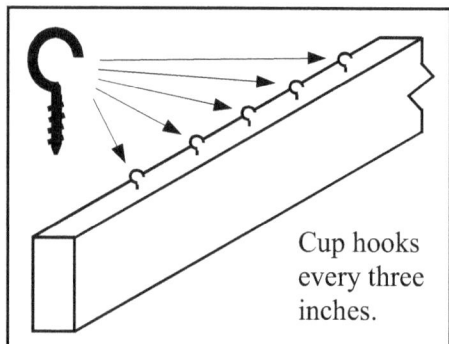

Cup hooks every three inches.

4. **Eye Screws:** An eye screw has an almost completely closed circle on its end. You may use eye screws spaced three inches apart on the inside of each piece of wood with the first eye screw about five inches from the end of the lumber. The eye screws must be on the inside of the frame facing the hide that will be stretched. The eye screws should have eye openings of at least 1/4 inch so the stretching cord can easily slip through the eye openings as you tighten and adjust the hide in the frame. The hole in the eye should be facing down the lumber so you could see through all the eye holes at the same time if you were looking down the length of the lumber.

5. **Cup Hooks:** A cup hook has a three-quarter circle on its end with an opening in one-quarter of the circle. Cup hooks should be spaced three inches apart with the first cup hook about five inches from the end of the lumber. The cup hooks should have openings of at least 1/4 inch so the stretching cord can easily slip into and out of the opening in the cup hook. The openings in the cup hooks should face outwards towards the flat side of the lumber as shown in the illustration.

Four Corner Eye Screws: You may wish to add four eye screws with hole openings of at least one-quarter inch. Screw one eye screw into each of the inside four corners of the rectangle. You will tie your stretching cords to these eye screws so the inside diameter of the eye screw should be at least a 1/4 inch hole opening. A bigger opening is preferred to a smaller opening so a 3/8 inch or a 1/2 inch opening would be preferred to a 1/4 inch opening.

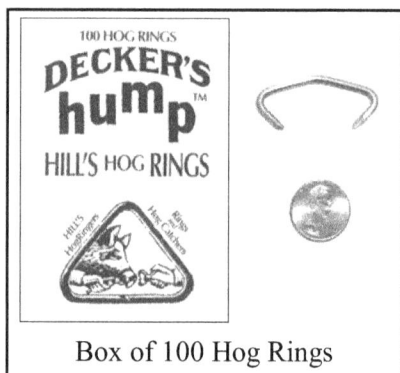

Box of 100 Hog Rings

Optional Hog Rings: A box of 100 hog rings may be purchased for approximately $3.00 at any hardware store that sells farm supplies, such as some Ace Hardware Stores. You will need approximately 70 hog rings. Each hog ring has two sharp ends so be careful when you handle each ring or you may cut yourself. Push one of the sharp ends of each hog ring though the outside edge of the wet hide at least 3/8 inch from the outside edge of the hide to give the hog ring something to hold onto without pulling its way through the edge of the hide. Space the hog rings about three inches apart along the outside border of the hide. This is the same distance between the fence staples or eye screws or cup hooks in your stretching frame.

Braided Cord or Rope: You will need 1/8 inch braided cord, twine, or rope. Braided cord is superior to twisted cord. Therefore carefully read the label on the cord, twine, or rope package before you buy it and make sure it is braided. Nylon cord, or polypropylene cord, or parachute cord are all excellent choices. You will need four cords or ropes. You will need two cords that are approximately 25 feet long for the top and bottom of the frame, and you will need two cords that are approximately 35 feet long for the right and left sides of the frame. Each side of the frame should have its own cord to make it easier to adjust the position of the hide inside the frame and to tighten each side as necessary. The longer cords will allow you to stretch any hide that will fit inside the frame including smaller hides because you can simply use more of the rope or cord on those smaller hides.

Tie one end of the cord to one of the corner eye screws. If you will not be using hog rings then allow the cord to hang loose until you are ready to tie a hide into the frame. If you don't have any hog rings then you will need to thread the cord through each individual slit or hole in the edge of the hide and then through your frame staple, or eye screw, one-at-a-time. It also requires more effort to tighten a hide in the frame because you must carefully adjust the cord at each slit or hole in the hide as you tighten the hide inside the frame.

If you will be using hog rings then loop the cord down about three inches and then back up and push it under the first staple or through the hole in the eye screw. Loop the cord down about three inches and then back up and push it through the second staple or eye screw. Continue this looping process until you reach the last staple (or eye screw) on one side and then allow the remaining free end of the cord to hang freely without tying it to anything at this time. Then repeat this process for the other three sides so that you have cords threaded along all four sides through all of the staples or eye screws. Each cord will be securely tied to one eye screw but the opposite end of that cord will remain loose until you begin to stretch a hide. When you need to stretch a hide on this frame you can adjust the loops and make them shorter or longer as necessary to fit the hide in the center of the frame. If you are using hog rings then you will not need to remove the cord from the fence staples each time you stretch a new hide because the cord should move freely inside the small gap between each staple and the wood frame (or the hole in the eye screw).

I recommend cup hooks and hog rings. If you use hog rings with cup hooks then you will loop the stretching cord around each hog ring and each cup hook combination, one at a time, until you reach the end of one side of the hide and then you will tie the stretching cord off to the edge of the frame. When you have finished stretching the hide the stretching cord will be easy to remove from the cup hooks and hog rings in order to release the hide from the stretching frame.

Your stretching frame is now complete and it is ready to be used.

How to Use a Stretching Frame

Safety Precaution: Always wear rubber, vinyl, or latex gloves when handling an animal hide.

Holes or Slits: Punch small holes or cut short slits around the entire outside edge of the hide with the holes or slits being approximately three inches apart and each hole or slit about 3/8 of inch from the outside edge of the hide. The stretching cord will be laced through these holes or slits. If you are using hog rings then the sharp end of the hog ring can be used to punch its own hole in the edge of the hide and the stretching cord will be looped around the opposite end of the hog ring.

Stretching needs to be done outdoors so the tanning solution from the wet hide can drip onto the ground.

The objective of softening and stretching is to separate the hide fibers so smoke can enter the pores of the hide and the smoke can completely penetrate the hide when the hide is smoked. You are not trying to stretch the hide to make it bigger. Softening and stretching also helps to prevent any glue that is still inside the hide from hardening and making the hide stiff.

When tying a hide inside a stretching frame the hide should be tied with enough pressure to keep the hide flat but do not stretch the hide with the ropes. In other words, the hide should have a relatively flat surface without any dips or creases in it. However, the hide should not be tied so tight that the hide is under tension and the hide is being stretched by the ropes. Later when you put pressure on the hide with the stretching tool the hide will stretch inside the frame but the rope tension should allow the hide to gradually shrink back to its original size when you remove the pressure of the stretching tool. This stretching and shrinking action is what causes the hide fibers to separate and become fluffy and soft.

Attach the neck end of the hide to the top of the stretching frame by placing a cord loop around the opposite end of each hog ring (or through a hole or slit in the hide). Adjust the top side of the hide so the top of the hide is at a convenient height for you to work on. Then tie the loose end of the top cord to the eye screw in the corner of the frame. Now loop the bottom cord through the hog rings (or through holes in the hide) in the tail end of the hide and pull the cord tight before tying its loose end to an eye screw in the corner of the frame. Repeat this process for each of the two sides. If necessary untie one of the cords and tighten the cord to stretch the hide tight inside the stretching frame. You are not trying to stretch the hide with the cords. You are just trying to put pressure on the hide to separate the fibers and pores in the hide so smoke can more completely penetrate the hide when it is placed into a smokehouse. Do not put too much pressure on the hide or you will create stretch marks in the hide.

Push on the hide with the hitting end of a baseball bat or the rounded end of your homemade stretching stick or the tapered end of your stick. Hold the baseball bat the same way you would normally hold the bat to hit a baseball but don't put the bat above your shoulder. Instead hold the bat straight out in front of you and push the opposite rounded end of the bat against the hide with the bat at a 90 degree angle to the hide. In other words, you will be standing directly in front of the hide and pushing into the hide with the opposite end of the baseball bat. The end of the bat should push into the hide about one or two inches and make an indentation just a little larger than the end of the bat. If you do not have enough arm strength to push the bat into the hide with your arms then you may use the weight of your body to push the bat gently into the hide. While applying pressure on the tool gradually slide the tool from the top of the hide towards the bottom of the hide in a straight line. Start at the left side of the hide and put the tool at the top of the hide. Apply pressure and gradually slide the tool in a straight line from the top to the bottom of the hide. Remove the tool from the hide and move it to the top of the hide a little to the right of the area you just stretched. Apply pressure and gradually slide the tool from the top to the bottom of the hide. Remove the tool and move it back to the top of the hide and a little to the right. Repeat this process until you have stretched the entire hide from top to bottom by gradually shifting your tool a little to the right each time. One side of the hide will take about four or five minutes of work. Some tanning solution will come out of the hide as you work the hide and the tanning solution will drip onto the ground.

Turn the stretching frame around so the other side of the hide is facing you and work that side for four or five minutes following the same procedure.

Wait about 20 minutes. Rotate the stretching frame onto its side so the neck is on the right and the tail is on the left. Put the tool on the edge of the hide that is facing up and work the hide from top to bottom, and from neck to tail, using a little more pressure for about ten minutes per side. This time the end of the bat should penetrate about two or three inches and make an indentation at least twice the size of the end of the bat. However, this time you will be sliding the tool across the hide in a 90 degree direction compared to before. When you have finished the first side put your stretching tool down and pick up your sanding block. Very gently sand the entire surface of the hide. Now turn the frame around so the other side of the hide is facing you and the tail is on the right and the neck is on the left. Pick up your stretching tool and work the hide again. When you have finished stretching that side of the hide switch to your sanding block and gently sand the entire surface of the hide that is now facing you. Gently sanding both sides of the hide will help the fibers to fluff up and the gentle friction will help some of the tanning solution to evaporate.

The hide will gradually stretch a little bit in all directions as you continue to push on the hide. Therefore you will need to periodically tighten all four stretching cords to keep consistent pressure on the hide across the entire surface of the hide. Wait until the hide has had a chance to shrink back towards its original size before you adjust the tension on the cords. Do not adjust the cord tensions immediately after a stretching session. Wait for the hide to shrink and then adjust the cord tensions uniformly. Adjusting the tension on the stretching cords is easy to do if you used hog rings to mount the hide because you only need to untie one knot on each side of the frame and pull on the cord and the hog rings will equally distribute the pressure evenly along that entire edge of the hide and then you can retie that one knot. Then do the next side of the frame. However, if you did not use hog rings and you put slits or holes in the outside edges of hide to receive the stretching cord then you will need to pull and adjust the stretching cord through each individual slit or hole in order to maintain consistent pressure around all four edges of the hide.

The neck area and both sides of the rump will usually dry slower than the rest of the hide and they will need to be stretched more often and with a little more pressure. Therefore as the hide gradually dries you will need to stretch the neck and each side of the rump area at least two or three times more than the rest of the hide before you switch to the other side of the hide or rotate the stretching frame. As the hide dries it will begin to turn white and it will be easier to see any damp spots because the damp spots will be darker in color. Work all of the damp spots more frequently than the areas that are already beginning to turn white. You can also move the scraping tool back and forth several times at a faster speed over the damp areas to increase the friction on those spots to help the hide to dry.

During stretching you should use your sanding block to remove any grainy spots or rough spots on either side of the hide as explained in the next chapter. In other words, when you see a spot that is thicker, coarser, or rougher than the rest of the hide you should put your scraping tool down and pick up your sanding block. Then sand the rough spot until you are satisfied that you have removed most of its roughness. Then put your sanding block down and pick up your stretching tool and continue the stretching process.

As the hide dries you can gradually apply more force on the stretching tool. You should also drag the tool with more pressure across any spots that have a crusty or rough surface to help scrape those stiff areas off the hide. However, always be careful when you approach an area that has a hole, or a cut, or that has been stitched closed.

The last time you stretch both sides of the hide with your stretching tool you can lean on the tool with all of your body weight and really push the stretching tool into the hide. But reduce the pressure around holes, cuts, and any area that has been stitched closed. As the hide dries these problem areas will become stronger but when the hide is wet these imperfections are still relatively weak.

The hide will gradually begin to dry on the stretching frame and become a little stiff. Continue to stretch the hide and allow the hide to dry completely on the stretching frame.

After the hide is dry and before you remove the hide from the stretching frame you should inspect it carefully for any remaining rough or crusty spots. If you discover some hard spots on the hide then you will need to sand those spots following the instructions in the next chapter while the hide is still on the stretching frame. After you have finished sanding any rough spots on the hide then you should gently sand the entire surface on both sides of the hide one final time to enhance the softness of the hide.

Chapter Twenty

Softening, Stretching, and Sanding - Part 3:
How to Use a Rock or Sandpaper

Sanding on a Rope or Cable: The hair side of a hide needs to be sanded while the damp hide is stretched over a rope or cable. The hide should be in the process of drying when it is sanded on the hair side. The sanding process should be done with the area that is to be sanded stretched out with nothing below the area to prevent the sanding process from removing too much of the thickness of the hide.

Sanding on a Stretching Frame: After the hide has completely dried on the stretching frame and while the hide is still on the stretching frame, the hair side of the hide should be carefully examined for rough or crusty spots. The rough spots may be sanded with a pumice stone, or a piece of sandpaper, on the hair side to remove any final residual membranes that might still be there. This sanding will also help to break up any "crust" that may begin to form on the hair side.

A piece of sandpaper or a pumice stone may be used to buff (or sand) the hair side of the hide. Wear an ordinary breathing mask, such as painter's mask or a doctor's mask, when using sandpaper or a pumice stone to buff a hide. If the hair side of the hide has some unusually thick crusty spots then you can sand them off with medium grade sandpaper attached to a handheld sanding block.

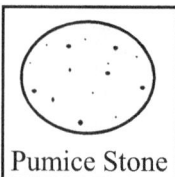
Pumice Stone

Pumice Stone or Rock: A pumice stone is a piece of volcanic rock that is approximately round. Pumice stones may be purchased at your local hardware store. One average size pumice stone with a diameter of about four inches may be used to sand the rough spots off approximately fifty hides before it will need to be replaced with a new stone.

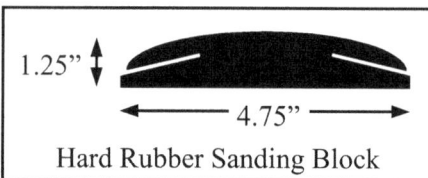
1.25"   4.75"
Hard Rubber Sanding Block

Sandpaper and a Sanding Block: Instead of a pumice stone an ordinary handheld sanding block may be used (see side view of block in illustration). These blocks are made of durable hard rubber. These handheld blocks may be purchased at almost any store that sells paint and sandpaper, including auto parts stores, hardware stores, and Walmarts. Look for them in the paint section of the store.

How to Use Sandpaper and a Sanding Block:

1. **Normal Sanding:** A piece of sandpaper is cut 2 5/8" wide and about 8" long and then aligned along the bottom flat surface of the block. The ends of the sandpaper are slipped into the slots at the right and left ends of the block and they are secured using the 3 short small pins that are inside each slot. Then the curved side of the block is held in the palm of the hand and the sandpaper on the flat bottom of the block is used to sand wood.

2. **Hide Sanding:** To use this same block on a hide the sandpaper should be placed over the top curved surface of the block, instead of along the flat bottom surface, and the two ends of the sandpaper are secured into the two end slots in the customary manner. Then the flat side of the block is held in the palm of the hand and the sandpaper on the upper curved surface of the block is used exactly like a pumice stone to smooth out and soften any rough or crusty spots on a hide. Use fine or extra fine sandpaper when sanding a hide.

Chapter Twenty-One

Introduction to Smoking a Hide

To Smoke or Not to Smoke

A few tanners will **not** smoke their hides in order to retain the white color of the original hide. When a hide is smoked the color of the hide will change from white to beige, to tan, to brown, or to some color in between based on how long the hide is smoked and the type of wood used to create the smoke. If a hide is not smoked then the hide will be relatively white. A tourist who does not understand the hide tanning process will usually not ask if a hide has been smoked. Instead a tourist will usually make his or her purchase decision based on the "appearance" of the hide. In most cases a tourist will pay more money for a "white" hide instead of one that is beige, or tan, or brown. Therefore, in order to increase their profits, some tanners will not smoke all their hides but they will offer their unsmoked hides to tourists at a higher price than their smoked hides. The majority of tourists are usually impressed with the white color of the hide and they are willing to pay a higher price for the white hide because they do not know that it has not competed the tanning process. Most tourists will simply display their hide for others to see and they will never realize that the hide they purchased cannot be made into clothing because the first time the white hide gets wet it will dry extremely stiff and it will no longer have the soft flexibility they originally admired. Therefore smoking is a necessary step in the tanning process and it should not be omitted.

Advantages of Smoking

Smoking provides all the following benefits:

1. It drives any remaining moisture out of the hide.
2. It neutralizes any residual tanning solution that is still in the hide, assuming the hide was tanned before smoking.
3. It helps to protect the hide from decaying.
4. It enhances the natural color of the hide.
5. It creates a slightly darker buckskin and this helps the buckskin to maintain its clean appearance longer when compared to a white buckskin because it only takes a very tiny amount of dirt to make a white buckskin look dirty.
6. Moths will eat a tanned hide but moths will ignore a smoked hide. This means you will not have to worry about moths eating holes in your buckskin clothing.
7. It makes the hide undesirable to a variety of other insects that would otherwise eat holes in the hide.
8. Wood smoke is also a natural insect repellent so the hide will be somewhat offensive to biting insects. This means you will attract fewer insects when you are wearing buckskin clothing.
9. It will soften the fibers in the hide and it will cause those fibers to shrink a little bit and move closer together. This helps the hide to repel insect bites even after the aroma of the wood smoke is washed out of the hide.
10. Smoking does not make a hide waterproof. However, it does permanently change the water retention properties of the hide. It helps the hide to repel water and therefore the hide will absorb less water when it does occasionally get wet.
11. It prevents the hide from hardening when it does become wet. It permanently conditions a hide so it will dry into a soft buckskin every time it gets wet.
12. If you don't smoke a hide then you will have to stretch the hide each time it gets wet or it will have a tendency to become stiff and hard as it dries. If you do smoke a hide then the hide will remain flexible every time that the hide does get wet and then gradually dries out.

Smoke, Moisture, and Heat

There are some major differences in the methods that are used to smoke meat for immediate consumption, and to smoke meat to extend is useful shelf life, and to smoke hides to create buckskin clothing. If you are aware of these differences then you will be less likely to make the mistake of trying to smoke everything the same way.

The variables of smoke, moisture, and heat need to be controlled differently for each of the following three applications:

1. **Smoking Meat so You can Eat it Now:** Requires some smoke, some moisture, and good heat.
2. **Smoking Meat for Long-Term Storage:** Requires some smoke, no moisture, and less heat.
3. **Smoking Animal Hides:** Requires thick smoke, no moisture, and almost no heat.

In this chapter we will be describing how to smoke animal hides so we will be trying to produce a lot of smoke, but no moisture, and almost no heat.

Smoking Hides versus Smoking Meat

Although wood smoke and a smokehouse may be used to smoke a hide and to smoke meat, the basic objectives of these two processes are totally different.

Smoking Meat for Long-Term Storage: When you are smoking meat the two primary objectives are: (1) to dry and cure the meat by removing the moisture from the meat, and (2) to enhance the flavor of the meat with the wood smoke. When you smoke meat you are not trying to cook the meat. Instead you are simply drying the meat to extend its shelf life so you can eat it safely at some future time. Depending on a variety of factors, the temperature at which you will smoke meat will usually be somewhere between 170 to 185 degrees Fahrenheit (°F) or 77 to 85 degrees Centigrade or Celsius (°C).

Smoking Hides: On the other hand, when you smoke a hide you are not trying to dry or cure the hide, nor are you trying to drive the moisture out in the hide, nor are you trying to cook the hide or make it smell better. The primary objective of smoking a hide is to break down the natural glues in the hide so those glues can be rinsed away. The temperature at which you will normally smoke a hide is somewhere between 105°F to 120°F (or 41°C to 49°C).

Once you understand the basic difference between smoking meat and smoking a hide then you will be able to successfully smoke either a hide or some meat based on what you are trying to accomplish and you will not use the same procedure for both even though you may use the same smokehouse for both (but at different times).

Smoke and Heat

There is a difference between burning wood to produce heat and burning wood to produce smoke.

1. **Heat:** When wood is burned to produce heat then very little smoke is desired. This is the objective when wood is burned inside a fireplace to heat a home.

2. **Smoke:** When wood is burned to produce smoke then very little heat is desired. This is the objective when wood is burned inside a smokehouse in order to smoke hides or to smoke meat.

The objective of smoking a hide is to produce smoke and not heat. Smoke is the result of the incomplete combustion of the wood. Smoke contains various gasses and formaldehyde. These chemicals in the smoke will bond with the fibers in the hide. The result is that the glues in the hide will be permanently neutralized. Later if the hide gets wet it will dry faster and it will remain relatively soft and it will not harden.

Wood Smoke and Humidity

Do not use wet wood or damp wood or freshly cut wood to create smoke because these types of wood will produce a lot of humidity and that is undesirable. The smoke needs to be a dry smoke in a very low heat environment.

However, some tanners prefer to use wood that is slightly damp because it generates more smoke. But that smoke is a high humidity smoke instead of a dry smoke. Those tanners believe that damp smoke does a better job of penetrating a hide when compared to dry smoke.

I personally recommend that you minimize the amount of moisture you use to create your smoke.

Different Types of Wood

1. Freshly cut wood is called "green wood" because it still contains moisture and it has not dried yet. Wood that contains moisture will smoke extensively when it is burned. For this reason most firewood is allowed to season, or dry, before it is used in a wood burning fireplace because dry wood will produce more heat and very little smoke. However, for smoking a hide neither green wood nor seasoned dry firewood should be used to produce smoke.

2. The best wood to use to create smoke is dry semi-rotten wood. Semi-rotten wood is called "punky" wood. Almost any type of dry, semi-rotten wood will produce a lot of smoke, almost no moisture, and very little heat.

3. Do not use wood that contains pitch, such as pine, because the pitch will be in the smoke and the pitch will get into the hide and the hide will feel sticky and stiff after smoking.

4. Dry corncobs or very dry leaves or dry sawdust may be used to create smoke.

Wood Types, Wood Chips, and Sawdust

Different types of wood will yield different amounts of heat and smoke. In other words, some types of wood burn hotter and some types of wood create more or less smoke than other types of wood.

If you use wood chips then the thickness of the wood chips should be between 1/2 inch to 3/4 inch. The width of the chips should be between 1 to 2 inches. The length of the wood chips should be based on the size of your fire pit or your Dutch oven. The wood chips should be at least one inch shorter than the minimum inside diameter of your fire pit or your Dutch oven.

Save the sawdust you create when you are cutting your wood and your wood chips. A little dry sawdust dropped onto hot coals will produce a good quantity of smoke for the smoking process.

Chapter Twenty-Two

Smoking an Animal Hide

Hair or Fur Still on Hide: Any hide that still has the hair or fur on it, such as a bearskin, will need to be smoked above a smoke pit and **not** inside a smokehouse. Only the **flesh** side of the hide should be exposed to the smoke. The reason is because smoke contains chemicals that will loosen the hair or fur and cause it to gradually fall off the hide. On the other hand, acids such as vinegar or animal brains will cause the hair to cling to the hide. Finally, the smoke will discolor the hair or fur if the smoke is allowed to make direct contact with the hair or fur.

Smoke One Side or Both Sides of the Hide: Some tanners, and some Native American Indians, only smoke the hair side of the hide because the smoke will penetrate all the way through to the flesh side of the hide during the smoking process. But most tanners smoke both the hair side and the flesh side of the hide to maximize the benefits of the smoking process.

There are two ways that an animal hide may be smoked:

1. **Above a Smoke Pit.** This method requires twice the amount of smoking time and it requires more labor for every hide that needs to be smoked.

2. **Inside a Smokehouse.** This method requires less total smoking time and it requires less labor for each hide that needs to be smoked.

Both of the above methods will be described in this chapter beginning with the smoke pit.

How to Build and Use a Smoke Pit

A smoke pit is the most popular and the most widely recommended method for smoking hides in all the hide tanning books that are currently available. Therefore this method will be described in detail. However, the reasons I personally do not recommend this method will be explained at the end of this section.

Hide Dryness: A hide must be dry before it can be properly smoked.

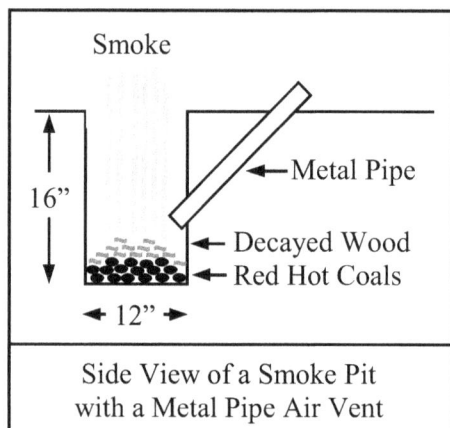

Side View of a Smoke Pit with a Metal Pipe Air Vent

The Hole: Dig a hole or pit in the ground about 12 inches in diameter and approximately 16 inches deep using a posthole digger (if you have one). The 16 inch deep hole allows less air to get to the fire in the bottom of the hole and this will help to create more smoke when you need it. The 12 inch diameter allows the smoke to be directed exactly where you want it.

Metal Pipe: One very practical enhancement to the traditional smoke pit is to push a stick or a metal rod from the top of the ground sideways through the ground at a 45 degree angle down into the smoke pit and then remove the stick or rod to leave an air hole. The air hole should be about twelve inches from the top opening of the smoke pit and the other end of the air hole should penetrate the side wall of the smoke pit about six inches above the bottom of the smoke pit. Then insert a hollow metal pipe into the air hole. This will allow you to control the flow of air into the smoke pit by blocking or unblocking the end of the pipe that is above the ground. If you block the end of the pipe then this cuts off the air into the smoke pit and the coals will begin to cool. If you unblock the end of the pipe then this allows air into the smoke pit and the coals will begin to heat up. You may use a fireplace wind billows (a hand operated air pump) to gently blow some fresh air into the top end of the metal pipe and into the bottom of the fire pit. The metal pipe will get very hot so be careful not to touch it.

The Fire: Build a small fire in the bottom of the hole. Gradually add some larger dry sticks that are about one or two inches in diameter. Wait for the large sticks to burn down into red hot coals. You will need a pile of red hot coals about two or three inches deep in the bottom of the smoke pit. You should be able to feel the heat of the coals about 12 inches above the ground but the heat should not burn your hand. Now drop some very dry decayed wood, or some suitable wood chips, onto the coals to create a lot of smoke. Keep a small bucket of water nearby so you can throw a **little** water on the fire if it flares up when you add wood and the wood begins to burn freely instead of smoking. You want smoke and not heat to smoke the hide.

Metal Can: If you wish you may place a metal can or stove pipe between the top of the smoke pit and the bottom of the smoking skirt (described next). This increases the distance from the smoke pit to the hide and it reduces the chance of the hide accidentally catching on fire. The metal can will need to have a larger diameter than the top of the smoke pit. The metal can will need to have its bottom removed so that the can is open on both ends. An old metal garbage can works well for this application. Place the can above the smoke pit and then drape the smoking skirt over the opening in the opposite end of the metal can so that the smoke travels up through the can, through the smoking skirt, and finally into the buckskin.

Smoking Skirt: A smoking skirt will need to be attached to the bottom of the hide. The skirt should be made from either cotton or wool and nothing else. Old ragged blue jeans may be cut and sewn together to make a skirt that is about 18 inches tall, with a diameter of about 18 inches so it will fit far enough away from the top of the smoke hole without touching the outside edges of the smoke hole. The skirt may be held against the ground with some rocks or it can be staked to the ground with several thin stakes.

How to Make a Blue Jean Smoking Skirt: Select an old pair of worn out blue jeans, preferably from an adult or a teenager. Either pin or sew the bottom of the two white pockets to the inside legs of the jean so the white pockets cannot fall down to the waist area when the jean is upside down. Close the zipper and then button or snap the waist closed. Look at the two legs and decide which one is in the worst shape based on holes and tears. Cut off that leg about half way between the crotch and the knee area. Fold the cut leg over onto itself twice to make a closed seam that is about 1/2 inch wide and either pin or sew the cut end of the leg closed at the new seam you just formed. Now cut the other leg that is still attached to the jean at the knee area so that you have about 18 or more inches from the waist to the knee. Cut patches from the jean pieces that you removed to the size required to cover any holes in the remaining jean that will be used as a skirt. Sew or pin those patches onto the jean to cover all the holes so smoke cannot easily escape from inside the jean. Place the waist end of the jean around the outside edge of the smoke pit and stake the jean to the ground using the belt loops around the waist of the jean. Position the jean so the leg that is still on the jean is directly above the smoke pit. Pin the leg opening in the jean to the temporary opening of the same size that you left on the bottom of hide. Since you will be creating the temporary opening in the bottom of the hide it is easy to make that opening the same size as the opening in the jean leg at its knee area. You now have a skirt that will direct most of the smoke from the smoke pit into the hide so the hide will be properly and thoroughly smoked.

Skirt Life: Each smoking skirt should only be used three or four times and then it will need to be discarded because it will have absorbed so many of the chemicals from the smoke that it could easily catch on fire if you continue to use it.

Tripod (illustration on next page): Build a tripod above the smoke pit so that the distance from the top peak of the tripod is about 12 inches higher than the combined length of the hide plus the smoking skirt. If you use a stove pipe or a metal can then the length of the stove pipe or metal can will need to be added to this distance.

Holes in the Hide: If there are any holes or cuts in the hide then they must be sewn or pinned closed to prevent the smoke from easily escaping through the holes or cuts.

Hide Smoke Sack: If you only have one hide then fold it in half with the hair side on the inside and use some straight pins or clothespins to secure the sides of the hide together. If you have two hides of approximately the same size then match them together at the necks and tails so that their hair sides are facing each other and then pin the hides together around their outside edges but leave an opening at the neck area for the smoke to enter.

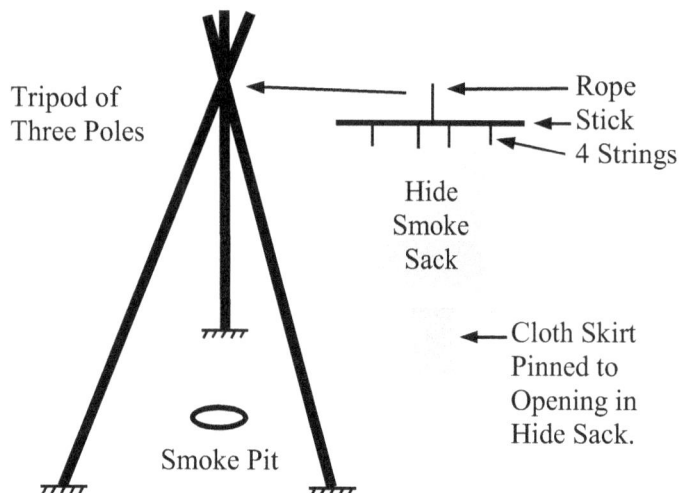

Tripod of Three Poles

Rope

Stick

4 Strings

Hide Smoke Sack

Cloth Skirt Pinned to Opening in Hide Sack.

Smoke Pit

Build a Three Pole Tripod centered above the Smoke Pit.
Fold One Hide in Half or Pin Two Hides together
to Make a Smoke Sack.
Pin a Cloth Skirt to Opening in Bottom of Hide Sack.
Tie Hide Sack (or 2 Hides) to Straight Stick with 4 Strings.
Tie Straight Stick with a Rope to Top Center of Tripod.
Adjust Rope Length until Cloth Skirt touches Smoke Pit.

Sewing Option: Instead of straight pins or clothespins you may sew the hide together around the outside edge. Sewing is the method recommended in all the currently available hide tanning literature. However, sewing requires some type of thread. And sewing takes more time than simply pushing a few straight pins into the outside edge of the hide. When you are finished smoking the hide it also takes more time to remove the thread than to simply pull out the straight pins.

Short Sticks: Place a few extremely dry short sticks between 6 inches to 12 inches long inside the hide to hold the inside of the hide open so smoke can reach the entire inner surface of the hide. Every four minutes while the hide is being smoked you will need to shift the positions of the sticks inside the hide that are keeping it propped open or the ends of the sticks will prevent those spots from receiving any smoke and they will not season properly. Do not use sticks with any moisture in them because they will begin to steam during the smoking process and the steam will leave spots on the hide. Do not use the same sticks more than once because they will become a fire hazard inside another hide if they are used a second time.

Hang Hide: Hang the hide above the smoke pit so the open area of the hide is approximately 18 inches above the ground and the top of the smoke pit.

Temperature: The smoke should be thick but not too hot. The objective is to smoke the hide but not cook the hide. Very carefully insert one of your fingers between the smoking skirt and the hide where they meet and test the heat of the smoke. If the smoke is so hot that you have to instantly jerk your finger out of the smoke then the smoke is too hot and it will burn the hide instead of smoking the hide. Remove the hide from above the smoke pit and wait for the fire to burn down and the smoke to cool off. Then replace the hide and test the temperature of the smoke again. Very carefully test the temperature of the smoke with one of your fingers every four or five minutes while the hide is being smoked.

Smoking the Hair Side: Smoke the hair side of the hide first. Continue to smoke the hair side of the hide until you can see the color on the flesh side of the hide beginning to change. If there are some thin spots or score marks on the hide then they will show color first. Wait until at least half of the outside flesh side of the hide has some color to it and then turn the hair side of the hide out and the flesh side of the hide in so the flesh side of the hide can be smoked as described next.

Smoking the Flesh Side: Remove the hide from above the smoke pit, turn the hide inside out so the hair side is on the outside and the flesh side is on the inside, and then place the hide above the smoke pit as before so the flesh side can be smoked.

Smoking Time: The total smoking time will be approximately 30 to 60 minutes. The hair side of the hide will usually take between 20 to 40 minutes to smoke properly. The flesh side of the hide will usually take about half the amount of time that the hair side required. The flesh side of the hide will need less smoking time because the entire hide will already be extremely dry and smoke saturated.

Observe Continuously: Never leave the hide unattended while it is being smoked, even for a short period of time. You must observe the hide smoking process continuously from beginning to end or you run the risk that your hide may be destroyed while you are absent from the smoking area.

Potential Fire and Wind Problems: The major problem with a smoke pit is that the smoldering fire in the bottom of the smoke pit can unexpectedly flare up and ignite the skirt or the hide. If this happens then instantly jerk the hide off the tripod and stomp on the hide to put the fire out. Part of the hide will be ruined but you will have saved the part of the hide that was not burned. Another problem is that a gust of wind may occur unexpectedly during the smoking process and this will blow the hide around above the smoke pit and cause the hide to smoke unevenly on the inside, or it could blow the center of the skirt over the top of the smoke pit and the skirt could catch on fire. Never smoke a hide on a windy day. However, even on an otherwise calm day the wind could increase after you start smoking a hide. If you hear the sound of a "crackling" fire inside the smoke pit then immediately remove the skirt and the hide from above the smoke pit and extinguish the flame. When you have the flame out and the pit smoking again then replace the skirt and the hide above the smoke pit.

Air Dry and Soak the Hide: Follow the instructions at the end of this chapter after the hide has finished smoking above the smoke pit.

In summary, the **advantages of a smoke pit** are as follows:

1. It is the traditional method that was been used by our ancestors and it is the method that is still used by most tribal groups worldwide.
2. It is the method most tanners still use and it is the method that is described in detail in all the currently available books on hide tanning.
3. It is the best choice if only one hide is going to be smoked and there is a very small chance that you will be smoking any additional hides at any time during the next few years.
4. It can be done almost anywhere that it is safe to build a fire.
5. It is appropriate if you are living a gypsy lifestyle and you move to a different camping area on a periodic basis.
6. It must be used if the hair or fur is still on the hide. Only the flesh side of the hide will be smoked above the smoke pit and the hair or fur on the hide should not be directly exposed to the wood smoke.

In summary, the **disadvantages of a smoke pit** are as follows:

1. The hide must be pinned or sewn together so it can be smoked. After smoking the pins or stitches must be removed. This step is not necessary when using a smokehouse.
2. Each side of the hide must be smoked. This means the hide must be turned inside out and smoked a second time so that both sides of the hide are properly smoked.
3. The sticks that are holding the hide open so the smoke can reach the entire inner surface of the hide must be repositioned every four minutes to allow the smoke to reach the parts of the hide where the sticks were previously touching the hide.
4. Twice as much smoking material is needed to smoke the hide.
5. More than twice as much time is needed to smoke a hide above a smoke pit when compared to a smokehouse.
6. A special smoke skirt must be constructed and the smoke skirt may only be used to smoke a few hides before it will have to be discarded and replaced.
7. There is a chance the hide will catch on fire above the smoke pit and all the work and effort that you have invested will be lost. You will have lost your hide and it will not be available to make buckskin clothing.

Because on the above disadvantages I do not personally recommend a smoke pit unless you only need to smoke one hide, or your are in a situation where you cannot build a simple smokehouse, or the hair or fur has been intentionally left on the hide.

How to Smoke a Hide (or Several Hides) Inside a Smokehouse

Any hide that still has the hair or fur attached must be processed above a smoke pit.

A smokehouse is a very practical option if you will be tanning more than one hide per year, or if you plan to smoke meat to extend the meat's shelf life. You should read Chapter 39 on how to construct a simple but practical smokehouse before you read the rest of this chapter. After you read the smokehouse chapter you may decide that it is more practical in your situation to build a small simple smokehouse instead of constantly investing the extra time required to smoke hides above a smoke pit.

Hide Dryness: A hide must be dry before it can be properly smoked.

Hanging Hides: Hang your hide, or hides, on horizontal (level) wires that run from front to rear, or from side to side, inside your smokehouse. The wires should be a few inches below the ceiling and six inches apart so that the smoke can easily reach and saturate both sides of all the hides hanging in the smokehouse. It is better to hang a hide, or hides, closer to the opposite wall of the smokehouse across from the Dutch oven. Do not hang a hide directly above the Dutch oven. Use ordinary wood clothespins to hang the hides on the wires.

A hide should not touch itself (it should not be folded in half over the wire) and a hide should not touch other hides inside the smokehouse during smoking.

The outside edge of a smoked hide will be trimmed off after smoking so you do not have to worry about the small outside edge of the hide that is making contact with the wire not being smoked properly.

The Dutch oven should be placed on top of a large flat rock, or a flat patio stone, about 12 inches from the small door opening at the bottom of the smokehouse.

The Fire: Start a small fire inside the Dutch oven using some small extremely dry sticks. Gradually add a few chucks of dry wood. Continue to add small chucks of dry wood until you have a nice bed of red hot coals about one inch deep in the bottom of the Dutch oven. Now you may add some very dry decayed wood, or any wood that smokes well, on top of the hot coals inside the Dutch oven and immediately place the lid on top of the Dutch oven so there is only a small opening on one side of the lid to allow air to enter the oven and heat and smoke to exit the oven.

It is now time to leave the smokehouse and close the smokehouse door behind you.

You may notice some of the smoke (and heat) escaping from the smokehouse around the edge of the roof where it is attached to the smokehouse.

The smoke should gradually become thick and dense inside the smokehouse. The thicker the smoke the better the smoke will saturate the pores of a hide.

You want maximum smoke and minimum heat and no moisture.

Smokehouse Temperature: Look at the temperature dial mounted on the exterior smokehouse wall to determine the interior smokehouse temperature. It is important to maintain an internal smokehouse temperature between 105°F to 120°F (or 41°C to 49°C) to properly smoke a hide.

Too Hot: If the temperature begins to get too hot then open the door of the smokehouse about two inches and this will allow some of the heat and smoke inside the smokehouse to escape. Close the door when the internal smokehouse temperature drops down below 105°F (or 41°C).

Too Cool: If the temperature begins to fall too low then open the small door at the bottom of the smokehouse near the Dutch oven. Use a Dutch oven lid lifter to transfer the lid from the oven to the ground. Toss two handfuls of dry decayed wood, or suitable wood chips, onto the coals in the Dutch oven. Wait approximately one minute and then replace the lid on the Dutch oven using your lid lifter but remember to leave a small air gap between one side of the lid and the Dutch oven. In other words, do not put the lid on the oven the same way you would do if you were cooking food inside the oven.

Time Required: The total hide smoking time can vary from 15 minutes up to about three hours depending on the thickness of the hide, the type of wood used, and the amount of smoke generated. Generally a little extra smoking time is better than not enough smoking time.

The first fill of the Dutch oven should be enough to keep the temperature and the smoke inside the smokehouse at reasonable levels for between 60 to 90 minutes. Depending on your hide, or hides, this will usually be more than enough time to complete the entire hide smoking process.

During the warm weather months the smokehouse will not be loosing much heat to the air outside the smokehouse. But during the cold weather months the heat loss through the smokehouse walls will be greater. Therefore it will usually take a little longer to smoke a hide during cold weather when compared to warm weather.

Finally, a thin hide will require less time to smoke than a thick hide.

When the hide is a little darker than it was when it was first put into the smokehouse then the smoking process is finished. If the hide is a lot darker then the hide will still be okay but you will need less time in you smokehouse for a similar type of hide in the future. However, a darker hide will be a little more water resistant later.

Save the Wood Ashes: The cold ashes inside the Dutch oven should be saved because they can be used in the hide soaking step that uses wood ashes (bucking). This is one of the advantages of using a Dutch oven because the cold wood ashes will be clean and easy to pour into a suitable storage container for future use when tanning hides or when making homemade soap. The procedure for making good homemade soap using wood ashes, animal fat, and rainwater is described in my book: **Grandpappy's Survival Manual for Hard Times.**

What to Do After Smoking a Hide Above a Smoke Pit or Inside a Smokehouse

Hide Color: The longer a hide is smoked the darker in color the hide will gradually become. If the hide is almost white to begin with then it will gradually turn slightly yellow, then slightly orange, and then a light shade of brown as the smoking time is increased.

Air Drying: After the hide has finished the smoking process, hang the smoked hide in the open air for one day to give the hide a chance to thoroughly dry and to release any moisture that may have become trapped in the hide during the smoking process.

Soaking: After the hide has been smoked and air dried, the hide should be soaked in a clean water bath for thirty minutes. This will rinse any smoke residue out of the hide, and remove most of the smoky smell from the hide, and it will allow you to verify that the entire hide will dry soft after it has become wet. Lay the hide down flat onto a flat surface by hand while it is still wet and then smooth out any wrinkles or folds by hand. As the hide gradually dries stretch it by hand every thirty minutes from side to side and from top to bottom. If the hide dries with hard spots on it then those spots will need to be sanded, brain tanned, and smoked again before converting the hide into buckskin clothing, or the cloth patterns will need to be strategically placed around those spots so the hard spots can be cut off and discarded when the buckskin is sewn into an article of clothing.

Chapter Twenty-Three

Final Hide Inspection and Deciding How a Hide Should be Used

Each hide is unique. No two hides will end up looking or feeling exactly the same even though you process them all exactly the same way.

Each hide began the tanning process with a different number of imperfections already in the hide, such as bullet holes, and knife cuts, and natural scars on the outside of the hide where the deer cut itself against a sharp long hanging tree branch or where it tried to go under the top wire of a barb wire fence. All of these imperfections will be present in the finished hide after you tan it. The number of imperfections, the position of those imperfections, and the size of the imperfections will influence how the hide should be used. For example, if the hide has almost no imperfections then it could be used for almost any large article of clothing. If the hide has a few imperfections that are far apart then it could be used for a medium size article of clothing. But if the hide has several imperfections scattered all around the hide, then it may be better utilized for some smaller articles of clothing.

One way to hide an imperfection is to include it in a seam or in a hem of the garment.

The thickness of the hide will also influence its final use. Thinner hides should be converted into warm weather clothing and thicker hides should be converted into cold weather clothing.

Be prepared for some of your hides to look and feel almost like velvet. Also be prepared for some of your hides to look like a disaster. You can still use a poor quality hide by converting it into a rope, or a whip, or a cap, or some gloves, or some moccasins.

Smaller thinner hides are more useful for shirts, skirts, or any article that will receive beads or embroidery as decoration.

Larger thicker hides are more useful for pants, dresses, jackets, and coats.

One of the easiest ways to evaluate a hide is to place it against your body, or the body of the person for whom you will be making clothing. This is called "draping." Is the hide wide enough to cover the entire back of the person? Is the hide long enough to fit from the person's waist to his or her ankles? Is the hide long enough to fit from a woman's neck down to her knees or her ankles? On shirts and dresses the sleeves may be added from a different hide if necessary.

Generally a garment should be made with the top or neck of the garment facing the neck area of the hide and the bottom of the garment facing the tail end of the hide. This will usually result in a garment that is a better fit and it will last longer.

Garments should always be designed to fit loosely at first in order to give the buckskin clothing some space in which it can shrink without making the garment too small to wear.

Now is the time to trim the small stretching holes off the outside of the hide. Chapter 36 contains detailed instructions on how to do this task so you can create a nice long buckskin strip that can be used as a thong, or as a strap, or as a lace.

Chapter Twenty-Four

Introduction to Homemade Buckskin Clothing and Animal Sinew

How to Begin

The first step in the construction of any type of buckskin clothing is always the same. Wash the hide that you just finished tanning is some warm clean water using a little pure soap that does not have any additives, such as Ivory brand soap. The soap will help to remove any residual chemicals that are still in the hide and it will wash a lot of the smoky smell out of the hide. Do not wash the hide in a washing machine. Wash the hide by hand in a large tub, such as a bathtub. Thoroughly and completely rinse all the soap out of the hide. Wring most of the water out of the hide by hand. Then lay the hide down on a flat surface so it can gradually dry. As the hide dries it will shrink into its new natural shape. This is critical because the hide must shrink into its finished shape before you cut it into pattern pieces to make clothing. In the future when you wash your buckskin clothing it will not shrink into a size that will not fit you. When the hide is completely dry then gently flex and bend the hide over a rope or cable to make the hide soft and flexible so it can be cut into pattern pieces, but do not attempt to stretch the hide again at this time.

Routine Washing and Drying of Buckskin Clothing

Always wash buckskin clothing by hand in warm or cool water using a mild soap. It is okay to use a soft bristle brush to help clean dirt and any stains off the clothes. A soft bristle brush, if used gently, will actually help to restore the soft texture of the buckskin.

When you are finished hand washing your buckskin clothing then gently wring most of the water out of the clothing by hand. Then lay the buckskin clothing on a flat surface to dry. After the clothing has dried you should very gently pull and stretch the clothing by hand in every direction to help soften the buckskin so it will feel comfortable against your skin.

Never wash buckskin clothing in water that feels too hot to your touch. If the temperature of the water is above 120°F (or 49°C) then the hot water will cook the buckskins and completely ruin your clothing.

Never hang buckskin clothing that is heavy with water on a clothesline. The weight of the water will pull and stretch the buckskin out of its original shape.

Never dry buckskin clothing in a clothes dryer because a clothes dryer will ruin buckskin clothing.

The Natural Smell of Buckskins

The natural smell of a buckskin will help to mask your human smell when you are hunting. If you know you will be hunting or trapping the next day, then you should consider wrapping your buckskin clothes around some fresh green pine needles before you go to bed at night. The smell of the green pine needles on your buckskin clothing will help to mask your natural human scent.

The Size of Buckskin Clothing

If you do not know if a hide will shrink when it gets wet, or if it will stretch after it has been worn several times, then it is better to make the garment a little bigger than it needs to be. After you have worn the garment for a reasonable period of time then you can always take the seams apart and remove some of the buckskin material and make the garment a little smaller so it fits you more comfortably. However, if the garment is too small then there is no easy way to make it bigger.

The same concept applies to the garments that you make for your growing children. Always make a child's garments a little bigger so the garment has some growing room in it.

Some General Guidelines for Making Buckskin Clothing

When possible an article of clothing should be made from a single hide. When this is not possible then try to select two or more hides that have the same approximate thickness, softness, and color. However, depending on the type of garment you may wish to select a hide with a slightly different color for specific parts of the garment, such as yokes, pockets, or fringe.

The Differences between Buckskin Clothing and Fabric Clothing

There are similarities and there are differences between clothing that is made from buckskins and clothing that is made from other materials, such as cotton, wool, or manmade fibers.

If you will closely examine conventional clothing then you will probably notice that there are a lot of different ways to make an article of clothing, such as a skirt. The skirt can be one long piece of material that is joined together, or it can be two pieces of material that are joined together, or it can consist of several pieces of material that are sewn together to make the skirt. The skirt may have buttons, or a zipper, or it may simply overlap from side to side in the front and be tied together in the rear or in the front.

The same concept applies to buckskin clothing. You may use any strategy you wish to create the article of clothing that you desire. This book will suggest some common simple strategies for making clothing but you may create your own clothing in any manner that pleases you.

Buckskins are extremely strong when compared to fabric made from cotton, wool, or manmade fibers. Therefore buckskin clothing does not need as many stitches per inch as clothing made from other materials. For example, most normal clothing has between six to twelve stitches per seam inch but buckskin clothing can be successfully made with four stitches per seam inch.

Buckskin clothing will last many, many years unless it is abused. Therefore you should try to make your clothing as comfortable as possible because you, or some member of your family, may be wearing it for a very long time. If the article of clothing fits well, and it is not too tight or too loose, and it flexes as you move without putting pressure on different parts of your body, then you will have created a high quality article of buckskin clothing.

The easiest way to create an article of clothing that fits you, or a member of your family, is to copy an article of clothing that you already own and that you are very happy with. If that article of clothing is almost worn out then you can remove the stitches in the garment and use the individual pieces of the garment as your pattern pieces. Just position those individual garment pieces on your piece of buckskin until you achieve both of the following objectives:

1. **Holes and Cuts:** If it is possible, move the pattern pieces around on the flesh side of the hide so that most of the holes and cuts are not inside a pattern piece. In other words, when the buckskin is eventually cut into pieces to make clothing those holes and cuts will be discarded as small scraps of buckskin.

2. **Hide Utilization:** Move the pattern pieces around to utilize as much of the hide as possible. In other words, try to position the pattern pieces so that very little of the buckskin will be discarded as scrap pieces. However, do not align pattern pieces in a diagonal line across the hide. If possible, align all the pattern pieces from neck to tail. If necessary, align some of the pattern pieces from the left side to the right side of the hide, if this is appropriate for the type of garment you will be making.

When you have the pattern pieces in their optimal positions to achieve the above objectives use a few simple straight pins to pin each pattern piece to the buckskin. Or trace around the outside edge of each pattern piece with a pencil. Then carefully cut the buckskin to match the pattern pieces. Then remove the pattern pieces and sew the buckskin pieces together to make the article of clothing that you just copied. When you are finished with the original pattern pieces then you should save those pattern pieces in a large paper envelope or cloth envelope so you can use them again in the future if you need to.

If the article of clothing you wish to copy is not worn out then you will need to make some paper patterns of the different pieces of the garment. Lay some large paper, such as a page from a flip chart tablet, or a large piece of brown wrapping paper, onto the garment and use a pencil to trace the shape of each pattern piece onto the paper. If the paper is not long enough to reach from one end of the garment to the other end of the garment then you can tape two or more pieces of paper together to make a bigger sheet of paper that will completely cover each part of the clothing. Then add one inch to the outside border all the way around each paper pattern piece to provide space for the seams that will hold the garment together. Then cut the paper pattern pieces out of the paper and pin them onto the huge piece of buckskin in the manner described above. When you are finished with your paper patterns you should save them in a large envelope and write the type of clothing on the outside of the envelope.

Cutting Buckskins

Hair Removed: If the hair was scraped off the hide then you may cut the hide using scissors or with a sharp knife. Scissors are easier to use and they will yield a cleaner smoother cut for sewing.

After you have the pattern pieces pinned to a buckskin, or you have traced the pattern pieces onto the buckskin with a pencil, then cut the buckskin using a sharp pair of scissors. Scissors will allow you to cut along a straight edge or a curved edge of a pattern piece and this will make it easier to fit those pieces together and sew them into a garment.

If your scissors become dull then you can easily sharpen them if you purchased the Pocket Pal Sharpening Tool that was recommended in Chapter 4.

Hair or Fur Still On: If the hide still has its hair or fur then you should not use scissors to trim the hide because the scissors will also cut off the hair and this will leave a "bald" spot at the edge of the hide where you made your cut. This may be desirable if that side will become part of a seam. But if that side will be visible then you will need to cut the hide carefully with a very sharp knife while holding the hide above the table so that you only cut through the hide and you do not accidentally trim off any of the hair or fur.

Sewing Buckskins into Clothing

The inside flesh side of the hide should always be towards your skin and the outside hair side of the hide should always be facing away from your skin. This is the way the hide was on the animal and it is the way the hide should be made into clothing. The hair side of the hide was designed to be exposed to the weather and to make the occasional contact with trees, brush, and rocks. The flesh side of the hide was not designed to make contact with foreign elements and it will more easily pick up stickers, burrs, and other small particles, such as dirt. Therefore always sew the flesh side of the hide so it faces inside the garment towards your skin.

Unraveling and Stretching

One of the nice qualities of buckskin is that it will not begin to unravel in a manner similar to most fabrics. Because most fabrics will gradually unravel and come apart along the edge of the fabric, a hem is placed in the edge of the garment to keep the fabric from unraveling. To prevent the unraveling the hem is double folded so the raw edge of the cloth is protected inside the hem.

One of the shortcomings of buckskins is that it will gradually begin to stretch along an exposed edge. As the buckskin stretches it will begin to look uneven along the edge of the garment even though it was cut smoothly in the beginning.

Therefore you will need to put a hem in the outer edges of your buckskin garments in order to maintain the original appearance of your buckskin clothing. However, the purpose of this hem will not be to prevent the buckskin from unraveling. Instead the purpose of the hem will be to help prevent the buckskin from stretching into an odd shape at the exposed edge of the garment. However, a buckskin hem is only single folded because the raw edge of the buckskin will not gradually come unraveled.

Summer and Winter Clothing

Most families will need clothing they can wear in warm weather and different clothing they can wear in cold weather. Keep this in mind as you create your buckskin clothing so each member of your family has the appropriate clothing to wear during the different seasons of the year.

Summer clothing should be made from thinner buckskins, such as the hides of females and young animals. Winter clothing should be made from thicker buckskins, such as the hides of males.

Summer clothing should fit loosely and it does not need to have closely fitted seams. Winter clothing should have overlapping seams that are securely stitched together to trap body heat inside the clothing and to prevent the winter cold from penetrating through the seams. Buckskin clothing is similar to regular clothing because two or more layers of clothing will keep you warmer than one thick layer of clothing.

Rainwear

Buckskin clothing is not waterproof. Therefore it is not acceptable rainwear. Buckskin clothing will absorb and retain water the same way cotton clothing does. Therefore you will need an outer garment, such as a rainproof plastic or rubber poncho, to wear over your buckskin clothing when it rains.

Sewing Machines

You do not need a sewing machine to create buckskin clothing. Buckskin clothing may be created using a needle and some thread or some sinew or some thongs.

Singer Model 66

However, if you wish to use a sewing machine then you will need a special sewing machine that is designed to sew leather, or you will need an antique sewing machine from the early 1900s. Sewing machines made in the early 1900s were designed to sew through thick materials, such as leather. These machines have fewer moving parts and those parts are made of heavy-duty strong materials. In addition, most of these antique machines are operated with a hand crank or a foot pedal. Therefore they do not sew as fast as modern electric sewing machines. If you are considering an antique sewing machine then may I suggest you consider the Singer Model 66 or the Singer Model 99, if you can find one available. Antique sewing machines are occasionally offered for sale on ebay.

Animal Sinew

Animal sinew may be used to sew pieces of buckskin together to make clothing. It is a good choice when the seam needs to be hidden or almost invisible, and when the seam will be subject to the same amount of normal wear or abrasion as the rest of the buckskin. Sinew will wear out at almost the same speed as buckskin. However, if the seam is exposed and the sinew thread is subject to continual abrasion then the sinew thread will wear out and the seam will come apart.

If you laid the sinew down flat when it was first acquired so it could dry properly then it will now be hard and brittle. The first step is to place a strand of sinew on a smooth flat rock and then gently pound the sinew with a smooth round rock to soften it up. Then place the strand of sinew into some hot, but not boiling, water. Allow the sinew to soak for a few minutes and then remove the strand of sinew and use an awl or a dull knife or your fingernails to separate each single individual thread of sinew from the strand. This is easier to do if you will first separate the large wide piece of sinew down the middle using your fingers to pull the two halves apart. Then separate one of the halves in half again by using your fingers to pull it apart. Continue separating the sinew into halves using your fingers until you have a thickness of sinew that is thin enough to be used as sewing thread.

A single thread of sinew will be about the thickness of a carpet thread or an embroidery thread. One thread of properly dried sinew can support a weight of up to 150 pounds. Although a single thread of sinew may be used as a bowstring, it is better to twist three strands of sinew together to make a reliable bowstring. When three strands are twisted together then it can also be used as a strong twine.

A single sinew thread should be moistened with saliva (spit) until it becomes pliable and then it should be twisted gently in one direction only between your fingers from end to end to improve its strength. Allow the thread to dry with a slight twist in the thread.

A single twisted sinew thread can be used to securely tie an arrowhead to the tip of an arrow, or to tie three split tail feathers to the other end of an arrow. As the sinew dries it will shrink and harden in place like glue.

Feathers tied with sinew to arrow shaft at both ends of the feather   Arrowhead tied with sinew

Although a needle is not required to use sinew thread, most people will thread one end of a sinew thread through the eye of the needle so it can be used in the same way as ordinary thread. However, since sinew thread is not very long and since it is very, very strong, do not use a double strand of sinew thread when sewing (the way you would do if you were using ordinary thread). Instead use a single strand of sinew thread in each stitch. Moisten the entire length of sinew with some saliva (spit) and hold the opposite end of the sinew and twirl it between your fingers until you have the sinew twisted in a gentle spiral from end to end. This will make the sinew thread even stronger when it is inside the seam.

If you do not have a needle then that is okay because a needle is not absolutely necessary when sewing with sinew thread. Simply moisten the entire thread with saliva (spit) until it becomes very flexible. Then twirl (roll) one end of the sinew thread between your fingers to form a point about one inch long. Twist the remaining long piece of thread gently between your fingers in one direction only to make the thread stronger. Allow the entire thread to dry with a slight twist from end to end in the thread. When the short end piece has dried the point will become stiff and hard and it will easily penetrate any hole that has been previously prepared using an awl or a small nail, such as the holes in seams in clothing or moccasins. Remoisten the long strip of thread with saliva to make it pliable so it can be used as thread but do not moisten the pointed tip.

After the sinew has been used as sewing thread it will quickly dry and shrink and this will form a tight seam in the clothing or moccasins. Because sinew hardens and adheres like glue it is not always necessary to tie the end of a sinew thread with a knot in the middle of a seam when a short length of sinew runs out. Just start a new piece of sinew about one inch before the place where the previous piece of sinew ran out so that you have a double stitch for approximately one inch along the seam.

Saliva (spit) is the preferred softening fluid for sinew because it contains natural body chemicals that react favorably with the sinew. Ordinary water does not contain these natural body chemicals and although water will gradually soften the sinew it will not react with the sinew to make it as pliable and useful as ordinary human saliva will.

Chapter Twenty-Five

How to Make Your Own Clothing Patterns

After investing a significant amount of your time and energy converting an animal hide into a soft piece of buckskin, you will be heartbroken if you ruin that beautiful piece of buckskin in a failed attempt to make a useful article of clothing. The simple way to avoid this tragedy is to carefully plan exactly how you are going to make the article of clothing you have in mind, and then carefully follow your plan.

Clothing is made by cutting cloth, fabric, or a buckskin into the individual pieces of a garment of the correct size and shape so those pieces can be sewn together to make a comfortable article of clothing. These pieces are called "patterns" and a garment is constructed by sewing all the appropriate "pattern pieces" together in the proper manner and in the correct sequence.

There are a three basic ways to acquire pattern pieces as follows:
1. You can purchase clothing patterns at stores that sell sewing supplies.
2. You can take an existing garment apart at its seams and use the individual garment pieces as pattern pieces.
3. You can create your own homemade clothing patterns by measuring a person and then drawing the appropriate pattern pieces on paper to match the dimensions of that specific person.

This chapter will discuss each of the above three options one-at-a-time.

Patterns Available at Sewing Stores

Most stores that sell cloth also sell patterns that can be used to make clothing. There are literally thousands of different patterns to select from and they include clothing for men, women, teenagers, and children in a variety of different styles and sizes. The patterns are usually sold inside a large paper envelope by size and style. In other words, after you select the article of clothing that you desire, such as a shirt, then you will also need to select the style of shirt you desire, and the size of shirt you desire. There are hundreds of shirt patterns to select from and you must choose the pattern that will fit you or your family member based on your clothing size (gender and height and weight). The pattern envelope will contain one or more large sheets of thin paper and the pattern pieces will be drawn on those pieces of paper. Each individual pattern piece is cut from the large sheet of paper. Then each pattern piece is pinned to some cloth and the cloth is cut to the shape of the pattern piece. (Note: Buckskin clothing will require that you add an additional 1/2 inch all the way around each pattern piece for the extra space required by a buckskin seam.) Then the paper pattern piece is removed from the cloth, and the cloth pieces are sewn together following the instructions that are included in the pattern package. The paper pattern pieces are then placed back inside their original paper envelope until the next time you need them.

Patterns Made from Existing Clothing

If you have an old garment that is almost worn out and you really enjoyed wearing that garment because it fit you really well then you can duplicate that garment using buckskin. Carefully remove the stitching from all the seams using a "thread ripper" or the tip end of some scissors. Discard the old thread but save the individual pieces of the garment. If you have an iron then dampen the garment pieces with a little water and iron the pieces flat with the seams stretched out flat. You may now use the flat cloth pieces as pattern pieces or you can create your own paper or cardboard pattern pieces using the cloth pieces as your templates. Any type of large paper or cardboard may be used, such as brown wrapping paper, or white flipchart paper, or a cardboard box that has been opened up and laid out flat. Trace the cloth pieces onto the paper or cardboard but add approximately 1/2 inch all the way around the outside border of each cloth piece because buckskin seams require a little more material than a cloth seam. You can save the cloth pieces and the paper or cardboard pieces inside a large paper or cloth envelope. Write the size and type of garment on the outside of the envelope before you put the envelope into storage.

Patterns Made at Home

You can make your own clothing patterns from scratch. A pattern is a flat two dimensional drawing of a garment that will properly fit the three dimensional form of a person. The flat drawing should not be judged based on how it looks on paper. Instead it should be evaluated on how well it conforms to the body's natural shape when it is placed on the human body.

To create your own pattern pieces you will need:
1. a flexible tape measure,
2. a yardstick or a long straight edge,
3. a compass for drawing circles,
4. a pencil or a pen, and
5. some large sheets of paper or cardboard. Any type of paper may be used, such as brown shipping paper for wrapping boxes, or white flipchart paper from a large pad of paper, or the pages from yesterday's newspaper, or the white inside surface of gift wrapping paper, or ordinary 8.5-inch by 11-inch copier paper that is taped together along its edges to make a large sheet of paper for each pattern piece to be drawn on.

Although we normally think of measurements in terms of straight lines, such as how tall a person is, when it comes to clothing we also need to think in terms of curved lines because the human body is curved and not straight.

The following measurements will be needed to make clothing that will fit a person comfortably. All the body's measurements are described below but when you decide on a specific article of clothing you will only need to collect the measurements that will be required for that specific garment. For example, if you are making a shirt then you will not need to know how long a person's legs are.

1. **Neck Opening or Neck Size:** The distance all the way around the bottom of the neck where it meets the shoulders.

2. **Neck Width:** The distance from side to side in a straight line across the front of the neck where it meets the chest.

3. **Shoulder Width:** The straight line distance across a person's back from the top of the left shoulder to the top of the right shoulder.

4. **Back Width:** The straight line distance across a person's back from the top of the left armpit to the top of the right armpit.

5. **Male Chest:** A single measurement all the way around the body at the widest part of the chest just below the armpits.

6. **Female Chest:** Six measurements will be required. First measure all the way around the body below the armpits and just above the breasts. Second measure all the way around the body a little below the armpits but include the fullest part of both breasts. Third measure all the way around the body a little lower under the armpits and just below both breasts (called the rib cage). Fourth measure the curved distance across the front of one breast beginning at one side of one breast, up and across the nipple, and down the other side of the same breast to the chest (called the cup size). Fifth measure in a straight line from the front tip of one breast to the front tip of the other breast. Sixth measure the straight line distance between the two breasts in front along the chest where each breast meets the chest.

7. **Male Waist:** The distance around the middle of the body about two inches below the navel. This is the position at which most men will wear the waist of their pants.

8. **Female Waist:** The distance around the smallest part of the middle of the body which is usually about one, two, or three inches above the navel.

9. **Hips:** The distance all the way around the buttocks at the widest and fullest part of the hips.

10. **Thigh:** The distance all the way around the top of the thigh just below the crotch.

11. **Knee:** The distance all the way around the knee at the center of the knee cap.

12. **Outside Leg Length (Out Seam):** The straight line distance from the waist of the pants down to just below the ankle.

13. **Inside Leg Length (Inseam):** The straight line distance from the middle of the crotch down to just below the ankle.

14. **Outside Arm Length:** The distance from the shoulder directly above the armpit down the outside of the arm to just below the wrist with the arm bent at a right angle at the elbow and the tape measure must go around the outside of the elbow to the wrist.

15. **Inside Arm Length:** The straight line distance from the middle of the armpit down the inside of the arm to just below the wrist.

16. **Sleeve Length:** The distance from the center of the neck at the back along the top of the shoulder and around the top of the shoulder curve and straight down the outside of the arm to the wrist. This measurement is used when specifying the size of commercially available shirt patterns and for specifying the size of long sleeve shirts (neck size and sleeve length). But this measurement will not be needed for creating homemade patterns because we will require more detailed measurements for the different pattern pieces.

17. **Shoulder Arm Opening:** The distance all the way around the very top of the arm beginning at the top of the arm where it meets the shoulder and going down around the arm and under the armpit and back up to the starting point at the top of the shoulder.

18. **Bicep:** The distance all the way around the upper arm at its widest point.

19. **Wrist:** The distance all the way around the wrist.

20. **Palm:** The distance all the way around the fullest part of the hand. This will be used for a sleeve opening to make sure the hand can fit through the end of the sleeve.

21. **Side Length (Side Seam):** The distance from the inside bottom of the armpit to the side of the hip directly across from the crotch.

22. **Male Neck to Crotch:** The straight line distance from the front of the neck where it meets the chest down the front center of the body to the crotch.

23. **Female Neck to Crotch:** The curved distance from the front of the neck where it meets the chest down the front center of the body to the crotch but the distance should include a curve that is across the top of the fullest part of the breasts in front. Do not include the curve below the breast. The distance should continue from the peak at the front of the breast straight down to the crotch.

24. **Female Waist to Knee:** The straight line distance from the top of the waist (at the point indicated for the waist measurement) to the position at the knee where the lady prefers to have her skirts end. This may be a little above the knee, or in the middle of the knee, or a little below the knee based on what the lady believes is appropriate.

25. **Female Waist to Ankle:** The straight line distance from the top of the waist (at the point indicated for the waist measurement) to just above the ankle, or in the middle of the ankle, or just below the ankle depending on what the lady believes is appropriate.

Creating the Pattern Pieces

Detailed information on how to use the above measurements to create patterns for underwear, bras, shirts, blouses, pants, skirts, dresses, ponchos, robes, and caps are in the next few chapters. The remainder of this chapter will discuss some sewing concepts that are universal in nature and that apply to many different types of garments.

Experiment with a "Practice Garment"

If you are using pattern pieces that you created yourself from an old article of clothing that you took apart and you know it was a perfect fit before you disassembled it, then this step is not necessary. But if this will be the first time you will be using a "new" pattern to create a garment you have not worn before then you should create a "practice garment" before you cut your buckskin into garment size pieces. You can use your "new" pattern pieces to create a practice garment using an old worn out bed sheet. Then put the practice garment on and see how it feels and how it fits. While wearing the garment, stand up, sit down, lie down, walk, run, bend over at the waist, and also knell on your knees. If the garment feels too tight in some places then you should add some more material to the appropriate pattern pieces. If the garment feels too loose in some places then you should consider removing a little material from the appropriate pattern pieces.

A Comfortable Loose Fit

After you cut the buckskin into the appropriate pattern pieces then sew the pattern pieces together at the seams using one stitch per inch. This is called basting. Then have the person try the garment on and make sure it fits comfortably and loosely when standing, bending over, kneeling on one knee, and when sitting. Regardless of how much planning and care you may have done up to this point, it is not unusual to discover that minor adjustments need to be made to the garment at one or more of the seams so that the garment fits the person more comfortably. It is not too difficult to remove the basting stitches and make a seam a little looser or a little tighter and then add a new basting stitch. However, please remember that it is better to have the garment fit a little too loose at first in order to allow for a little shrinkage if it should occur.

After you have achieved a slightly loose fit of the garment on the person then you can begin sewing the garment together at the seams with the basting stitches still in the seams. When you have finished sewing a seam then you can remove the basting stitch and begin working on the next seam.

Draping

If you do not have a pattern to follow but you have a good idea of the type of garment that you wish to make, then you can simply drape the buckskin on the person's body and use a pencil to mark the outline of each pattern piece on the hair side of the buckskin. But remember to add 3/4 inch for each hem and each seam. If you have not done draping before then you should allow an additional 1.5 inches around the border of each pattern piece to allow for fitting issues that you did not anticipate as you were draping the buckskin on the person's body. If you cut a piece a little too big then you can always trim a little off the piece to make the garment fit better, but you can't stretch a piece that was cut too small to make it fit.

Chapter Twenty-Six

Needles, Hems, Seams, and Stitches

Needles and a Needle Threader (Thread Guide) and a Thimble

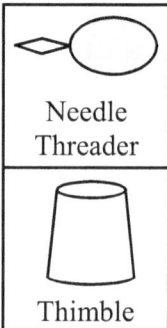

Craft Needles

Needle Threader

Thimble

Any handheld sewing needle may be used to sew buckskins if the eye hole in the needle is large enough to accept the diameter of thread you are using. A handheld sewing needle has the point at one end of the needle and the thread eye hole at the other end of the needle. Craft needles are bigger and they are useful when sewing with sinew.

Most people find it easier to sew with a handheld sewing needle that is a little bigger than average and that has an eye hole a little bigger than average so it can be easily threaded. The reason is because buckskin is thicker and stronger than most fabrics and you need to be able to firmly grasp the sides of the needle in order to push it through the buckskin. A slightly larger needle is easier to hold and to control and therefore it requires less effort to push it through buckskin. However, there is a tradeoff between needle diameter and the strength required to push it through the buckskin. A small diameter needle is hard to grasp but it requires the least amount of strength to push it through the buckskin because the hole that it makes is relatively small. A large diameter needle is easy to grasp but it creates a larger hole and it requires more effort to push the needle through the buckskin. Therefore a medium size sewing needle will usually achieve the best compromise between being easy to hold and easy to push through the buckskin.

The easiest way to push the end of a piece of thread through the eye of a needle is to use a special needle threader or thread guide. The flexible thin wire end of the needle threader is pushed through the eye of the needle. The opening between the two wires will expand after being pushed through the needle eye. The end of the thread is placed between the two wires and the needle threader is withdrawn from the eye of the needle. This pulls the end of the thread through the eye and the needle is now properly threaded.

A thimble is worn on the tip end of one finger. A good thimble is made of metal and a cheap thimble is made of plastic. A thimble is used to help push the point of a needle through the buckskin by applying pressure on the opposite end of the needle with the thimble.

Punching Holes in Buckskins

If you are using a needle then the needle will penetrate the buckskin as you are sewing. However, if you will be using thongs or thin strips of rawhide then you will need to punch a small hole in the seams of the buckskin for the thong to enter and exit. The appropriate tool to use to punch a hole in a buckskin is an awl. The diameter of the awl should be the same diameter as the thong you will be sewing with. The tip of the awl should have a smooth round tapered sharp point that looks like the point of a large quilting needle except it should be very sharp. It is possible to make your own assortment of awls with different diameters and different points by using some heavy-duty nails of different sizes and then shaping the nail point with a metal file. Use a hammer to drive the point of the nail through the buckskin about 1/8 inch into a flat board at the spot where you need a hole and then remove the nail with the claw end of the hammer. Although there is now a hole in the buckskin the hole will close up around the thread or thong after it has been inserted through the hole. This type of hole is appropriate for most normal sewing tasks.

Another option for punching holes is to use a leather punch. A leather punch removes a small round piece from the inside of the hole in a manner similar to a paper punch when you punch three holes in the side of a piece of paper to put it into a three-ring binder. This type of hole will always be open and it will not close up around the thread or thong. This type of hole is appropriate in a leather belt but not in most seams.

Hems

There is a difference between a hem and a seam as follows:

1. **Hem:** A hem is placed in the edge of a single piece of material by folding the edge of the material over onto itself either once or twice.

2. **Seam:** A seam is used to join two pieces of material together along a common edge in both pieces of material. The two pieces of material may or may not be folded together at the seam.

Buckskin is a lot thicker than most fabrics and buckskin does not unravel like most fabrics. Therefore the type of hem that is appropriate for buckskin is not the same type of hem that is appropriate for most fabrics.

1. **Cloth or Fabric Hem:** Because most cloths and fabrics are relatively thin and they have a tendency to gradually unravel, the hem in the edge of piece of fabric is usually doubled over onto itself so that the raw edge of the fabric is captured inside the hem where it cannot easily unravel. The entire hem is then stitched closed as shown in the illustration.

Cloth Hem - Double Fold

2. **Buckskin Hem:** Buckskin does not unravel but the edge of a buckskin does have a tendency to gradually stretch into an unusual shape. Buckskin is also thicker than most fabrics. Therefore the hem in the edge

Buckskin Hem - Single Fold

of a piece of buckskin is usually folded over once and then it is stitched down as shown in the illustration.

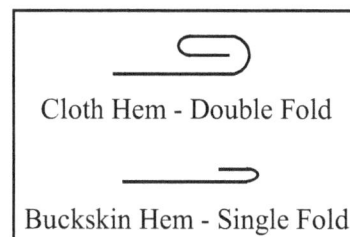

Seams

There are four basic types of hems and seams that are commonly used when making buckskin clothing:

1. **Hemmed Edge:** The edge of one buckskin is folded over onto itself so the short folded piece is on the inside of the garment. A running stitch is then put into the entire length of the hem. This prevents the exposed edge of the buckskin from stretching out of its original shape. Or, if you prefer, you may use a whip stitch around the exposed inside edge of the hem to make the hem stronger.

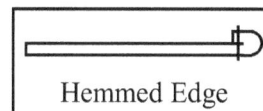

Hemmed Edge

2. **Invisible Seam or Hidden Seam:** Two pieces of buckskin are placed on top of one another along the entire edge of both buckskins so that the outside faces of the buckskins are touching one another and the inside faces of the buckskins are facing out. Either a running stitch or a whip stitch is then put into the entire length of the seam. The two pieces of

Invisible or Hidden Seam

buckskins are then unfolded so the stitched seam is on the inside of the garment and the folded seam is on the outside of the garment. The stitches will be invisible from the outside of the garment.

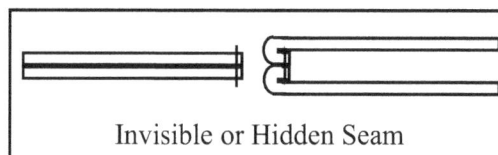

3. **Overlapping Seam:** Two pieces of buckskin are placed together along one of their edges. The insides of both buckskins are facing up and the outsides of both buckskins are facing down. Either a running stitch or a cross stitch is then put into the entire length of the seam. The seam and the stitches will be visible on the inside of the garment and on the outside of the garment.

Overlapping Seam

4. **Flat Seam or Butted Seam:** Two pieces of buckskin are placed side by side with their edges touching along the entire length of the seam. A baseball stitch is then put into the entire length of the seam. The baseball stitch looks exactly the same from the inside of the garment and from the outside of the

Flat or Butted Seam

garment. This seam may be used to eliminate the extra material needed with the other types seams so that all the material is used in the garment. This may sometimes be necessary when fitting a garment to a person and discovering that you cut the pattern pieces just a little too small. This may allow you to finish the garment without having to discard all the work you have invested up to this point.

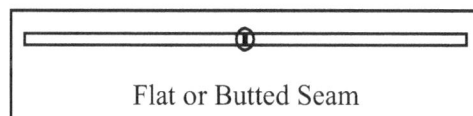

Stitches

There are seven basic types of stitches that are commonly used when making buckskin clothing:

1. **Running Stitch or Top Stitch, Single or Double:** See page 48.

2. **Whip Stitch or Overcast Stitch:** See page 48.

3. **Buttonhole Stitch or Blanket Stitch:** See page 48.

4. **Basting Stitch:** A basting stitch is similar to a single running stitch except that it is a temporary stitch and the individual stitches are approximately 1 inch to 1.5 inches apart. The purpose of a basting stitch is to just barely hold a garment together at its seams so a person can try the garment on to determine if the garment fits, or if some adjustments will be needed in specific areas in order to improve the comfort and appearance of the finished garment. A basting stitch is sometimes left in the seam to hold the seam together until the final stitching has been added to the seam and then the basting stitch is carefully removed from the seam and discarded.

5. **Cross Stitch or "X" Stitch:** This is a decorative stitch and it is also a very strong stitch. It is equivalent to a double row of stitches. It is very pretty and it is very distinctive when a contrasting thread color is chosen that compliments the buckskin and the thread color does not exactly match the color of the buckskin.

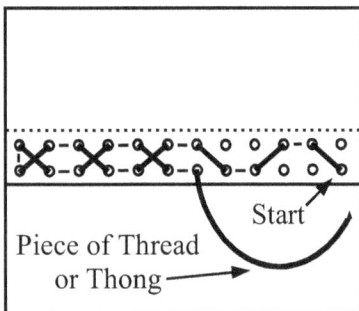

Start
Piece of Thread or Thong

This stitch may be used with an **overlapping** seam or it may be used to temporarily lace and unlace the right and left sides of a garment together in the front.

If you are using a needle then you may punch the holes as you go. If you are not using a needle then you will need to punch holes in both sides of the seam directly across from one another. The holes should penetrate both pieces of buckskin an equal distance from their edges. In the illustration the solid line from left to right is the edge of the top piece of buckskin and the dashed line is the edge of the bottom piece of buckskin which cannot be seen when looking down on the two pieces from the top as shown in the illustration. Start at one end of the seam and below the seam, such as on the right in the illustration. Cross over the top of the seam and go down through the next hole. Go under the seam on the same side and come up through the next hole. Then cross over the top of the seam and go down through the next hole. Go under the seam on the same side and come up through the next hole. Continue to the end of the seam. Then go straight up under the seam to the hole directly above the seam and come up through that hole. Now cross over the seam and form an "X" with a previous stitch and go down through the hole on the other side of the seam. Go under the seam on the same side and come up through the next hole. Continue this process to the end of the seam. When you are finished you will see a row of "Xs" on the top side of the seam which should always be visible on the outside of the garment and you will see a "running stitch" on the under side of the seam on the inside of the garment.

6. **Zig Zag Stitch:** This is a decorative stitch. It is very pretty and it is very distinctive when a contrasting thread color is chosen that compliments the buckskin and the thread color does not exactly match the color of the buckskin.

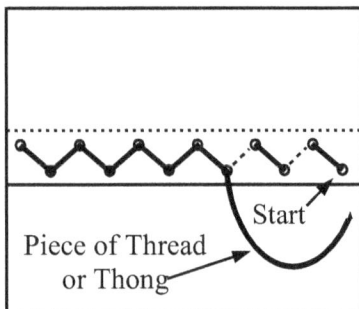

Start
Piece of Thread or Thong

This stitch may be used with an **overlapping** seam or as a decorative stitch on a hemmed edge.

If you are using a needle then you may punch the holes as you go. If you are not using a needle then you will need to punch holes in both sides of the seam at an angle across from one another. The holes should penetrate both pieces of buckskin an equal distance from their edges. In the illustration the solid line from left to right is the edge of the top piece of buckskin and the dashed line is the edge of the bottom piece of buckskin which cannot be seen when looking down on the two pieces from the top as shown in the illustration.

This stitch is formed by using an offset running stitch from the right to the left of the seam, and it is finished with an offset running stitch from the left to the right of the seam back to its starting position using the same holes that were used the first time across the seam. This forms a connected series of "Vs" on the top of the seam and on the bottom of the seam.

Start at one end of the seam and below the seam, such as on the right in the illustration. Cross over the top of the seam and go down through the next hole on the top. Go under the seam on the back side and come up through the next hole on the bottom. Then cross over the top of the seam and go down through the next hole on top of the seam. Go under the seam on the back side and come up through the next hole on the bottom. Continue to the end of the seam. Then immediately reverse and go under the seam across the back of the seam and up through the next hole on the bottom of the seam. Now cross over the seam and form a "V" with a previous stitch and go down through the hole on the top side of the seam. Go under the seam on the back side and come up through the next hole on the bottom. Cross over the seam and form a "V" with a previous stitch and go down through the hole on the top side of the seam. Continue this process to the end of the seam. When you are finished you will see a row of "Vs" on the top side of the seam which should always be visible on the outside of the garment and you will see a row of "V's" on the under side of the seam on the inside of the garment.

6. **Baseball Stitch:** This stitch may be used with a **flat** or **butted** seam.

If you are using a needle then you may punch the holes as you go. If you are not using a needle then you will need to punch holes in both sides of the seam across from one another. Select one long piece of sinew or a thong and fold it in half. Start at one end of the seam and below the seam, such as on the left in the illustration. Pull one end up through the top hole and pull the opposite end up through the bottom hole. Match the two ends together and pull to form the first stitch under the seam so that both ends of the thread or thong are the same length above the seam. Push the end that is extending out of the first top hole between the seam and below the seam and then come up out of the second hole on the bottom of the seam. Now push the opposite end that is extending out the first bottom hole between the seam and below the seam and then come up out of the second hole on the top of the seam. Repeat this process until you reach the end of the seam. The seam will look like a series of "Vs" on the top side of the seam and on the bottom side of the seam. You will be able to see half of each stitch on the top side of the seam and when you turn the seam over you will be able to see half of each stitch on the bottom side of the seam. This stitch will hold two pieces of buckskin together without any overlap at the seam and the seam will lay almost flat against your body. This is a good choice for the shoulder seams of shirts and dresses.

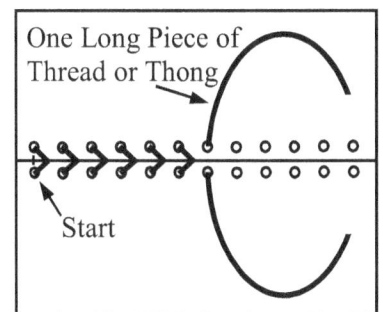

Chapter Twenty-Seven

Buttons, Buttonholes, Drawstrings, Ropes, Suspenders, Belts, and Belt Loops

Buttons and Buttonholes

The same buttons that you use on ordinary clothing may also be used on buckskin clothing. If you do not have any plastic or metal buttons then you can make your own buttons using small flat pieces of wood, or scrap pieces of plastic, or some scrap pieces of metal. The material you select should be hard enough to maintain the shape of a button without bending, splitting, or cracking but it should be pliable enough to be cut into a button shape.

Drill two small diameter holes in the wood, plastic, or metal about 1/4 inch apart. Then cut or carve around the two holes to form a round button of the desired diameter. Although other button shapes may be used for decorative purposes the most practical and useful shape is the round flat button.

Commercially made buttons typically have four holes in the center of the button but only two holes are needed. If you drill four holes into a homemade button then you may weaken the button in the area between the four holes and the button may fall apart. Therefore I suggest you be content with two holes in the middle of the button instead of four.

Make sure the outside edge of the button is smooth and that it does not contain any sharp edges, burrs, or splinters that could cut or injure your fingers when pushing the button through the buttonhole.

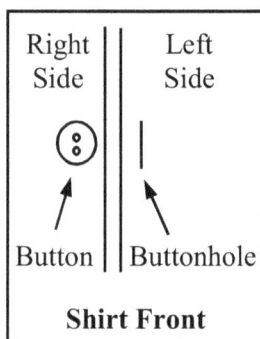

Right Side		Left Side
Button		Buttonhole

Shirt Front

Right Waist	Left Waist
Button	Buttonhole

Pants Front

A buttonhole may be cut into buckskin clothing using the tip end of a sharp knife. The buttonhole should be cut in a straight line the same length from end to end as the diameter of the button that will be inserted through the buttonhole. The reason is because the buttonhole slit in a buckskin will gradually stretch and become a little longer. Use a steel ruler or other flat straight metal surface to guide your knife blade as you make the cut.

The buttonhole should be cut directly across from the position of the button in the other side of the garment as shown in the two illustrations. You may put the button on either side of the garment you wish. However, traditionally on men's shirts the button is placed on the right side of a shirt and the buttonhole on the left side of a shirt. On ladies' blouses the button is placed on the left side of a blouse and the buttonhole is placed on the right side of the blouse.

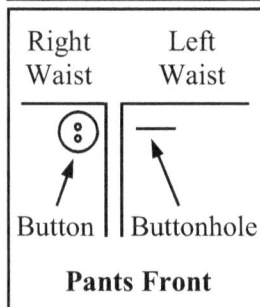

On both men's and ladies pants the button is traditionally placed on the right side of the waist opening in the front center of the pants and the buttonhole is placed on the left side of the waist opening. If you will be using buttons instead of a zipper to close the front of the pants then the buttons should continue in a straight line down the right side of the opening and the buttonholes should be lined up across from the buttons on the left side of the opening.

As mentioned in a previous chapter, buckskin has a tendency to stretch instead of unraveling. This means you will still need to reinforce all the buttonholes that you cut but not for the same reason as a buttonhole in an ordinary cloth garment. On an ordinary cloth garment a buttonhole stitch is used around the inside edges of the buttonhole to prevent the buttonhole from tearing and from unraveling. A buttonhole stitch is also used around the entire inside edge of a buttonhole in a buckskin garment but the reason is to prevent the buttonhole from stretching and to help the buttonhole retain its shape and hold the button firmly in position when it is being used.

Drawstrings

A strip of leather or a thong may be inserted into the hem at the bottom of each leg panel in some pants, or in the waist hem of some pants, or in the cuff hem of a shirt sleeve, or in the bottom hem of a shirt or blouse. The ends of the strip of leather or thong should extend at least eight inches beyond the end of each seam so the ends can be pulled to tighten the garment to your body. The ends can then be tied in a bow so they can be easily untied when you wish to remove the garment. Do not sew the thong with the stitches. The thong should move freely inside the hem from one end of the hem to the other end of the hem so it can be used as a drawstring. Insert the drawstring into the hem before you sew the hem closed.

Soft Flexible Rope

Instead of a drawstring or a belt you may use a soft rope of the appropriate length to hold your pants up. Push the rope through the belt loops of your pants and tie the rope into a bow knot at the front of your waist. This is the same type of knot you would use to tie one of your shoes.

Belt or Suspenders

If your widest waist measurement is **less than** your widest hip measurement around your buttocks, then a belt will hold your pants up and prevent your pants from sliding down on your hips as you walk or work. Or you may use suspenders if you prefer.

If your widest waist measurement is **equal to or more than** your widest hip measurement around your buttocks, then suspenders will hold your pants up and prevent your pants from sliding down on your hips as you walk or work. A belt will not work well because the waist of your pants will be constantly shifting down around your hips as you walk or work, and you will be continually pulling your pants (and your belt) back up to your waist.

Suspenders

Suspenders may be used instead of a belt to hold your pants up. Suspenders may be made from two pieces of leather or buckskin that are sewn together where the two pieces of leather overlap as shown in the illustration. Suspenders may also be cut from the center backbone section of a soft buckskin because there is very little stretch in a buckskin along its backbone from neck to tail. A button is placed at the end of the four leather straps and those buttons may be placed through buttonholes that you cut in the waist area of your pants. The two buttonholes in the rear of your pants are close together but the two buttonholes in the front of your pants should be further apart with one on each side of your waist. The buttonholes in your pants should go up and down and not from side to side. The suspenders are worn over your shoulders with the crossover area in the rear and the two front straps extending straight down your chest to your pants.

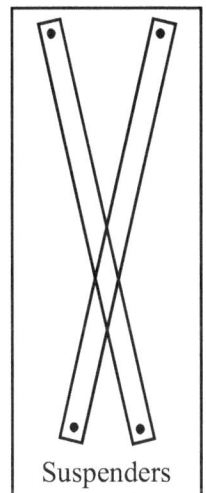

Suspenders

If you prefer, you may put the buttonholes on the suspenders and buttons on your pants. The buttonholes on suspenders should go up and down the length of the suspenders and not across the width of the suspender. Buttons are then placed on the front and rear of the pants.

Belts

Belts should be made from leather or rawhide instead of buckskin because buckskin is flexible and it will stretch but leather and rawhide will not stretch. Sew a double running stitch around all four outside edges of the leather or rawhide belt.

However, if you do not have any leather then two identical strips of buckskin may be used as a belt if both are cut from the center backbone area of a hide. Match the two pieces of buckskin together and sew the two strips of buckskin together using a double running stitch around all four outside edges of the belt. A buckskin belt may have a buckle or it may have a button at one end of the belt and one or more buttonholes at the other end of the belt. The belt is then held closed by placing the button through the appropriate buttonhole.

The width of the belt may be anywhere from 1/2 inch wide up to 2 inches wide. The most common width is one inch. Many people prefer a belt that is 1.5 to 2 inches wide because the surface of the belt has more area that will make contact with your waist and therefore it does not "dig" into your waist in the same manner as a slimmer belt.

The minimum length of the belt should be six inches wider than your waist at its thickest width. If you loose weight you can always punch some new holes in the end of the belt. But if you should gain a little weight then you cannot increase the length of the belt.

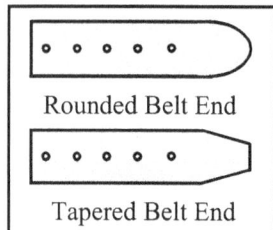

Rounded Belt End

Tapered Belt End

The holes in the belt should be punched (or drilled) in the loose end of the belt after you have attached the buckle to the opposite end of the belt. The first hole is usually punched two inches from the end of the belt halfway between the top and bottom of the belt. Additional holes are punched one inch apart on centers. A minimum of five holes are usually punched in the end of the belt but you may punch more holes or fewer holes as you believe appropriate. To help the loose end of the belt quickly and easily fit into the opening of the belt buckle, the loose end of the belt is cut into an oval or round shape or into a tapered shape as shown in the illustrations.

The buckle end of the belt will need to have a hole punched or drilled approximately one inch from the end of the belt to provide a place for the swivel piece. Then the end of the belt is folded around the buckle at the hole so the swivel is in the hole and the leather is sewn together along the dashed lines as shown in the illustrations to hold the belt to the buckle. There are three basic buckle designs: single, double, or wire.

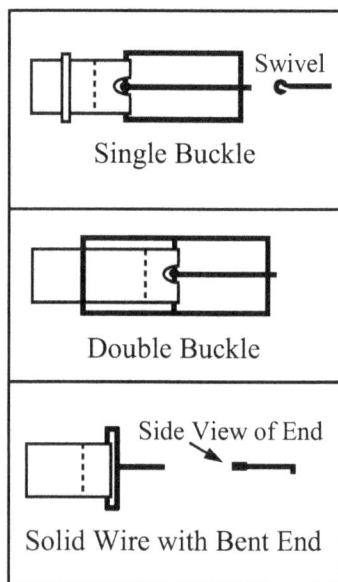

Single Buckle

1. **Single:** A rectangular metal wire has a swivel belt hole catch attached on the left side of the rectangle. The loose end of the leather belt is placed up under the right side of the metal rectangle, and the belt is pulled to a comfortable position around the waist, and then the catch is inserted through the nearest hole in the leather belt. This type of buckle works well if there is a leather belt loop on the left side of the leather belt to hold the loose end of the belt.

Double Buckle

2. **Double:** A rectangular metal wire has a center wire that holds the swivel belt hole catch. The loose end of the belt is placed under the right end of the rectangle, and pulled up over the center piece, and then the catch is placed through the appropriate hole in the leather belt. The loose end of the belt is then pushed under the left end of the metal rectangle.

Solid Wire with Bent End

3. **Solid Wire:** This design does not require a hole in the buckle end of the leather belt. A strong solid wire is welded to a piece of rectangular wire. The opposite end of the solid wire is bent at a 90 degree angle towards the body. The loose end of the belt is placed under the sewn end of the belt and then the bent wire end is pushed down into the appropriate hole in the loose end of the leather belt.

A belt buckle will normally last a lot longer than the leather belt to which it was originally attached. If you have an old belt that is worn out then the metal buckle may still be in very good condition. You should remove the metal buckle from the old belt and use that buckle on a new leather belt that you make yourself.

Belt Loops

Belt loops may be cut from the scrap pieces of buckskin that are left over after you have cut all the major pattern pieces from the hide. Belt loops may be any length and thickness but the most common size is 3 inches long by one-half (0.5) inch wide. Three-fourths (0.75) inch wide is a good choice for buckskin belt loops.

Belt loops are placed about 3 or 4 inches from the right waist opening and about 3 or 4 inches from the left waist opening and in the exact middle of the rear of the pants. Additional belt loops are then added around the waist of the pants at intervals of between four to six inches.

There are two common ways to attach belt loops to the waist of pants:

1. **Bottom of Loop Sewn on the Outside**: Fold the top of the belt loop over and stitch it even with the top waist of the pants. Fold the bottom of the belt loop over and stitch it to the pants.

2. **Bottom of Loop Sewn on the Inside:** Lay the bottom of the belt loop down flat against the pants so the bottom of the belt loop is the proper distance from the top waist of the pants and the top of the belt loop is extending down towards the bottom of the pants. Sew the bottom of the belt loop to the pants. Lift the belt loop up off the pants, fold the top of the belt loop over, and sew the top of the belt loop to the pants so it is even with the top waist of the pants.

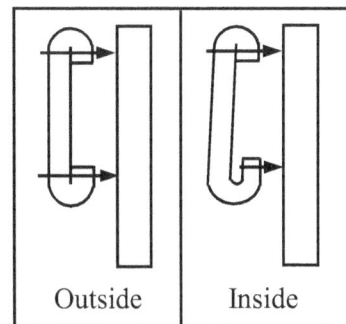

Outside   Inside

Chapter Twenty-Eight

Darts, Pockets, Sleeves, Fringes, Tassels, and Yokes

Darts

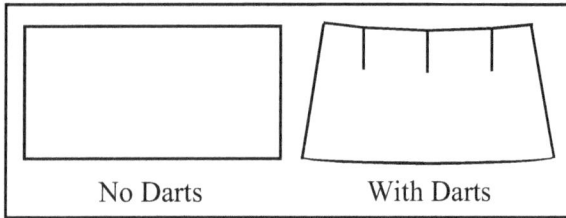

Darts may be inserted in any garment when it is necessary to remove some material at a seam or hem. The most common example is on the back side of pants or along the waist of a skirt. When a person's waist measurement is smaller than his or her buttock measurement then less material is needed at the waist and more material is needed for the buttocks. One way to achieve the desired measurements at the waist and at the buttocks is to gather some of the material at the waist and sew a short "V" shaped seam, or dart, in the material with the top of the "V" at the waist and the bottom of the "V" pointed towards the buttocks.

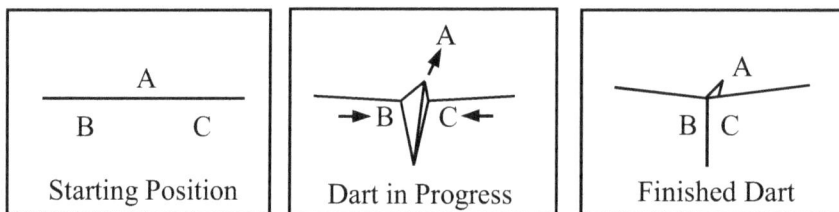

Instructions for Creating a Dart: Pinch the material at "A" and pull in the direction "A" while pushing the material together from directions "B" and "C." The objective is to decrease the measurement at the top and not change the measurement at the bottom.

Sew the finished dart closed along the straight line that is between B and C on the inside of the material so the stitching is invisible from the outside of the material. You may also fold the dart over so that A is lying flat on the inside "C" side of the garment and then stitch the dart to the material.

Pockets

The easiest way to attach a pocket to a shirt, pants, skirt, or dress is to sew the pocket onto the outside of the garment. This type of pocket is sometimes called a patch pocket.

The pocket may have a straight bottom, or a pointed bottom, or a rounded bottom, as shown in the illustrations below. The top of the pocket may be left open or a buttonhole may be sewn in the pocket and a button sewn on the shirt so the pocket may be buttoned closed.

Pockets may also have a flap added above the pocket, if you wish. The flap may simply hang down over the pocket, or the flap may have a buttonhole and a matching button on the top of the pocket.

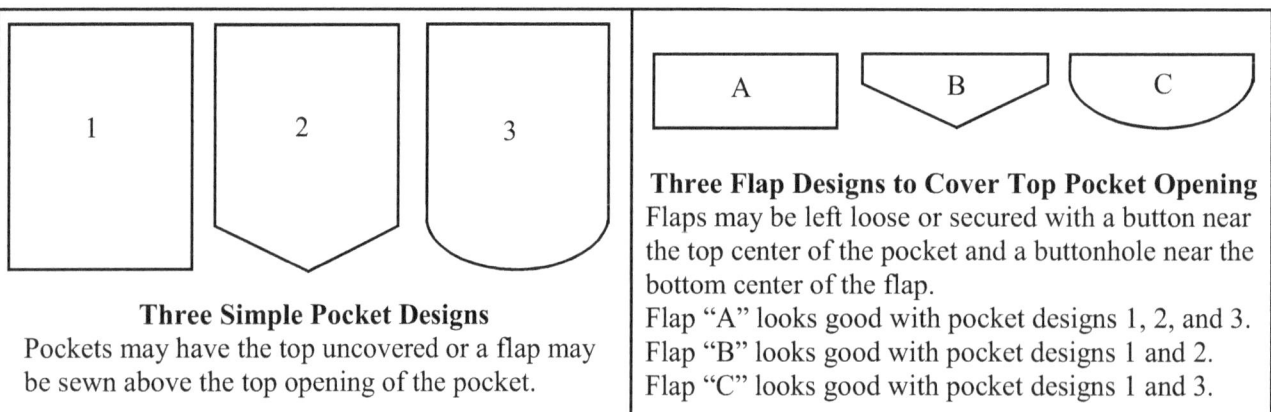

Three Simple Pocket Designs
Pockets may have the top uncovered or a flap may be sewn above the top opening of the pocket.

Three Flap Designs to Cover Top Pocket Opening
Flaps may be left loose or secured with a button near the top center of the pocket and a buttonhole near the bottom center of the flap.
Flap "A" looks good with pocket designs 1, 2, and 3.
Flap "B" looks good with pocket designs 1 and 2.
Flap "C" looks good with pocket designs 1 and 3.

Patch pockets may be sewn on the right and left sides of the front of a shirt, and on the right and left rear of pants, and on the right and left front of pants, and on the right and left front of skirts and dresses.

Cut the pocket 1/2 inch wider around the entire outside edge of the pocket to allow for the seam. Hem the top of the pocket by folding 1/2 inch over on the top of the pocket towards its inside and then stitch the folded seam closed with a running stitch or a whip stitch. Now fold the other edges under the outside edge of the pocket and pin the pocket onto the garment in the location you want it. A pocket with a pointed bottom may need to have a straight line cut 1/2 the distance down the inside of the "V" on the inside of the bottom hem so the folded hem will lay flatter on the garment. Sew around the outside edges of the pocket using a whip stitch but do not sew across the top of the pocket which will be left open. Keep the stitches close together when sewing the whip stitch around the outside edge of the pocket because the pocket will be used to hold things and it needs to be tight and secure against the garment.

Do **not** pull the top of the pocket taunt against the garment and then sew the sides of the pocket to the garment. Instead allow a very small gap along the top opening of the pocket so you can put stuff into the pocket. You should be able to insert your fingers into the pocket opening at the top of the pocket without any difficulty. However, the pocket opening should not be so loose that a crease or a wrinkle will appear later in the top of the pocket.

Cargo Pockets

A cargo pocket is a big rectangular pocket with a larger top than a bottom. To create a cargo pocket the buckskin must be cut as shown in the illustration where the top of the pocket is larger than the bottom of the pocket. The edges of the pocket are therefore cut at an angle as shown in the illustration.

The cargo pocket is sewn onto the garment by gathering the top of the pocket together and pinning the sides and the bottom of the pocket on the garment so that the sides of the pocket are in a straight line down the garment. Then both sides of the pocket and the bottom of the pocket area sewn onto the garment and then the pins are removed.

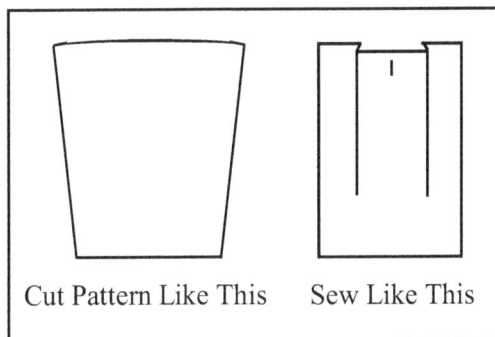

Cut Pattern Like This   Sew Like This

The top of the cargo pocket is usually folded as shown in the illustration.

Because of the looseness of the top of the pocket you may wish to sew a buttonhole at the top of the pocket as shown in the illustration and then sew a button onto the garment directly behind the buttonhole. This will allow you to button the pocket closed when it is empty, or when there are only a few small items in the pocket. When the pocket is being used to carry larger items the button is not used and the pocket is allowed to hang open away from the garment.

Jean Front Patch Pockets

A special design pocket is sometimes put on the front of work jeans or pants. The curved top pocket opening is designed to make it easier to reach into the pocket with the hand. The top of the pocket is sewn about two inches below the top waist band of the pants and the side of the pocket is sewn even with the seam on the outside of the leg of the jean. Only the bottom of the pocket is functional for holding items. This design puts the pocket opening at a convenient height for the hand and the bottom of the pocket is designed to be at the lowest point the hand can reach while standing straight up. This makes it easier to retrieve items from the pocket.

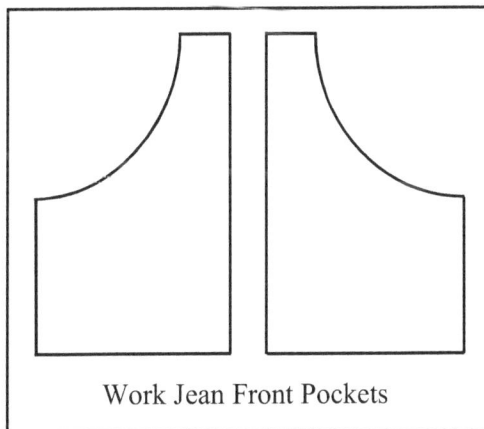

Work Jean Front Pockets

Sleeves

A sleeve may be added to any upper body garment, such as a shirt or a blouse, by taking the following measurements:

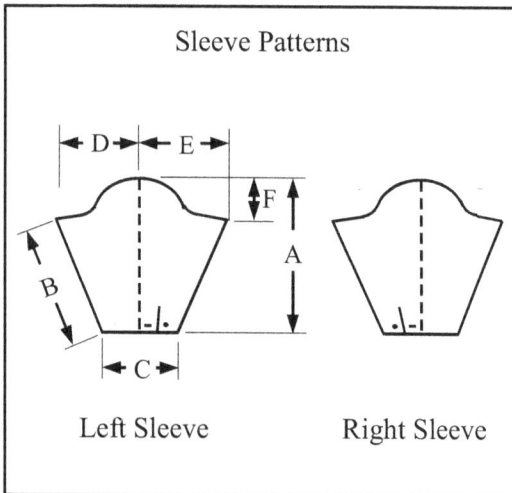

Sleeve Patterns

Left Sleeve   Right Sleeve

Measurements

A = outside length of arm from top of shoulder to wrist plus 1/2 inch for a seam, plus an additional 2 inches

B = inside length of arm from armpit to wrist plus 1/2 inch for a seam, plus an additional 2 inches

C = diameter of arm at wrist plus 1/2 inch for a seam, plus an additional 4 inches

D = one-half the diameter of the upper arm at the top of the shoulder straight down under armpit plus 1/2 inch for a seam, plus an additional 1 inch

E = one-half the diameter of the upper arm at the top of the shoulder straight down under the armpit plus 1/2 inch for a seam, plus an additional 3 inches

F = one-fourth the diameter of the upper arm at the top of the shoulder straight down under the armpit plus 1/2 inch for the shoulder seam

The plus additional inches above are for an adult male or female. Reduce the plus additional inches by 25% for a teenager and by 50% for a child.

A shirt sleeve is not symmetrical on both sides of its vertical axis (the dashed line in the illustration). The side of the sleeve (E) that will be attached to the back of the garment is a little wider than the side of the sleeve (D) that will be attached to the front of the garment.

If the garment will be a shirt, blouse, or other garment that is worn next to your body then the above dimensions are correct.

If the garment will be a robe, jacket, or coat that will be worn over your other clothing then add another two inches to dimension A, and add another one inch to dimension B, and add another two inches to dimension C, and add another two inches to dimensions D and E.

The above length dimensions allow for approximately one inch of shrinkage in the sleeve because the sleeve may shrink after it has been worn and washed several times. If the sleeve does not shrink after several washings then the sleeve can be easily shortened by removing a little material from the wrist opening.

If the length of the sleeve should shrink more than was originally allowed then you may add a cuff to the sleeve to increase the sleeve length as appropriate.

In most situations the sleeve pattern should be cut from a single piece of buckskin. If necessary, a sleeve may be cut from two pieces of buckskin along the dashed line as shown in the illustration with 1/2 inch added at the dashed line on both halves of the sleeve for the seam. If you use a baseball stitch to join the two sleeves halves together then you do not need to add the extra 1/2 inch to each sleeve half.

The wrist end of the sleeve will need to contain a slit with a button and a buttonhole so the wrist end of the sleeve will fit over the hand when putting the garment on. After the garment has been put on then the wrist slit may be buttoned closed. If you do not wish to add a slit with a button and a buttonhole, such as the sleeve for a robe, jacket, or coat, then the diameter of the wrist should be changed to the diameter of the widest part of the hand plus 5 inches.

If you wish you may shorten the sleeve and then add a separate cuff to the sleeve.

Fringes

A fringe is a series of long thin strips of buckskin that hang down from a seam. A fringe may be added to a shirt yoke and the strips would hang down the shirt towards the waist. Or a fringe may be added to the out seams on pants and the individual strips would hang down and overlap one another on the outside of the leg.

A fringe may be cut into some extra material that extends beyond a seam. But this is not the best way to add a fringe because the cuts in the material will slowly and gradually tear their way up into the seam and this will weaken the seam.

A better way to add fringes is to cut the fringes into one long piece of narrow buckskin. Or fringes may be cut into several shorter pieces of scrap buckskin that are joined together inside a seam. When that extra piece of buckskin that contains the fringes is sewn into a seam it is called a "welt."

The bottom edges of fringes may be straight or they may be uneven where they match the outside jagged edge of a hide that is used for this purpose.

Fringes should be cut using sharp scissors. Most fringes are three inches long or less. A good average fringe length is 2.5 inches. Depending on how often you wear your buckskin clothing, and the type of work you do when you are wearing your buckskin clothing, the ends of the fringes will gradually wear off and each fringe will gradually become a little shorter.

Fringes should not be cut too thin. Thin fringes will gradually get pulled off the garment and you will have bare spaces in the fringe area. On a buckskin of average thickness and average flexibility, a fringe width of 3/16 inch will usually last as long as the clothing.

The two locations where fringes cause problems are on sleeve cuffs and pant cuffs. You use your hands all the time and sleeve cuff fringes will interfere with everything you try to do. Fringes on the bottom of a leg cuff will collect dirt and they will always look dirty.

Yoke Fringes and Pants Out Seam Fringes

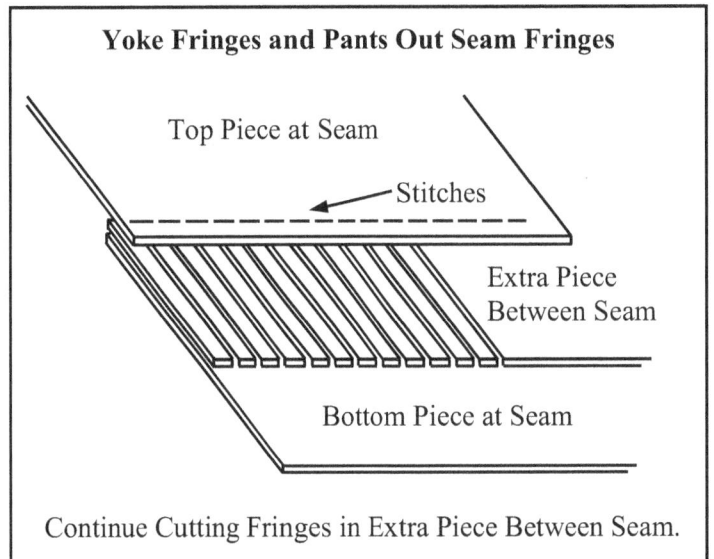

Top Piece at Seam

Stitches

Extra Piece Between Seam

Bottom Piece at Seam

Continue Cutting Fringes in Extra Piece Between Seam.

Skirt Bottom Hem Fringes

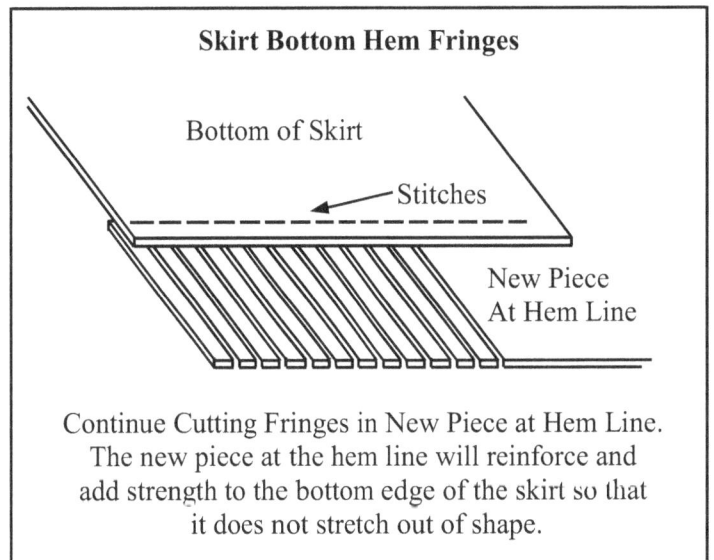

Bottom of Skirt

Stitches

New Piece At Hem Line

Continue Cutting Fringes in New Piece at Hem Line. The new piece at the hem line will reinforce and add strength to the bottom edge of the skirt so that it does not stretch out of shape.

Tassels

Tassels are decorative strips of buckskin, approximately 3/16 inch wide, that are tied to small holes that are punched in a garment. Fold the strip in half and insert the two ends of the strip through a hole in the buckskin. Then insert the two loose ends through the loop as shown in the illustration on the right, and pull the tassel tight against the buckskin. If you wish, a knot may be tied in each of the two loose bottom ends of the tassel to add a distinctive appearance to the tassel.

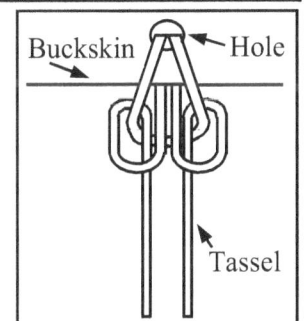

Buckskin — Hole

Tassel

Yokes

Yokes are pieces of material that are sewn to the upper part of a shirt, blouse, dress, jacket, or coat. These pieces of material are called yokes because they are added to the right and left shoulder areas of a garment in the same way that a yoke, or harness, is added to the neck and shoulders of a horse, mule, or ox so that it can pull a plow or a wagon.

Originally yokes were added to the garments of men who did hard physical labor that involved the use of their shoulders, such as carrying objects on their shoulders or using their shoulders to push heavy burdens. These yokes added another layer of material around the shoulders to help protect the shoulders from abrasion and to help pad the shoulders to make the work a little more comfortable to do and to reduce fatigue.

Today a yoke may serve any of the following purposes:

1. When a yoke is added as an additional piece of material to the shoulder area of a garment then it strengthens that part of the garment because that part of the garment will now be twice as thick. However, since there are now two pieces of material in the shoulder area this will require more material and overall material utilization will be lower.

2. When a yoke is added as a separate piece of material to the shoulder area of a garment instead of the original piece of material that would have been used in that location then the shoulder area is only one piece of material thick. This allows for better utilization of the material because the main body piece will be a little shorter and it can be fitted more strategically onto the existing material (or buckskin) and the yoke may be cut from a different area of the material (or buckskin) to achieve better utilization of the material by more strategically arranging the individual pattern pieces on the large piece of material (or buckskin). This can be a significant advantage with buckskins because buckskins are of a fixed length and they may sometimes contain holes or cuts in an undesirable location. By reducing the length of the main body pieces, the body pieces may be more strategically placed on the buckskin to use a much of the buckskin as possible while avoiding the cuts or holes. The yokes can then be cut from another piece of buckskin that was left over from a previous sewing project.

3. When a yoke is added for fashion reasons then it enhances the appearance of the garment.

When creating buckskin clothing the yokes are usually of a darker color, or shade of color, than the main body piece on the lower part of the same garment. This is more visually appealing to the eye. This means that yokes are frequently cut from unused pieces of a darker buckskin than the buckskin being used to make the current garment. In addition, a darker thread color should be used to sew the lower part of the yoke to the rest of the garment in order to emphasize the design of the yoke on the garment.

Yokes that are added to a woman's garment may be attached with any color of thread that is appealing to the eye of the lady who will be wearing the garment.

Straight yokes and curved yokes may be easily sewn to a garment that has a matching straight line or curve.

Yokes with points are usually sewn to a garment that has been cut in a straight line where the yoke will be attached. The yoke is then matched to this straight line so the point of the yoke extends down below the straight line onto the garment. The yoke is then sewn to the garment along the shoulder seam and along its bottom edge.

Yokes with special fashion designs are usually sewn to a garment that has a normal full front panel. The yoke is matched to the shoulder seam and the special design of the yoke extends down the front panel. The yoke is then sewn to the garment along the shoulder seam and along it special design on the bottom of the yoke.

Several common yoke designs are illustrated on the next page. The front yoke design and the corresponding back yoke design are shown side-by-side in the illustrations.

Yoke Examples

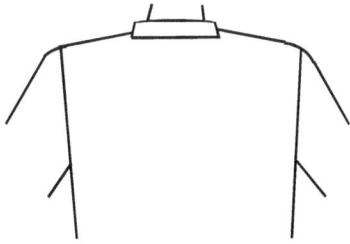 

No Yokes

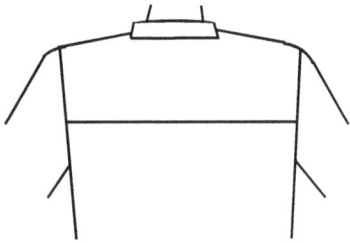 

Straight Yokes

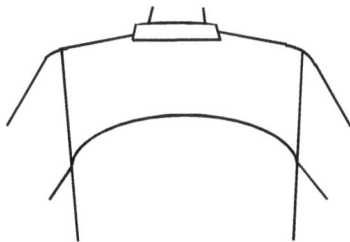 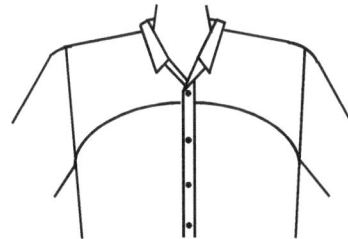

Curved Yokes

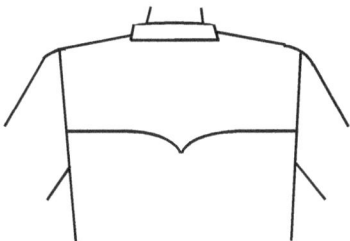 

Pointed Yokes

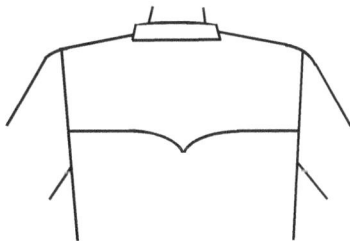 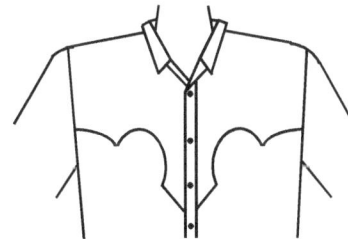

Fashion Yokes

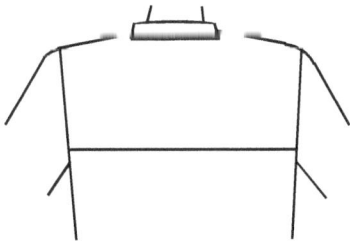 

Deep Yokes

Chapter Twenty-Eight: Darts, Pockets, Sleeves, Fringes, Tassels, and Yokes

Chapter Twenty-Nine

Undergarments: Loincloths, Underwear, Halters, and Bras

Loincloths or Breechcloths

A loincloth, also know as a breechcloth, is a simple one piece covering for the groin area. It hangs down in the rear from your waist to below your buttocks and it hangs down in front from your waist to below your groin area.

Loincloths must be made from the softest, most flexible buckskins you have available or you will not be comfortable wearing one.

At the beginning of the year 2012 all the available literature in reference books and on the internet describe and illustrate a loincloth as being a long rectangular piece of material that is placed between the legs and then pulled up in the front and in the rear and then draped over a waist rope or a belt and allowed to hang down freely in the front and in the rear. In my opinion nobody could wear a rectangular loincloth in this fashion for very long because the middle of the loincloth between your legs would be bunched up into a uncomfortable mass and it would quickly wear blisters on the insides of your legs and on your genital area. Therefore I must depart from all the current published wisdom about loincloths and recommend a more practical loincloth design in this chapter.

The middle of the loincloth is wrapped under your groin from front to rear and the approximate middle of the loincloth should be trimmed to a width of about two inches so it fits comfortably between your legs and it does not rub blisters on the insides of your legs when you are walking. The inside curve of the loincloth must be trimmed to fit each person comfortably so that the loincloth makes contact with the skin without folding over and rubbing against the skin to cause a blister. The rear of the loincloth should be just a little longer than the front of the loincloth so it will properly cover the curve of your buttocks.

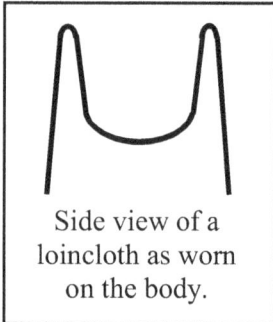

Side view of a loincloth as worn on the body.

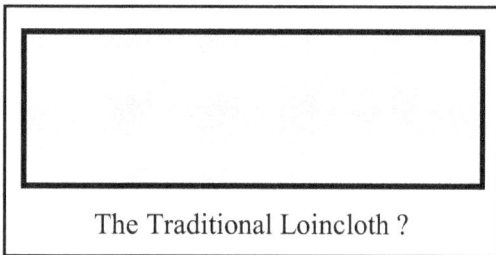

The Traditional Loincloth ?

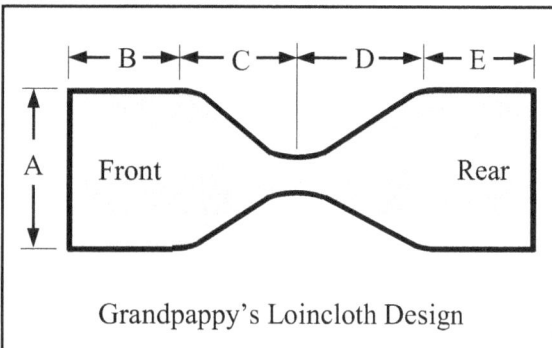

Grandpappy's Loincloth Design

Measurements:

A = curved distance around the entire waist where the top of the loincloth will be worn multiplied by 0.35
B = straight line distance from waist down to approximately one-half way between the crotch and the knee
C = curved distance from center of the crotch between the legs up to the front waist
D = curved distance from center of the crotch between the legs up around the buttocks to the back of the waist
E = curved distance from waist around the back of the buttocks to one-half way between crotch and knee

The loincloth may be looped over a belt or a soft thick rope that is tied around your waist. Or thongs or straps may be sewn to the waist area of the loincloth on both the right and left sides and those thongs or straps may then be tied together on the right hip and on the left hip to keep the loincloth in position. The front and rear of a loincloth should extend about halfway down to your knees in the front and in the rear. After you have worn a loincloth for a reasonable period of time you may shorten it if you wish. However, do not start with a really short "Tarzan" loincloth because you will probably not be comfortable in it when you sit down.

Underwear

Instead of a loincloth most people will find that ordinary underwear is more comfortable and more practical to wear as a covering for the groin area. Underwear must be made from the softest, most flexible buckskins you have available or you will not be comfortable wearing the underwear.

The basic functions of a groin undergarment are as follows:

1. Protect the genital area from the constant rubbing and friction that would be caused by the outer garment when you are walking, working, sitting, or standing.
2. Catch and contain very minor *unintentional* discharges of urine and gas (poop) so the stains are on the undergarment and they do not get on the outer garment.
3. A male will need underwear to comfortably hold the genitals in a stable position when walking or running.
4. A female of child bearing age will need comfortable underwear to hold absorbent pads or some other absorbent material close to the middle of her groin area during her monthly menstrual cycle. During hard times women have used a variety of disposable materials for this purpose. They have also used soft materials that could be washed, sterilized in boiling water, and then reused, such as the soft absorbent cloth material that is used to make cloth baby diapers. During hard times any soft cotton material could be used, such as old soft white cotton t-shirts that are cut and hemmed into a suitable size for this purpose.

Conventional underwear is made from material that is elastic. The material stretches. The waist band and sometimes the leg bands of the underwear are made of elastic that easily stretches and then contracts back to its normal shape so it is easy to put the underwear on and to take it off.

Unfortunately, buckskin is not elastic. Even if you sew a piece of ordinary elastic around the waist of some buckskin underwear the buckskin itself will not stretch and then return to its normal size. Therefore buckskin underwear will need to be made using a different design than conventional underwear.

The simple solution is to use the same design as a loincloth but eliminate the front and rear pieces of the loincloth that hang down in the front and in the back. Allow a little more length in the rear of the underwear so it will cover the curve of your buttocks. Then sew a strap or thong onto each of the four corners of the underwear. Tie the straps or thongs together in a bow on the left hip and on the right hip after you have the underwear in a comfortable position.

Side Tie Straps

Front   Rear

Underwear with Side Ties

Instead of the side tie straps, if you have some elastic then sew a short strip of elastic to the right and left side of the underwear to join the front and rear panels at the top. The side elastic will stretch and it will allow you to put the underwear on and to take it off. Do not sew the elastic all the way around the waist. Just sew the elastic to the top of the open right side and to the open left side of the underwear.

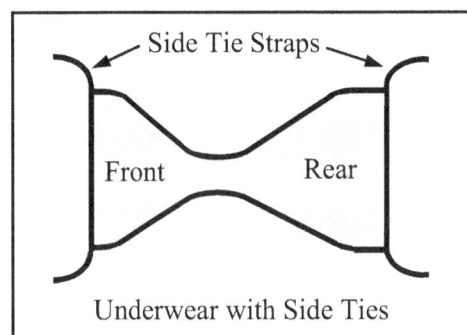

Halters

A halter is worn by a female on her upper body to support her breasts. The halter is frequently made from a single piece of buckskin but it may be created using two or more pieces of buckskins that are sewn together. The middle section of the halter is wrapped around the back and each end of the halter is pulled under the armpits and then under and over each breast to support and hold each breast. The end of the halter that covers the right breast is draped over the left shoulder at the neck. The end of the halter that covers the left breast is draped over the right shoulder at the neck. Then the two ends of the halter are tied in a bow knot behind the neck so that the halter feels comfortable to the woman who is wearing it.

Bras

There are a variety of different bra designs, such as:

1. **Snap in the rear or in the front:** Bras that snap in the rear are usually put on with the snap in the front,

and then the bra is snapped together in the front, and then the bra is rotated around the body so the snap is now in the rear and the cups of the bra are in the front.

2. **Straps or no straps:** Most bras have shoulder straps because they aid in the support of the breasts. Bras that do not have shoulder straps require wires or stiffer support below the breasts to support them.

3. **Padded or not padded:** Some bras have additional material in both cups to create a fuller figure for a woman who desires larger breasts.

This chapter will describe how to create a comfortable bra that is buttoned in the front, and it has shoulder straps, but it will not have any padding in the two cups.

Although the human body appears to be symmetrical, it is not perfectly symmetrical. Generally one foot will be just a little bigger than the other foot. And one breast will usually be just a little bigger than the other breast. However, these differences are ignored when making shoes and when making bras.

Measurements:
The bra will be symmetrical and each side of the bra will be a mirror image of the other side of the bra. Therefore cup pieces 1 and 2 are mirror images of those pieces on the other half of the bra.

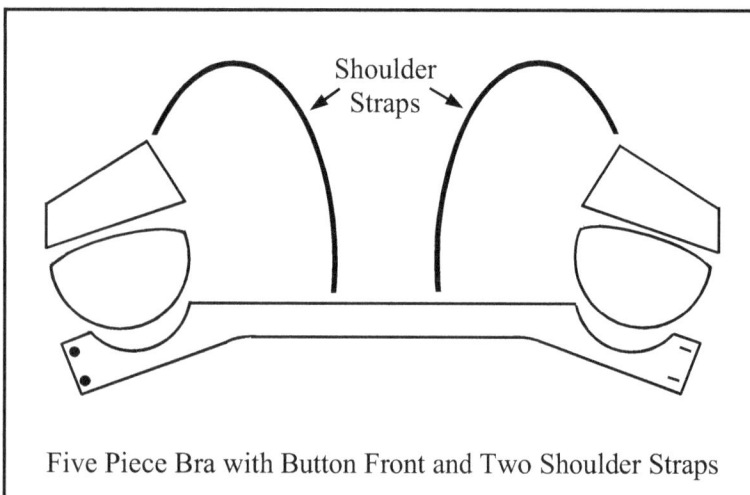

Five Piece Bra with Button Front and Two Shoulder Straps

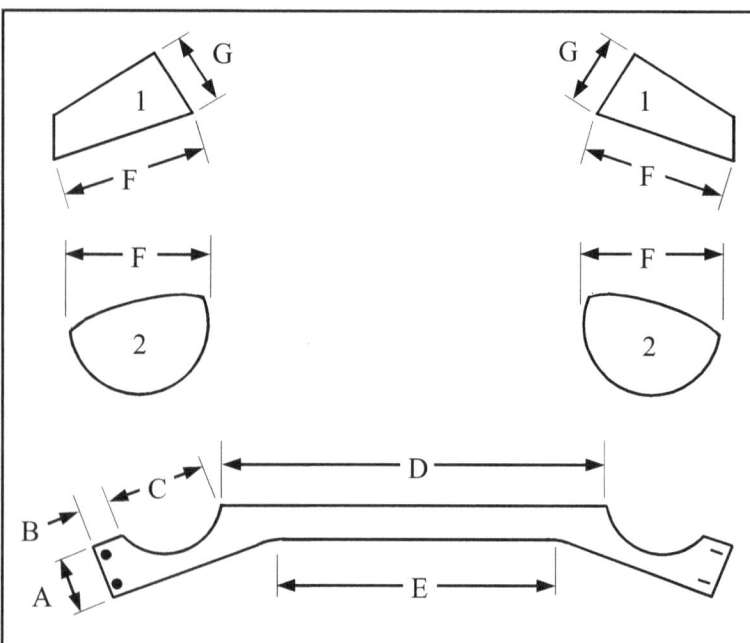

A = 1.5 inches

B = one-half of the distance between the two breasts in the center of the chest plus 1/2 inch for the button overlap

C curvature = the straight line distance from one side of the breast to the other side of the breast measured flat against the chest below the breast and this will be the diameter of curve C and the radius of curve C will be one-half of its diameter

C straight line from left to right = (the straight line distance from one side of the breast to the other side of the breast measured flat against the chest below the breast) multiplied by 0.80 because this opening will not extend halfway up the bottom part of the bra

D = straight line distance from the outside of one breast, under the armpit, straight across the back, under the other armpit, to the outside of the opposite breast

E = straight line distance from the center beneath one armpit, straight across the back, to the center below the other armpit

F = distance across the front of one breast beginning at one side of one breast, up and across the nipple, and down the other side of the same breast to the chest (called the cup size)

G = measurement "F" multiplied by 0.40

How to Draw and Cut the Two Cup Pieces:

1. **Cup Piece Number 1:** This piece will be flat when it is cut but it will be partially curved when it is sewn to cup piece number 2. Measurements "F" and "G" should be drawn accurately. But the other two sides of cup piece number 1 should be drawn straight but they may be estimated so the piece has the same general appearance as the illustration. The angles are not critical. However, the two angles that touch side "F" should be less than 90 degrees and the two other angles should be more than 90 degrees.

2. **Cup Piece Number 2:** This piece will be flat when it is cut but it will be curved when it is sewn onto the bra. Use a compass to draw a circle that has a diameter of measurement "F" and a radius that is equal to one-half of measurement "F." Set the compass to the radius because the point of the compass will be in the middle of the circle. Draw a freehand line across the top of the circle from one side to the other so the center of the line is about one inch above the center of the circle and the outside edges of the line are about 3/4 inch above the center of the circle on both the right and left sides of the circle.

How to Sew the Bra Together:

Cup piece number 2 will need to be sewn into the circular opening "C" in the long piece of the bra. However, the curve on cup piece number 2 is bigger than the curve "C" opening. Therefore the bottom part of cup piece number 2 will need to be gathered or pinched together along its bottom curve to make it fit into the "C' opening. Use a whip stitch to attach cup piece number 2 beginning at the bottom center of curve "C' and the bottom center of cup piece number 2. Then gradually pinch and sew the cup into the curve opening until you reach one side of curve "C." Then return to the center of cup piece number 2 and sew the other half of the cup piece to the other side of curve "C." Cup piece number 2 must be pinched together between each stitch to create the required cup opening for the breast above curve "C."

After cup piece 2 has been attached you can attach cup piece number 1 to cup piece number 2 along their common measurement "F." Since cup piece 1 has a straight bottom it will need to be bent gently so it can be sewn to the slightly rounded cup piece 2 using a double running stitch where cup piece 1 overlaps the top of cup piece 2 by approximately 1/4 inch. The top point of cup piece 1 will not be directly above the center of cup piece 2.

Buckskin straps of the correct length will need to be sewn to the top point on cup piece 1 and to the back of the bra. The length of the shoulder straps will need to be determined by trying the bra on and cutting the straps to the proper length.

Finally, two buttons and two buttonholes should be sewn to the front of the bra between the two cups so there is approximately 1/2 inch of overlap in the front where the left and right sides of the bra button together.

How to Adjust the Bra Cups for a More Comfortable Fit:

If you are happy with the way the bra fits and the way the cups feel then no adjustments need to be made to the bra. However, if the cups feel a little bit too loose then you can add one or two darts to each cup to make the cups fit more comfortably. Page 98 describes how to add a "V" shaped dart to a garment. The dart will either begin or end at the center of the cup near the nipple in Cup Piece Number 1.

1. **Cup Feels Too Loose Around the Outside of the Breast:** If the point of the "V" shaped dart ends near the center of the cup and the wide end of the "V" ends at the outside edge of the top of the cup then this will result in a reduction in the cup size and the cup will fit more snuggly to the outside of the breast next to the chest.

2. **Cup Feels Too Loose Around the Center of the Breast Near the Nipple:** If the wide end of the "V" shaped dart ends at the center of the cup and the pointed end of the "V" is near the outside edge of the top of the cup then this will result in a cup with an outside dimension that is almost the same size as before but the center of the cup will have a more pointed appearance as it approaches the nipple because there will be less material in the center of the cup. Because the wide end of the "V" shaped dart will end just beyond the edge of Cup Piece 1 near the center of the cup, it will be necessary to sew a matching dart into Cup Piece 2 with the pointed end of the "V" ending approximately 1/2 way towards the bottom of Cup Piece 2.

Chapter Thirty

Pants, Jeans, and Leggings

When making any garment that will be worn on your legs you want the length of the garment from your waist down to remain the same and not stretch. On the other hand, you want the width of the garment that goes around your waist, and your rear end, and your legs to stretch a little bit when you walk, or sit down, or stand up. The hide of an animal contains both of these desirable qualities. From the neck to the tail of the animal along its backbone there is very little stretch. However, from the right side of the animal to the left side of the animal there is more stretch. The reason for this is simple. The distance along an animal's backbone remains constant after it becomes an adult. Therefore there is very little stretch in the animal's hide from its neck to its tail. On the other hand, each time an animal eats its stomach area expands a little bit. As it gradually digests its food its stomach area contracts a little bit. And as the animal walks and runs the skin that is on the sides of the animal will flex and stretch with the animal's movement. This means an animal's hide has more stretch in it from side to side than from neck to tail. This is important when placing the pattern pieces of pants on the hide. The length of the pants' leg should extend from the neck towards the tail. This means the width of the pants' leg will be aligned from the right side to the left side of the hide. The end result will be a pants leg that has almost no stretch from your waist down towards your ankle but that same pants leg will have a little bit of stretch around your waist, hips, and legs. Therefore it is important to position the pants leg pattern pieces on the hide so the length of the pants' leg is aligned from the neck of the hide towards the tail of the hide. If the hide is big enough then place the left pants leg on one side of the spine and the right pants leg on the other side of the spine on the same hide.

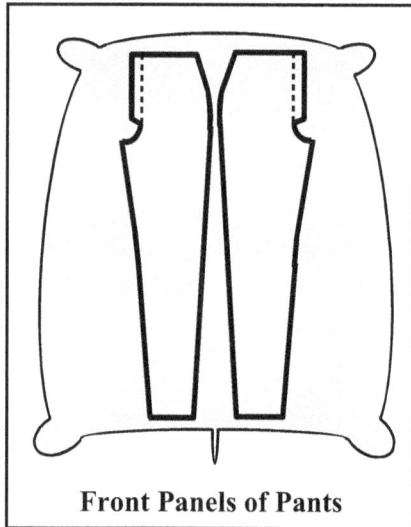

Front Panels of Pants

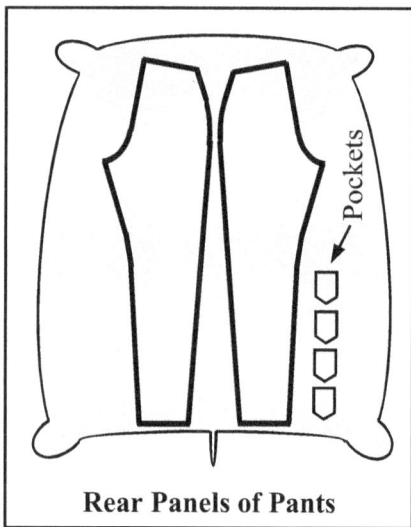

It is usually better to cut pants legs at least one or two inches longer than they need to be. When you first begin wearing the pants you can roll the bottom of each leg up into a cuff. After the pants have been worn and washed several times then you can make a final decision about the length of the legs. If the garment has shrunk then the legs may now be the right length. If the garment didn't shrink, or if is stretched a little bit, then you can trim off the extra length around each leg and put a final hem into the bottom of each leg.

Rear Panels of Pants

Pockets

There are three basic types of pants that can be worn to protect your legs: leggings, britches, and pants.

Leggings or Chaps

The purpose of leggings or chaps is to protect your legs when walking through thick underbrush. A chap is a garment for one leg. There is a separate chap for the right leg and a different chap for the left leg. A chap does not have a groin area or a buttock area. The chap begins on the outside of the leg about halfway between the navel and the crotch and continues down the leg to the ankle. A chap is made from a single piece of buckskin that is wrapped around the leg, and cut to the correct size, and then sewn together down the inside of the leg or the outside of the leg. Chaps normally have three or four loops at the top that a belt is pushed through to hold them onto each leg. A thick soft rope may be used instead of a belt. Chaps may be worn with a loincloth or chaps may be worn over your normal breeches or pants to protect your breeches or pants when doing difficult work or when walking through an area that might damage or stain your clothing.

The illustration for leggings on the right has the seam down the inside of the chaps along the inseam of the leg for the following two reasons:

1. The seam will be on the inside of the leg instead of the outside of the leg and this will protect the seam and the stitching from the wear and tear that the outside of the chaps will encounter when walking between bushes and in heavily overgrown areas.

2. The seam on the inside of the leg is at an angle to the ground whereas the seam on the outside of the leg is straight up and down. When you are standing straight up in a normal standing position and you look down at your legs then you will see that there is an almost straight line from your hips down the outside of your leg to the outside of your ankle, but there is an angled line from your crotch down to the inside of your ankle. Therefore a pattern that utilizes the straight line down the outside of the leg in the exact center of the pattern is an easier pattern to draw and it is also an easier pattern to sew together along the inseam of the leg.

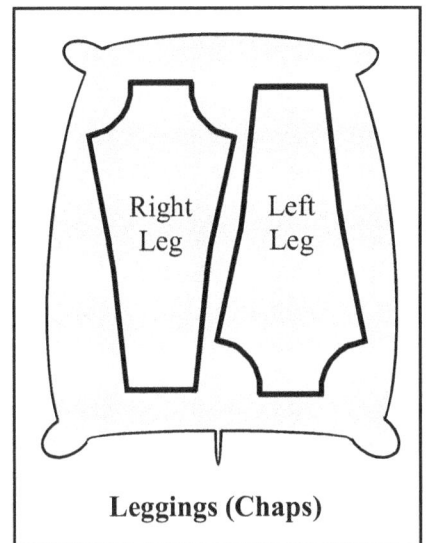

Leggings (Chaps)

Measurements:

A = straight line distance from waist to below ankle plus 1.5 inches for two hems, plus 0.5 inch for shrinkage (C + D + E)

B = straight line distance from crotch to below ankle plus 0.75 inches for one hem at bottom of leg, plus 0.5 inch for shrinkage (D + E)

C = straight line distance from waist to crotch plus 0.75 inch for one hem at waist

D = straight line distance from crotch to knee plus 0.25 inch for shrinkage

E = straight line distance from knee to below ankle plus 0.75 inch for one hem at bottom of leg, plus 0.25 inch for shrinkage

F = diameter of the top of the thigh at the crotch plus 0.75 inch for one seam, plus 3.25 inches for comfort

G = one-fifth of the diameter of the waist at the top of the leggings

H = diameter at knee plus 0.75 inch for 1 seam, plus 2.25 inches for comfort

I = diameter of foot opening around ankle plus 0.75 inch for one seam, plus 1.5 inches for comfort (wide enough for heel of foot to enter)

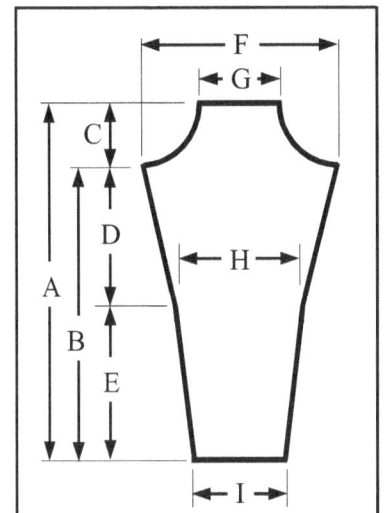

How to Sew Leggings (Chaps): Both legs may be cut using the same pattern. Sew the inseam on the left side of the pattern to the inseam on the right side of the pattern using an overlapping seam of 3/4 inch and a double running stitch. Sew a 3/4 inch hem in the top waist and a 3/4 inch hem in the bottom leg opening using a whip stitch. Reinforce the curve in front and the curve in the back by sewing a double running stitch along the entire curve 1/2 inch from the curve. Sew three or four belt loops to the hair side of the buckskin along the waist. Wear the chaps with the hair side facing out.

Half Leggings: In some areas the surrounding brush and grass grows no taller than the knee. In this type of environment a half legging may be worn to protect the lower half of the leg from briars, thorns, and short shrubs. A separate legging is worn on the lower half of each leg. The legging is usually tapered from top to bottom to match the diameter of the leg.

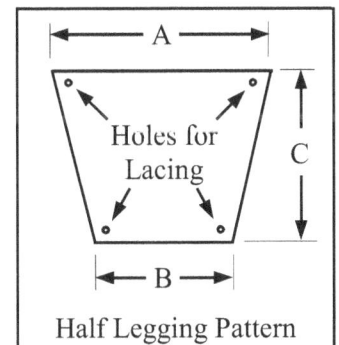

Half Legging Pattern

Measurements:

A = the diameter around the leg just below the knee plus four inches

B = the diameter around the ankle plus two inches

C = the distance from just below the knee to the ankle

Chapter Thirty: Pants, Jeans, and Leggings

How to Sew Half Leggings: Sew a double running stitch around all four sides of each legging to prevent the legging from stretching and to help the legging retain its original shape. Punch a small hole in each of the four corners about 3/4 inch from the corner to receive the lacing that will be used to secure a half legging to the lower half of each leg.

How to Wear Half Leggings: The leggings are simply a flat piece of clothing that is wrapped around the lower part of the leg and then secured to the leg with lacing that begins at the two holes in the legging at the ankle end and wraps around the legs four or five times before reaching the knee area. The two ends of the lacing are then placed through two small holes that have been punched in the top of the legging and then wrapped one more time around the top part of the leg just below the knee before tying the two lace ends together in a bow. The lacing should not be so tight that it cuts off or hinders the blood circulation in the lower legs and feet. But the lacing should not be so loose that the leggings slide down the legs. Half leggings may be successfully worn over your bare skin, or over your pants, by both men and women. However, for half leggings to stay on your legs the upper part of your leg just below your knee should be at least one inch smaller in diameter than the thickest part of your lower leg. This will help to keep the legging from sliding down your leg to your ankle.

Britches or Breeches

Breeches are short loose fitting pants with extra room in the waist and rear. This allows more freedom of movement when working and bending over. Each leg is cut off at the knee or about halfway between the knee and the ankle. This prevents the lower legs of the breeches from dragging on the ground and from getting wet when walking through a grassy area that is wet from the rain or from the morning dew. Britches may be made using the measurements for the pants pattern below but the legs will be shorter.

Pants or Jeans

Pants are usually about one or two inches wider than your waist and they extend down just below your ankle. They are generally tailored to fit your body comfortably without being too tight or too loose. Pants should allow you to walk comfortably, to sit down, to bend over at the waist, and to kneel without causing you discomfort. Pants should also be loose enough at the waist so that you can eat a normal meal without feeling uncomfortable. If you have some old worn out pants, or blue jeans, that you really like then very carefully remove the stitches from all the seams. Use the separate pieces of material as pattern pieces for your buckskin pants. However, add approximately 1/2 inch to the outside edge all the way around the pattern piece because buckskin seams are a little thicker and wider than the seams in ordinary clothing. Instead of a zipper you can install four or five buttons down the front of the pants to make the pants easier to put on and to take off. The waist of buckskin pants will gradually stretch after you put them on and you will need belt loops and a belt (or a soft rope) to hold your pants in position. Belt loops can be made from the extra scrap pieces of the hide that are not used to make the major pattern pieces.

The crotch area of pants is the most challenging area to sew. The crotch must fit comfortably at the bottom of your groin area, and the two leg openings at the crotch must be large enough to fit comfortably around the top part of your thighs so that you are comfortable when walking, sitting, or bending over. After you get the crotch area to fit comfortably then you should adjust the buttock seam to get a comfortable feel in the seat of the pants. Then you can hem the waist around the entire top part of the pants with an opening in the front. Then you can overlap the front of the jeans and insert a zipper or a few buttons down the front. Finally, you can sew the inseam of the right and left panels. Then you can sew the out seams of both legs. Finally you should hem the bottoms of the right and left legs. The legs should be a little longer than necessary so you can fold or roll the lower part of each leg up into a cuff. You can make a decision about adjusting the length of the legs after you have worn the pants for a few weeks and washed them several times. You may also sew "patch pockets" on the front and rear of the pants as you see fit.

An illustration for a typical pants pattern is on the next page along with instructions on how to collect the appropriate measurements.

Four Piece Pants Pattern

Diagram labels: E, D, K, C, L, H, I, J, A, B, Back Right, Front Right, Front Left, Back Left, G, F

Right Inseam — Right Out Seam — Right Inseam — Left Inseam — Left Out Seam — Left Inseam

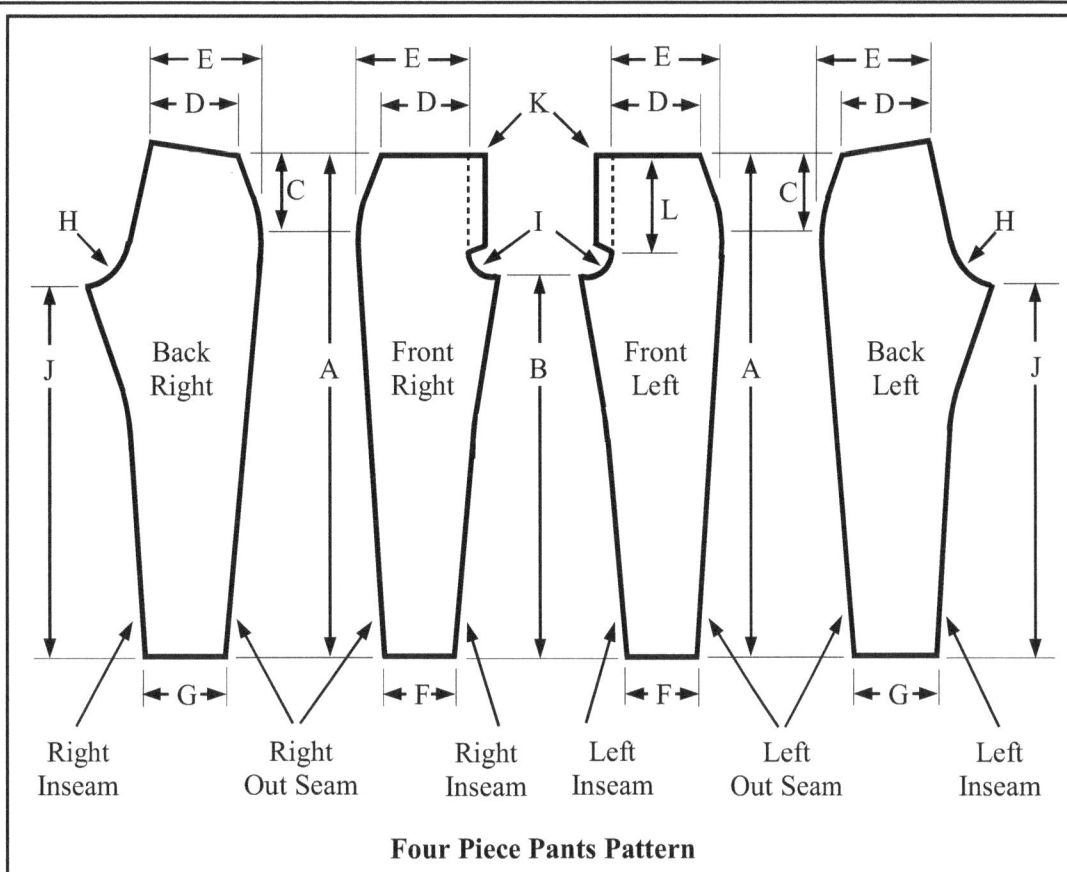

Measurements:

A = straight line distance from waist to below ankle (out seam) plus 1.5 inches for two hems, plus 1 inch for shrinkage

B = straight line distance from crotch to below ankle (inseam) plus 1.5 inches for one hem and one seam, plus 1 inch for shrinkage

C = straight line distance from waist down to the widest part of the hips plus 0.75 inch for one seam, plus 0.25 inch for shrinkage

D = one-fourth of the distance around the waist at the position where the pants will be worn plus 1.5 inches for two seams, plus 0.5 inch for comfort, plus 0.25 inch for shrinkage

E = one-fourth of the distance at the widest part of the hips plus 1.5 inches for two seams, plus 0.5 inch for comfort, plus 0.25 inch for shrinkage

F = 0.55 multiplied times the distance around the bottom hem of the leg plus an additional 1.5 inches for two seams and you must determine how big a bottom leg opening you believe is fashionable (see page 113)

G = 0.45 multiplied times the distance around the bottom hem of the leg plus an additional 1.5 inches for two seams and you must determine how big a bottom leg opening you believe is fashionable (see page 113)

H = radius of the curve at the rear of the crotch under the buttocks which is usually at least four inches or more (radius is one-half of the diameter of a circle)

I = radius of the curve at the front of the crotch which is usually at least two inches or more (radius is one-half of the diameter of a circle)

J = distance "B" minus one-half of the radius "H"

K = distance for the right and left overlap at the center of the pants for a zipper or for buttons. This distance is 2 inches for adult pants and about 1.5 inches for children pants.

L = straight line distance in front from the waist down to the crotch, without adding or subtracting any distances. This will allow enough space for the waist hem and it will put the beginning of the top of the crotch curve at the correct height on the front of the pants.

Note 1: After you have drawn the right front panel you may flip it over and it will be the left front panel. After you have drawn the right back panel you may flip it over and it will be the left back panel.

Note 2: The right out seams of the right front and the right back will be sewn together so the curves and lines down both out seams should be mirror images of one another. The left out seams of the left front and the left back will be sewn together so the curves and lines down both out seams should be mirror images of one another. In addition, the right front out seam should be exactly the same as the left back out seam, and the left front out seam should be exactly the same as the right back out seam. Therefore, after you have drawn any one of the four out seams you may use it as the model for the other three out seams, but you will need to flip it over for two of those out seams.

Note 3: The top waist of the right and left front panels are flat (horizontal) and the front of both panels is vertical, or straight up and down.

Note 4: The top waist of the right and left back panels are elevated towards the center of the back and the seat line of the back panel is angled down the back panel towards the bottom of the buttock curve. The degree of waist elevation and the degree of buttock angle should both match the straight line angle from the waist to the fullest part of the buttocks in the rear.

How to make a simple adjustment to the pattern so it will fit the person more comfortably: Create a paper pattern of one back panel and one front panel. You will only need one of each because the other panels are created by simply flipping the paper panels over so each one is a mirror image of the original panel.

The inseams must be matched together first and they will require some patience to match them correctly because the back panel inseam has a different curve than the front panel inseam due to the curvature of the buttocks. Place the front panel on top of the back panel and match the bottom of the front leg panel to the bottom of the back leg panel and pin them together so the inseam curve is aligned along the inseam of both panels. Match the bottom of the inseam crotch curve of the front panel to the bottom of the inseam crotch

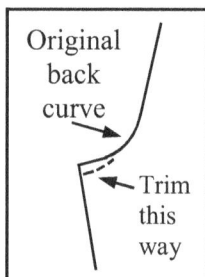

Original
back
curve

← Trim
this
way

curve of the back panel. The two pieces of paper will not lay down perfectly along the inseams because the inseams have different curvatures. You will probably need to bend the inseam of the paper back panel to get it to match the inseam curve of the front panel. Depending on the curvature of the buttocks it may be necessary to trim a little of the length off of the back panel inseam but do not trim any of the width off the back panel. Do not trim any material off the front panel because it has the correct inseam for the person and the front panel will not need any of its length removed. Only the back panel should be adjusted so the curved length of the back panel inseam is the same as the curved length of the front panel inseam.

How to sew the four pieces together:

1. Match the bottom of the inseam of the right front panel and the right rear panel. Use a basting stitch to sew the inseams together from the foot opening to the crotch area. Repeat this process for the left front panel and the left rear panel.
2. Match the left and right legs together at the top of their inseams at the middle of the crotch area. Use a basting stitch to join the right front panel to the left front panel along the front crotch curve and stop at the top of the crotch curve at the spot where the zipper or button front will begin.
3. Use a basting stitch to joint the right back panel to the left back panel beginning at the inseam and continuing up the buttock curve to the waist.
4. At this point the left and right out seams will still be open. Put the partially sewn pants onto the person and verify that the inseam length will be correct when the cuff hem is added later, that the buttock curve fits correct around the rear of the person, and that the front crotch curve is not too tight in the front. If the pants are too tight in an area then remove the basting stitch and put less material into that seam. If the pants are too loose in an area then remove the basting stitch and add a little more material into that seam. Try the pants on again and verify a reasonable fit.
5. Now use a basting stitch to sew the right front out seam to the right back out seam. Repeat the process for the left front out seam and the left back out seam.

6. The pants are almost complete except for the waist hem and the leg opening hems. Have the person try the pants on and verify that the pants are comfortable when standing up, when sitting down, when bending over at the waist, and when kneeling on the knees. If any adjustments are necessary then remove the appropriate basting stitches and either add or subtract a little material in the appropriate seams.

7. When the pants fit comfortably, sew all the seams together using a double running stitch. Then you can remove the basting threads.

8. The front zipper or button area will now need to be completed:
   Zipper: If you have a zipper then install each side of the zipper to the pants so that the right front lays flat against the body and the left front is folded over before sewing the zipper to it. Then complete the crotch area so it meets the zipper in front.
   Buttons: If you have buttons then sew a one inch hem down both the right and left front openings. Now sew buttons on the left front panel hem and cut buttonholes on the right front panel hem directly across from the buttons. The buttonholes should be cut horizontally and not vertically up and down the front. A minimum of four or five buttons will be needed to properly join the two front panels together.

9. Finish the pants by adding a 3/4 inch wide hem at the waist and a 3/4 inch wide hem on each leg opening.

Waist, Hips, and Buttocks: The rear of the pants must allow extra room for the buttocks. This can be done by using either one of the following two construction methods:

1. **Pants Method:** This is the method described on Page 111. The top of each back panel is cut along an inclined straight line at the waist to add the extra room required by the buttocks. If the waist is too big in the back when the person tries the pants on, then one or two darts can be sewn in the top of the left back panel and one or two darts can be sewn in the top of the right back panel to make the waist smaller. This is the normal construction technique for pants.

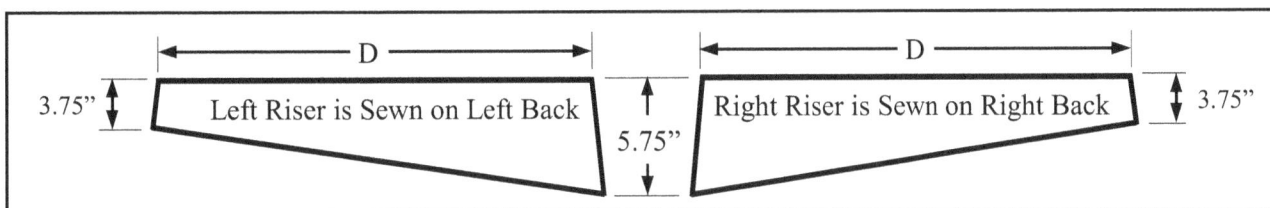

2. **Denim Blue Jeans Method:** The waist of both back panels is cut along a level straight line instead of the inclined straight line as illustrated on Page 111. Distance "A" and distance "C" on the back panels are each reduced by 3 inches. Do not reduce "A" and "C" on the two front panels. Then two extra separate pieces of material are cut. These two extra pieces of material are called "risers." Each riser is sewn onto the top of one of the rear panels of the legs. The riser allows more room in the buttock area than in the waist because of the way it is shaped. This is the normal construction technique for denim blue jeans.

Optional Waistband: A waistband may be sewn around the entire waist opening before belt loops are sewn onto the pants. The length of the waistband should match the waist opening. The waistband should be cut 3 inches wide. Then fold the waistband in half to make it 1.25 inches wide and sew it around the entire waist as shown in the illustration.

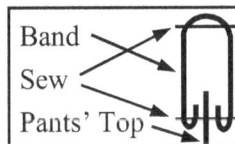

Ankle and Foot Openings: The size of the bottom of the leg opening varies based on the style of the pants and what is in fashion at the current time. There are three basic options: narrow, average, and large.

1. **Narrow:** The bottom of the leg is just a little bigger than what is required to comfortably insert the foot through the bottom of each pants' leg. This normally results in a slightly tapered appearance from the knee down to the ankle.

2. **Average:** The bottom of the leg has several inches of clearance so it is easy to insert the foot through the bottom of each pants' leg. This usually results in an almost straight line from the knee down to the ankle.

3. **Large (Flair, Bell Bottoms):** The bottom of the leg is approximately double the diameter of the leg at the knee. This results in a very loose fit at the ankle and the bottom legs of the pants will swing back and forth against your ankles as you walk.

Chapter Thirty-One

Shirts, Blouses, and Halters

A Halter Top

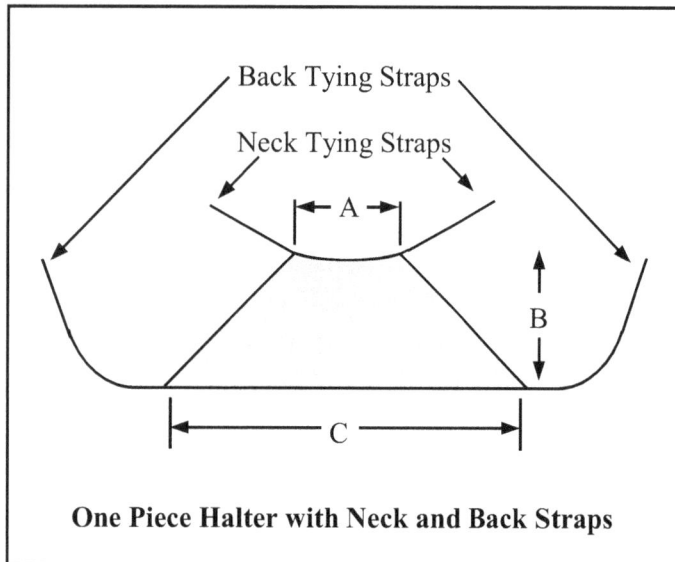

Back Tying Straps

Neck Tying Straps

One Piece Halter with Neck and Back Straps

A halter top is a simple covering for the top front half of the female body and it may be made from a single piece of buckskin. Four buckskin straps or leather straps should be sewn to the four corners of the halter top so it can be tied around the neck and around the back.

The purpose of a halter top is to simply cover the top front of the female body. It does not provide any significant support for the breasts.

Measurements:
A = Distance below neck from side to side in front
B = Distance from neck over breasts to below breasts
C = Distance from under right arm to under left arm

Shirts and Blouses

A shirt or a blouse should have sleeves if it will be worn during cold weather and it should be cut from a thicker hide. If the shirt or blouse will only be worn during warm weather then it does not need sleeves and it should be cut from a thinner hide. Most buckskin clothing that is intended for summer wear does not have short sleeves as is common on conventional warm weather clothing.

A shirt or a blouse may be worn so that it hangs loosely around the outside of your pants or skirt, or it can be tucked inside your pants or skirt. If the garment will be tucked inside your clothing then it should extend down to your groin in the front and in the back. This will allow enough of the garment to be caught under your belt so that it does not pull out when you sit or when you bend over. If the garment will be worn so that it hangs loosely from your shoulders then it needs to be at least long enough to extend down past your navel halfway to your groin in the front and in the back.

A shirt or a blouse with sleeves will usually require three hides of the same approximate thickness, softness, and color. The two front panels of the shirt will be cut from the first hide, the back panel and the pockets of the shirt will be cut from the second hide, and the optional sleeves will be cut from the third hide.

The length of a shirt sleeve should extend from the neck towards the tail. This means the width of the shirt sleeve will be aligned from the right to the left side of the hide. The end result will be a shirt sleeve that has almost no stretch from your shoulder down to your wrist but that same shirt sleeve will have some reasonable stretch at your shoulder and elbow. Therefore it is important to position the shirt sleeve patterns on the hide so the length of the shirt sleeve is aligned from the neck of the hide towards the tail of the hide. If the hide is big enough then place the left shirt sleeve on one side of the backbone and the right shirt sleeve on the other side of the backbone on the same hide.

It is usually better to cut shirt sleeves at least one inch longer than they need to be. When you first begin wearing the shirt you can roll the bottom of each sleeve into a cuff. After the shirt has been worn and washed several times then you can them make a final decision about the length of the sleeves. If the garment has shrunk then the sleeves may now be the right length. If the garment didn't shrink, or if is stretched a little bit, then you can trim the extra length off each sleeve and then put a final hem into the cuff of each sleeve.

The same concept applies to the front and back panels of a shirt or blouse. If possible align the shirt panels in the center of the hide with half of the shirt panel on each side of the spine. The neck of the shirt panel may face the neck of the hide or the tail of the hide. But the neck of the shirt panel should not face towards the right or left sides of the hide. You should also cut the front and back panels at least one or two inches longer than you think they need to be. If the garment shrinks then it will still fit okay.

Men's Basic Shirt Pattern (before the addition of two sleeves and an optional collar)
(The illustration below is for an average adult of average weight and average height. If the adult weighs more or less than average, or is taller or shorter than average, then the appearance of the finished pattern will look different but the dimensions will still be determined as explained in the instructions.)

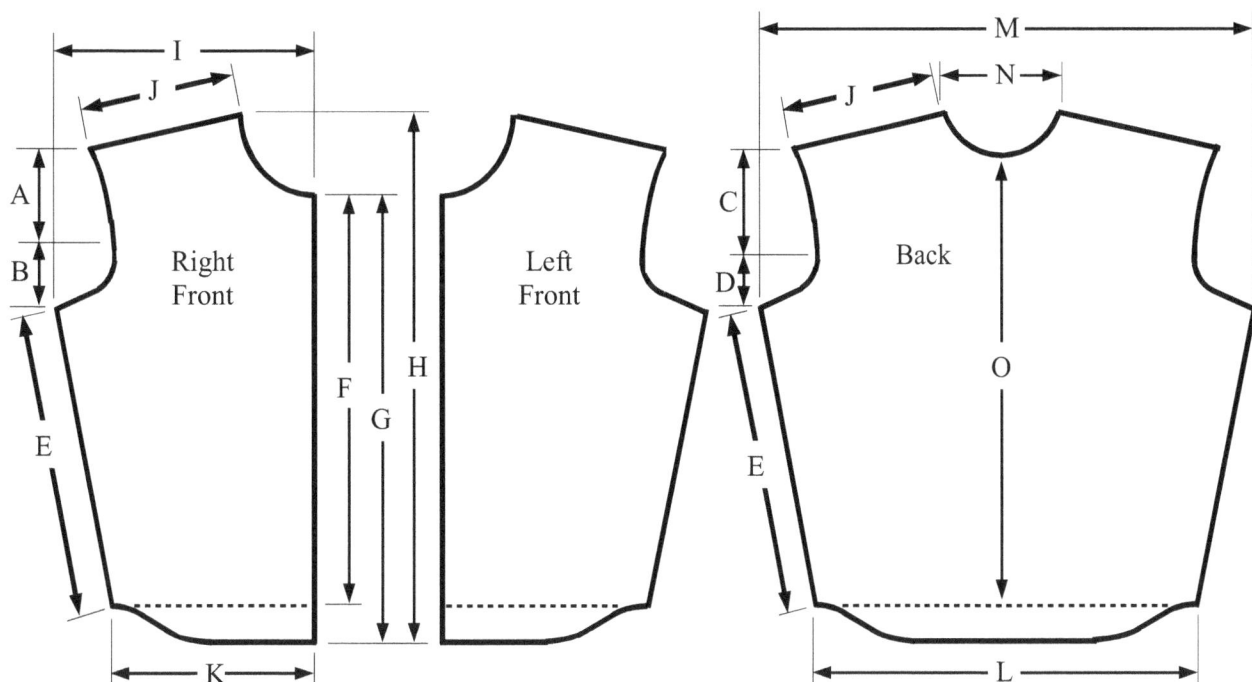

Measurements:

A = 2/3 of the straight line distance from the top of the shoulder to the bottom of the armpit plus 1.5 inches for flexibility, plus 1/4 inch for possible shrinkage

B = 1/3 of the straight line distance from the top of the shoulder to the bottom of the armpit plus 1.5 inches for flexibility, plus 1/4 inch for possible shrinkage

C = 2/3 of the straight line distance from the top of the shoulder to the bottom of the armpit plus 2.5 inches for flexibility, plus 1/4 inch for possible shrinkage

D = 1/3 of the straight line distance from the top of the shoulder to the bottom of the armpit plus 2.5 inches for flexibility, plus 1/4 inch for possible shrinkage

E = straight line distance from the center of the armpit down the side to the widest area around the buttocks plus 1.5 inches for one seam and one hem, plus 1 inch for possible shrinkage

F = curved distance from the front bottom center of the neck down over the chest to the widest area around the buttocks plus 3/4 inches for the bottom hem, plus 1 inch for possible shrinkage

G = curved distance from the front bottom center of the neck down over the chest to the crotch plus 3/4 inch for the bottom hem, plus 1 inch for possible shrinkage

H= curved distance from the middle of the side of the neck down over the chest to the crotch plus 3/4 inch for the bottom hem plus, 1 inch for possible shrinkage

I = curved distance from the center of the armpit around the chest to the center of the chest plus 3/4 inch for one side seam, plus 1 inch for the center hem, plus 1.5 inches for overlap down the front of the shirt, plus 1 inch for flexibility, plus 1/2 inch for possible shrinkage

J = straight line distance from the side of the neck down the center of the shoulder to the top of the shoulder directly above the armpit plus 3/4 inch for one seam at the sleeve, plus 1/4 inch for possible shrinkage

K = 1/4 of measurement "X" plus 3/4 inch for one side seam, plus 1 inch for the center hem, plus 1.5 inches for overlap across the front of the shirt, plus 1 inch for flexibility, plus 1/2 inch for possible shrinkage

L = 1/2 of measurement "X" plus 1.5 inches for two side seams, plus 2 inches for flexibility, plus 1 inch for possible shrinkage

M = curved distance across the back from the center of the left armpit to the center of the right armpit plus 1.5 inches for two side seams, plus 2 inches for flexibility, plus 1 inch for possible shrinkage

N = straight line distance across back at base of the neck at the widest point of the neck where it meets the shoulders plus 1 inch for flexibility

O = straight line distance from the back bottom center of the neck straight down the back to the widest area around the buttocks plus 3/4 inches for the bottom hem, plus 1 inch for possible shrinkage

X = use the distance around the hips at their widest area around the buttocks, or use the distance around the waist at its widest area if the waist measurement is wider than the hip measurement

Fitting Notes:

1. **"E" Side Seams:** The side seams on the front and back panels will need to be the same length because they will be sewn together.

2. **"J" Shoulder Seams:** The shoulder seams on the front and back panels will need to be the same length because they will be sewn together.

3. **Neck Opening:** The neck opening in the two front panels will curve down lower in the front than the neck opening in the back panel.

4. **Armhole Opening:** The left and right armhole openings in the back panel will be about two inches longer than the armhole openings in the front panels.

5. **Curves:** The curves for the neck opening and the armhole openings will need to be drawn by hand because they will not be perfect circles.

6. **Back Panel Mirror Image:** Either the left half or the right half of the back panel can be drawn first and then it can be folded over and duplicated on the opposite side of the back panel as a mirror image.

Shirt Bottom Design: The shirt may have a straight bottom or a curved bottom as illustrated. If the shirt will be tucked into the pants then a curved bottom is recommended. If the shirt will be worn on the outside of the pants then a straight bottom yields a more pleasing appearance. If a straight bottom is preferred then the shirt should be cut along the bottom of each panel at the dashed lines instead of the curved bottom lines and dimensions G and H should be reduced by the amount that will be removed from the bottom of the shirt.

How to sew a shirt together:

1. Use a basting stitch to sew the front panels to the back panel at the side seams and the shoulder seams. Then have the person try the shirt on. Have the person bend over at the waist and also twist his or her upper body from side to side. Make any adjustments that may be necessary so the shirt feels comfortable to the person in all the different positions in which he or she normally moves the upper part of the body.

   Too Big? To make the shirt a little tighter you can trim a little material out of each of the matching seams on the right and left sides of the body.

   Too Small? To make the shirt a little looser you can decrease the amount of material that are in the matching seams on the right and left sides of the body. If necessary you can use a flat seam at the left and right side seams along with a baseball stitch to add the maximum amount of material to the body of the shirt.

2. When the shirt fits the person comfortably, sew the right front side seam to the matching back side seam using a double running stitch and an overlapping seam. Then sew the left front side seam to the matching back side seam using a double running stitch and an overlapping seam. Sew the right front shoulder seam to the matching back shoulder seam using a baseball stitch and a flat or butted seam. Sew the left front shoulder seam to the matching back shoulder seam using a baseball stitch and a flat or butted seam. You may now remove the basting stitches. Have the person try the shirt on again and verify that it is a comfortable fit.

3. You may leave the neck opening as it is, or if you wish, you may now attach an optional collar. A variety of different collar designs is on the next page. If you do not add a collar then sew a buttonhole stitch around the entire neck opening to help it retain its shape and to minimize stretching.

Sleeves

You have the choice to leave the armhole openings open for summer weather, or you may attach short sleeves for slightly cooler weather, or you may attach long sleeves for winter weather. Sleeves may be added to a shirt or a blouse by following the directions on page 100 in Chapter 28. If you do not add sleeves then sew a buttonhole stitch around both arm openings to help them retain their original shape and to minimize stretching.

Lady's Shirts and Blouses

A shirt made using the same procedure as a man's shirt will still fit a lady but, depending on the lady's waistline, it may not fit as snuggly as she would prefer. In some cases a man's shirt that has enough material in the chest area will have too much material in the waist area but it will still fit in the hip area. Therefore the shirt will need to be modified for a lady to reduce the amount of material in the middle section of the shirt.

Front Panels: The simple solution is to add two long darts to the front of the shirt. The small end of each dart should begin at the tip of each breast and continue straight down to the smallest measurement around the lady's waist which is usually one or two inches above the navel and this is where the large end of each dart will terminate. In this situation each dart will be in the shape of an upside down "V." Another "V" shaped dart should begin at the spot where the first dart ended with the wide end of the "V" matching the wide end of the "V" that was just made. The pointed end of the "V" should be further down the shirt somewhere between two to four inches below the navel. When you are finished there will be four darts in the front of the shirt with the wide end of the darts meeting a little above the navel at the smallest measurement around the waist, and the opposite pointed ends of the darts ending at the tip of each breast and at a few inches below the navel.

Back Panel: The back panel can be easily adjusted so that there is less material in the midsection of the back along each of the side seams. In other words, instead of having a straight side seam in the back like a normal man's shirt, the side seam in the back can be curved in towards the middle of the back panel at the location of the smallest measurement around the lady's waist. This is shown by the dashed lines in the illustration. In order to get the back panel to fit properly it will need to be held against the lady's back and the correct curves drawn in pencil on each side of the back panel while still allowing enough distance in the back panel so that the bottom hem of the shirt will be even with the bottom hem of the front panels of the shirt.

Neck Openings: Some different options for the neck opening of a blouse are on page 123 in Chapter 32.

Lady's
Back
Panel

Collar Designs

Shirt collars on cotton or polyester or wool shirts are usually made from four pieces of material that are sewn together. However, the collar on a buckskin shirt may be made from a single piece of buckskin because buckskin is heavier than most other fabrics. On the other hand, if you prefer the four piece collar design then you may use that type of design instead of the one piece collars that are described below.

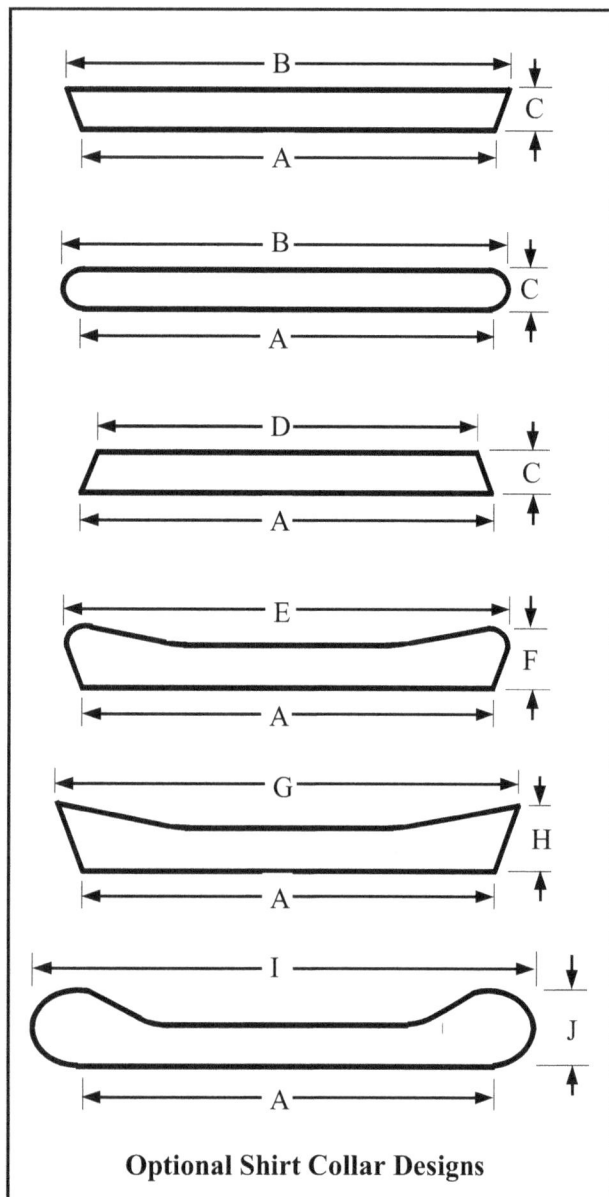

Optional Shirt Collar Designs

Measurements:

A = distance around bottom of neck at its widest point where it meets the shoulders plus 1.5 inches for comfort. This distance must exactly match the neck opening in the shirt or blouse.

B = distance "A" plus 1 inch

C = between 1 inch to 1.5 inches based on personal preference

D = distance "A" minus 1 inch

E = distance "A" plus 1.5 inches

F = 2 inches

G = distance "A" plus 2 inches

H = 2.5 inches

I = distance "A" plus 3 inches

J = 3.5 inches

Note: By simply changing the shirt collar design you can create a new look on an old pattern. Or you can replace an existing shirt collar on an old shirt with a different shirt collar design and create the appearance of a different shirt because most people look at your face when they are talking to you and the collar of your shirt is what they normally see and remember.

How to sew a collar onto a shirt or blouse: One piece collars are attached to a buckskin shirt or blouse after the body of the shirt has been finished and fitted to the person. Although the shirt collar is cut straight along its bottom, this distance must match the circular neck opening of the garment because the collar will be sewn to the neck opening. Therefore it is usually a good idea to cut the collar approximately one-half inch longer than you think you will need because it is relatively easy to trim just a little material off the bottom of each end of the collar to make it match the neck opening in the garment but it is not easy to add length to the bottom of the collar. Begin in the middle of the back neck opening and lay the collar on the garment so that the hair side of the collar is lying flat on the outside hair side of the garment. If you wish for the collar to always lie down flat against the garment then use a buttonhole stitch to sew the collar to the neck opening from side to side. If you wish for the collar to be more flexible so that you can lift the collar up to cover the bottom part of your neck then use a baseball stitch to attach the collar to the garment.

Chapter Thirty-Two

Skirts and Dresses

Ladies' clothing can be made in a variety of different ways depending on the activity the lady wishes to engage in and her personal preferences in clothing. A lady may wear pants and either a shirt or a blouse. Or a lady may wear a skirt with either a shirt or a blouse. Or a lady may wear a dress that covers the upper and lower parts of her body. Buckskin skirts and dresses will be described in detail in this chapter.

Bottom of a Skirt or a Dress

The bottom of a lady's skirt or dress may be cut straight, or it may be cut in a gentle curve, or it may be cut in any shape you desire, such as the wavy shape in the illustration. The wavy shape may match the natural curve in the edge of the buckskin or it may be intentionally cut into the dress pattern. The wavy shape may be symmetrical as illustrated. Or it may be of an irregular shape to create a more primitive backwoods appearance.

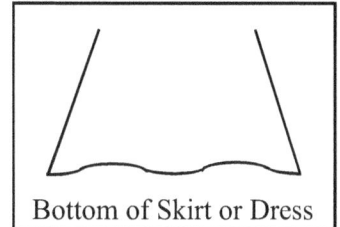

Bottom of Skirt or Dress

Skirts

A skirt covers the lower part of the body. A skirt may fit loosely and hang straight down the sides, or it may be tailored to fit the natural curves of the body.

Wrap Around Skirt

This skirt is extremely practical and it is also very fashionable. And it can be easily made from a single buckskin or from the unused pieces of five different buckskins. The front of the skirt overlaps itself. The two top ends of the skirt may be tied to one another in the back or in the front using thongs that are sewn onto the skirt. Or two buttons and two buttonholes may be placed in the waist of the skirt so that both of the loose ends of the top of the skirt may be buttoned at the waist.

One Piece
Wrap Around Skirt
with Two Buttons

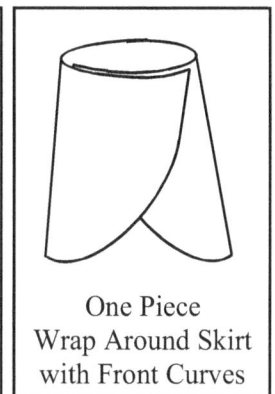

One Piece
Wrap Around Skirt
with Front Curves

This skirt allows for complete freedom of movement of the legs while walking, running, or sitting. The skirt can also be easily removed, or simply lifted up, when the lady needs to relieve herself. This skirt will always fit extremely well even if the buckskin stretches or shrinks a little bit with each washing, or if the person adds a little weight or loses a little weight with the passage of time.

One easy way to create this skirt is to wrap a buckskin around the lady's waist and use a pencil to mark where the buckskin needs to be cut so that it extends the correct length from her midsection down her legs to the length that she prefers. Also mark the right and left edges of the skirt. Remember to allow 3/4 inch for each of the four hems. There will be a hem at the waist, and at the bottom, and on the right side, and on the left side. Or you can use the following measurements:

Measurements:

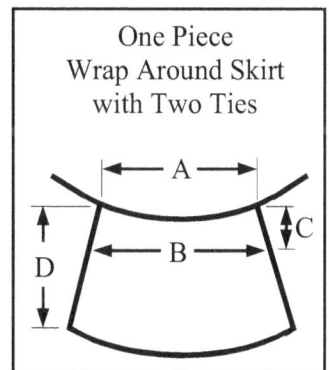

One Piece
Wrap Around Skirt
with Two Ties

A = the curved distance around the waist at it smallest measurement multiplied by "E" plus 1.5 inches for two side hems

B = the curved distance around the widest hip measurement multiplied by "E" plus 1.5 inches for two side hems

C = distance from waist to widest part of hips plus 1 inch for the waist hem

D = distance from waist to the knee plus 1 inch for the waist hem, plus 3/4 inch for the bottom hem

E = use 1.25 for a straight front skirt or use 1.4 for a skirt with front curves

A basic Wrap Around Skirt can be easily enhanced by adding fringes along the waist hem, or along the bottom hem, or along both the waist hem and the bottom hem. Another alternative is to use a decorative cross stitch around the entire waist hem using a contrasting color thread or a buckskin lace that contrasts attractively and distinctively against the color of the buckskin.

Five Piece Wrap Around Skirt with Two Ties

Five Piece Skirt with Two Ties

This is a basic wrap around skirt but it is made from five separate pieces of buckskin instead of a single piece of buckskin. This will allow you to create a very nice skirt using some left over pieces of buckskin from some of your other sewing projects. The five pieces of buckskin may all be of a similar color. However, a more attractive skirt is sometimes possible if the five pieces of buckskin are of different shades or colors. Alternate the five pieces using a lighter shade, then a darker shade, then a lighter shade, then a darker shade, and so on.

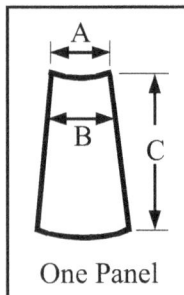

One Panel

Measurements of One of the Five Skirt Panels:
(Allows skirt to overlap by 1/4 of the waist measurement in front)
A = 1/4 of the smallest waist measurement usually just above the navel. Add an additional 1.5 inches for the side seams, plus 1/2 inch for comfort
B = 1/4 of the widest hip measurement around the buttocks which is usually about 9 inches below the waist. Add an additional 1.5 inches for the side seams
C = Desired length of skirt from waist to bottom hem of skirt. Add an additional 1 inch for the waist hem and add 3/4 inches for the bottom hem

How to Sew: Sew the five panels together using an overlapping seam of 3/4 inch between each panel. Overlap the five panels as shown in this illustration =
A running stitch will work well but a zig zag stitch with a contrasting color thread will add a distinct pattern to the skirt. If the skirt is made from some unused pieces from five different buckskins then each skirt panel will be a slightly different color than the other panels and this will enhance the natural beauty of this skirt.

Skirts with Two Long Ties

Allow the top waist of the skirt to fold over once or twice until it is in a comfortable position around your waist but above your hips and then tie the ends of the two ties together in front of your waist. This is usually just below your navel. This will allow you to more comfortably sit down and stand up without the waist of the skirt causing you discomfort in your midsection.

Three Piece Fitted Skirt

This skirt is designed to fit the curvatures of the body by using three pieces of material: a singe front piece and two back pieces.

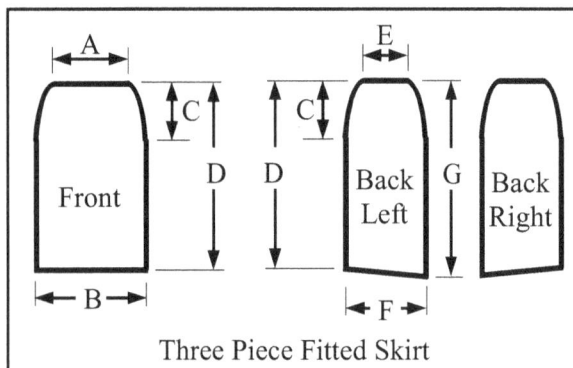

Three Piece Fitted Skirt

When standing straight up if you look down to your feet you will probably notice that the front of your body is relatively straight from your waist down to your knees. This means the front can be made from a single piece of material. But if you look at yourself sideways in a mirror then you will probably notice that your buttocks extend out further in the rear than your waist and the backs of your legs. Therefore the back of the skirt will need to be made in two pieces in order to allow for the curvature of your waist around your buttocks and back down to your legs.

Measurements:

A = one-half of smallest waist measurement plus 1.5 inches for two side seams, plus 1 inch for comfort

B = 4/10 of widest hip measurement plus 1.5 inches for two side seams, plus 1 inch for comfort

C = distance from waist to widest part of hips plus 1 inch for the waist hem

D = distance from waist to the knee (or ankle) plus 1 inch for the waist hem, plus 3/4 inch for the bottom hem

E = one-fourth of smallest waist measurement plus 1.5 inches for two side seams, plus 1/2 inch for comfort

F = 3/10 of widest hip measurement plus 1.5 inches for two seams, plus 1/2 inch for comfort

G = D plus one-third of the difference between the widest hip measurement and the smallest waist measurement, or $G = D + [1/3 \times (hip - waist)]$

How to Sew: If you are right handed then sew the right side seam from the bottom hem up to just below the widest part of the hips and stop. Then put a hem in the remaining distance on the front panel and on the right back panel. If you have a zipper of the correct length you may install it between the two hems, or you may install buttons and buttonholes on the two hems. Sew the left side of the skirt from the bottom hem up to the waist. (Note: If you are left handed then you may wish to put the zipper or buttons on the left side of the skirt instead of the right side of the skirt.)

Now sew a basting stitch in the two back panels to hold the left back panel to the right back panel. Try the skirt on and see if it fits well when standing, when sitting, and when walking. Use a full length mirror to look at the way the back of the skirt fits you in the rear. If necessary you may add or subtract some material from the center back seam from your waist down to below your buttocks to make the skirt fit better in that area. Or you may need to add two or more darts to the waist area of the two back panels to make the waist a little smaller. When you have made the appropriate adjustments you should sew the back seam together using a double running stitch and then you should remove the basting thread. To complete the skirt, sew a 1 inch wide hem around the waist and a 3/4 wide hem around the bottom edge of the skirt.

Knee Length Dresses

If possible align the dress panels in the center of the hide with half of the panel on each side of the backbone. The top of the panel may face the neck of the hide or the tail of the hide. But the top of a dress panel should not face towards the right or left sides of the hide. You should also cut the front and back panels at least two or three inches longer than you think they need to be. If the dress shrinks then it will still fit okay.

A knee length dress can be made from two different hides of approximately the same thickness, softness, and color. One hide will be used for the front panel of the dress and the other hide will be used for the back panel of the dress.

Ankle Length Dresses

The average buckskin is approximately 48 inches long from neck to tail. If the distance from the front of the lady's neck to her ankles is greater then the length of the buckskin you are using then you can still make an ankle length dress but the dress will need to be made from three different hides of approximately the same thickness, softness, and color. The two longest hides will be used for the front dress panel and the back dress panel. The third hide will be draped over the shoulder and it will form the shoulders and front and back yokes of the dress, and the sleeves of the dress, if appropriate. (Note: Some summer dresses do not have sleeves.)

The yokes will reduce the length of the front and back panels of the dress by approximately 10 inches each. This means you will be able to cut the front bottom panel of the dress from the chest down to the ankles from one buckskin, the back bottom panel of the dress from a second buckskin, and the front and back yokes from a third buckskin or from unused pieces of other buckskins that you have left over from other sewing projects. A few yoke designs are illustrated at the end of this chapter on page 123 and some different yoke designs are illustrated on page 103 in Chapter 28.

Dresses are frequently decorated with fringes along the bottom hem and along the front and back yokes, and sometimes the shoulder/sleeve seams. These fringes are made from the unused pieces of the same hides that the dress panels were cut from. Fringes are illustrated on page 101 in Chapter 28.

Straight Two Piece Dress

This basic dress hangs straight down from the shoulders to the knees (or lower if you prefer). This design is a good choice because it is easy to make and it looks nice on most women, even if the woman no longer has her teenage figure.

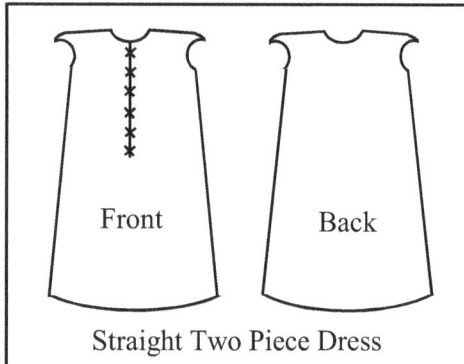

Straight Two Piece Dress

Measurements:
1. The front top middle slit will be laced together each time the dress is put on and unlaced when the dress is removed.
2. The front piece should be a few inches wider than the back piece just below the armholes to allow room for the breasts.
3. The buttock area of the back piece should be a little wider than the matching front piece to allow room for the buttocks.
4. The armhole openings in the back piece should have about 1.5 to 2 inches more curve than the same armholes in the front.

How to Sew: Sew the front and back pieces together down the right and left sides and across the top of the right and left shoulders. Hem but do not sew the bottom, neck, two armholes, and front slit.

Buttons or Zipper: Instead of the front lace you may install buttons or a zipper down the front opening.

Cool Weather Dress: A sleeveless summer dress can be converted into a cool weather dress by sewing sleeves onto each armhole. Instructions for adding sleeves are on page 100 in Chapter 28.

Two Piece Summer Dress with Shoulder Straps

This is a simple dress to make and it will fit the natural curvatures of your body.

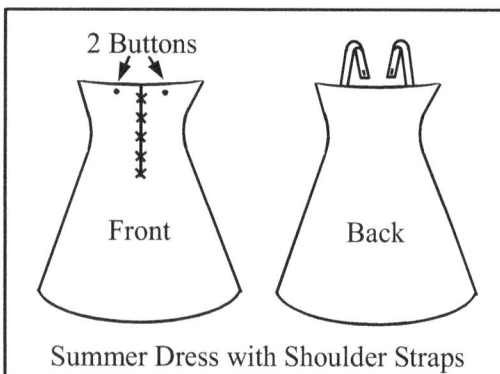

Summer Dress with Shoulder Straps

Measurements:
1. The front top middle slit will be laced together each time the dress is put on and unlaced when the dress is removed.
2. The front piece should be a few inches wider than the back piece along the top to allow room for the breasts. If necessary, the front piece can be made to fit comfortably around the breasts by sewing some extra material on both sides of the front slit opening.
3. The buttock area of the back piece should be a little wider than the matching front piece to allow room for the buttocks.

How to Sew: Sew the front and back pieces together down the right and left sides. Hem but do not sew the bottom, the top back, the top front, and front slit. Sew Straps onto the back and sew a buttonhole at the end of each strap with the length of the buttonhole going up and down the strap and not across the strap. Then sew a button on each side of the front to attach the straps in front.

Buttons or Zipper: Instead of the front lace you may install buttons or a zipper down the front opening.

Optional Bows: If you wish you may add a bow on the top center of each shoulder strap.

Sleeveless Two Piece Summer Dress

This is an easy dress to make and it will fit the natural curvatures of your body.

Measurements:
1. The front top middle slit will be laced together each time the dress is put on and unlaced when the dress is removed.
2. The front piece should be a few inches wider than the back piece just below the armholes to allow room for the breasts.
3. If necessary, the front piece can be made to fit comfortably around the breasts by sewing some extra material on both sides of the front slit opening.
4. The buttock area of the back piece should be a little wider than the matching front piece to allow room for the buttocks.
5. The armhole openings in the back piece should have about 1.5 to 2 inches more curve than the same armholes in the front.

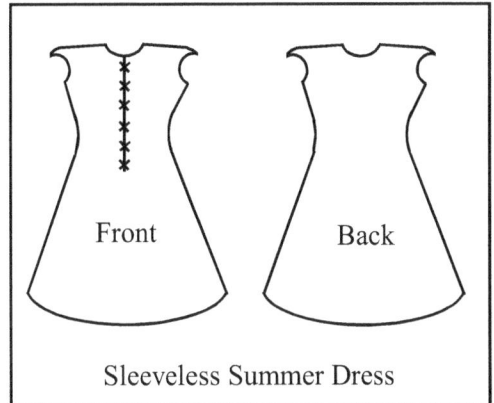

Sleeveless Summer Dress

How to Sew: Sew the front and back pieces together down the right and left sides and across the top of the right and left shoulders. Hem but do not sew the bottom, neck, two armholes, and front slit.

Buttons or Zipper: Instead of the front lace you may install buttons or a zipper down the front opening.

Cool Weather Dress: A sleeveless summer dress can be converted into a cool weather dress by sewing sleeves onto each armhole. Instructions for adding sleeves are on page 100 in Chapter 28.

Optional Neckline Openings for Dresses and Blouses

Simply changing the neckline on an old pattern, or changing the neckline on an old buckskin garment, will create a totally new look because most of the time other people are looking at your face and the upper half of your body. A variety of different neckline options are illustrated below.

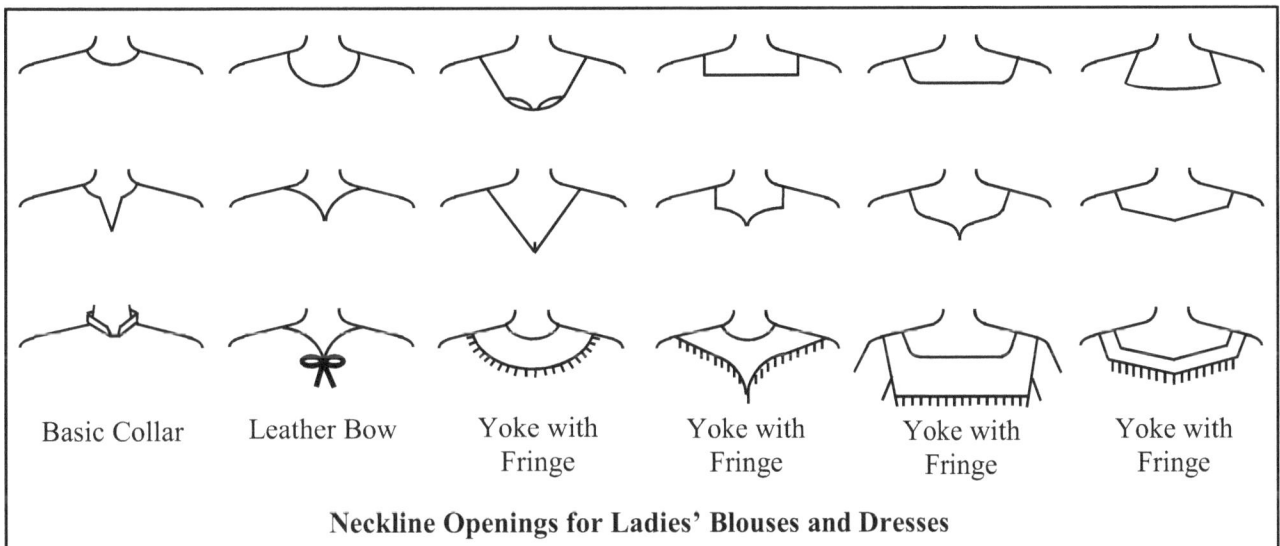

| Basic Collar | Leather Bow | Yoke with Fringe | Yoke with Fringe | Yoke with Fringe | Yoke with Fringe |

Neckline Openings for Ladies' Blouses and Dresses

Chapter Thirty-Three

Ponchos, Robes, Jackets, Coats, and Blankets

Ponchos

A poncho is an outer garment that is usually worn over other garments, such as a shirt or a dress. The purpose of a poncho is to protect its wearer from the wind and from cool weather. It can be taken off at night and then used as a simple blanket to cover the body to keep most of the body warm while sleeping.

Ponchos do not have sleeves. The left and right edges of the poncho simply hang down over the arms on both sides. These edges are not gathered together under the arms nor are they tied together with straps on the sides. A poncho simply hangs down from the neck and shoulders to cover the upper part of the body.

The length of a poncho may be whatever you wish it to be. The minimum poncho length would be down your front and your back to a point about halfway between your navel and your crotch. A longer poncho may extend down to your crotch, or midway down your upper thigh, or to your knees. Ponchos generally do not extend down to the ankles because their simple hanging design can interfere with walking and running.

A primitive poncho can be made by cutting an oval shaped slit in the center of a buckskin and then placing the cut area over the head and around the neck and then wearing the buckskin without any further modification. The most common exception would be to cut off the tail if it is still attached to the buckskin.

A modern poncho is usually rectangular. The poncho is cut as a rectangle from a single buckskin to utilize as much of the material from neck to tail, and from side to side as possible. The neck opening is cut like the opening in a pullover shirt with a long oval from side to side and a short half circle in front. The inside of the neck opening should be buttonhole stitched to prevent it from stretching. The outside edges of the poncho may be hemmed if you wish for the poncho to retain more of its original rectangular shape. Either a running stitch or a whip stitch may be used for the hems on the poncho.

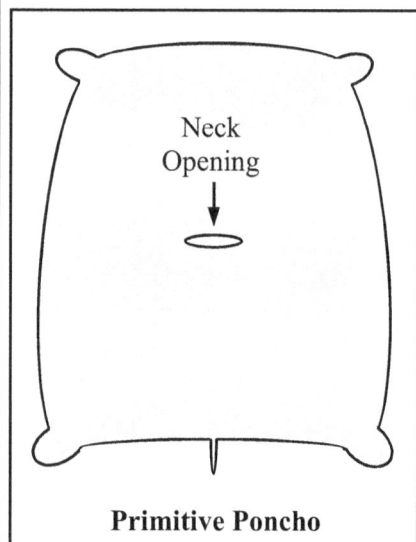

Primitive Poncho

Neck Opening

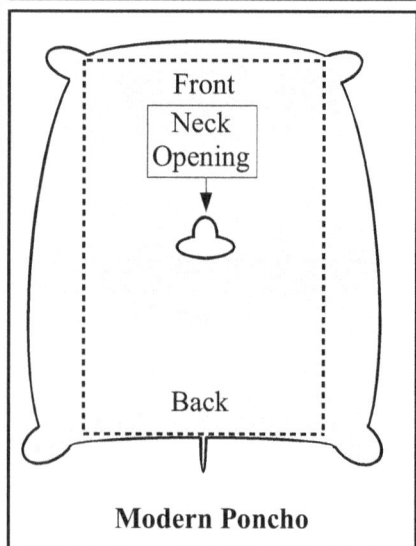

Modern Poncho

Front

Neck Opening

Back

Robes

Robes are traditionally worn during cool and cold weather for warmth. A robe is worn on top of all your other clothing as an outer garment. Some native American Indian tribes would sleep in their robes during the cold weather months when the temperature would drop 20 or more degrees during the night.

The robe hangs down from your shoulders to your ankles. A robe has two sleeves. It has an overlapping front and therefore the right and left front panels must be cut so they can overlap by about four to six inches in the front. This means the total combined width of the two front panels will be more than the width of the back panel by approximately four to six inches. In other words, the right front panel will be one-half the width of the back panel plus two or three inches. The left front panel will be the same width as the right front panel. The robe may be buttoned half way down the front or it may be tied half way down the front with several short

Back

Right Front Left Front

Back Panel for a Robe

Two Front Panels for a Robe

Two Sleeves for a Robe

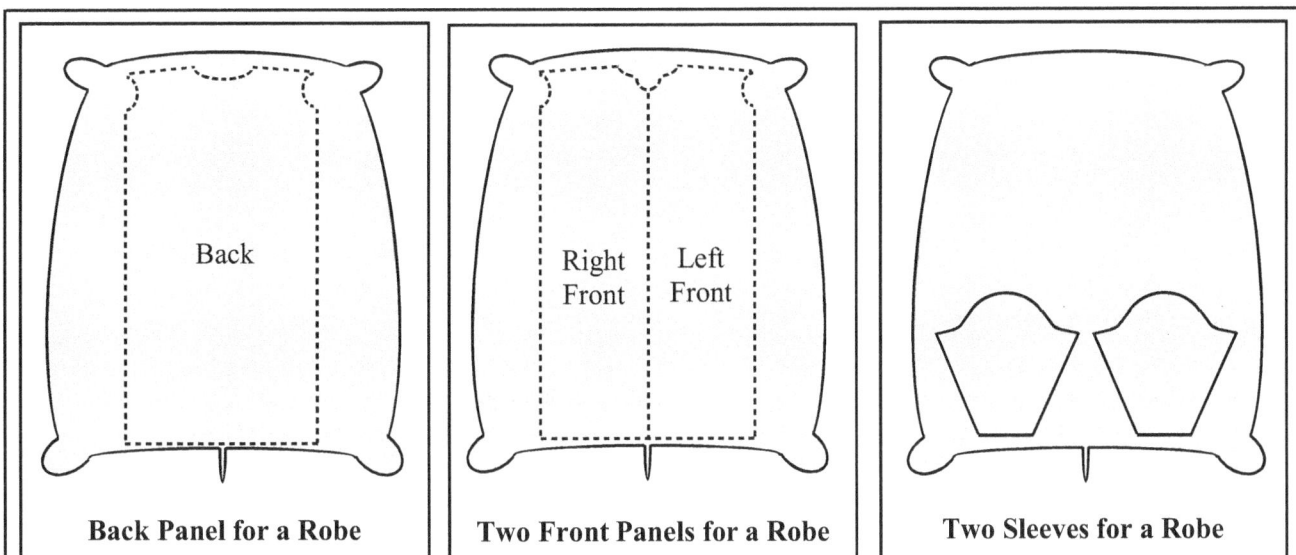

ties that are sewn opposite one another on the right and left front panels. Or the robe may be held closed with a soft buckskin belt that is wrapped around the waist and tied in front.

A robe will usually require three large buckskins. The back panel will be cut from one buckskin, two front panels will be cut from a second buckskin, and two sleeves will be cut from approximately one-half of a third buckskin. Instructions for creating sleeves are on page 100 in Chapter 28. A robe is similar to a poncho because it simply hands down around your body and it is not designed to follow the shape of your body, except that it must be wide enough and long enough to properly cover your body.

Either a whip stitch or a running stitch may be used to sew the robe pieces together. The shoulders are sewn together across the top of the robe except for the neck opening. Then the two sides are sewn together down the right and left sides except for the arm openings. The top of each sleeve is then sewn to the arm hole openings in the top of the robe. Then each sleeve is sewn down the seam of the sleeve to form the normal sleeve shape. A hem is then sewn into the wrist end of each sleeve.

Finally a hem is sewn around the neck opening and a hem is sewn around the entire bottom of the robe.

Jackets and Coats

A jacket usually extends down to the crotch area. A coat usually extends down to the middle of the thigh, or to the middle of the lower leg, or to just above the ankle.

A jacket or a coat is made following the same procedure that is described in Chapter 31 for making shirts. The major difference is that the length of a coat is whatever you desire it to be. You will also need to add an additional one or two inches to most of the other measurements so that the jacket or coat may be worn on top of your other clothing.

Blankets or Quilts

A single buckskin may be cut into a blanket of the proper size for a child. But a single buckskin is too small to serve as a blanket for an adult. Therefore more than one buckskin will be needed to make an adult size blanket. Since multiple buckskins will be required to make a blanket, the most practical way to create a blanket is to use the same method that is used to make quilts. After you have accumulated a lot of left over pieces of buckskin that are at least six inches square or bigger, then you can sew all the small pieces of buckskin together using a baseball stitch to make a homemade buckskin quilt of the size that you require. All the pieces do **not** need to be square or the same size square. Some of the pieces may be rectangular and different size rectangles. Simply take the time to fit the pieces together the same way you would a jigsaw puzzle except this is usually easier to do since the edges of all the buckskin pieces will be straight lines.

Chapter Thirty-Three: Ponchos, Robes, Jackets, Coats, and Blankets

Chapter Thirty-Four

Hoods, Caps, Ski Masks, Mittens, and Gloves

Old Proverb: "If your feet are cold and you are wearing two pair of socks, then put on a hat. If your feet are still cold, then put on another hat."

When people become civilized they gradually forget many things that were of critical importance to their ancestors. Today hoods, hats, and caps are usually not given much thought by people who live in prosperity, except in relation to a fashion statement.

However, after a person is fully clothed then the two areas where a person will continue to lose body heat are through the hands and the head. Gloves can be used to protect your hands from heat loss, and a hood or hat or cap can be used to protect your head from heat loss. If you are properly clothed, but you are not wearing some type of head covering, then approximately 90% of your body's heat loss will be through your head. However, because your feet are so far away from your heart and your main body mass, your feet will frequently get cold in addition to your nose and ears. The way to get warm is to put on a hood or hat or cap or ski mask to reduce the heat loss from your head.

Beaver hides are the best hides to use when making hoods, caps, and ski masks.

Hoods

A hood is a covering for the head and the neck. I designed this hood so that when it is worn it will drape down in front to just above the eyebrows. This unique hood design has all three of the following benefits:

1. It will keep the front of your forehead warm on cold days and on windy days.
2. On cold sunny days it will help to shade your eyes from the sun.
3. On cold rainy days it will help to direct rainwater off the front of the hood so the rainwater drips down in front of your body and not on your face.

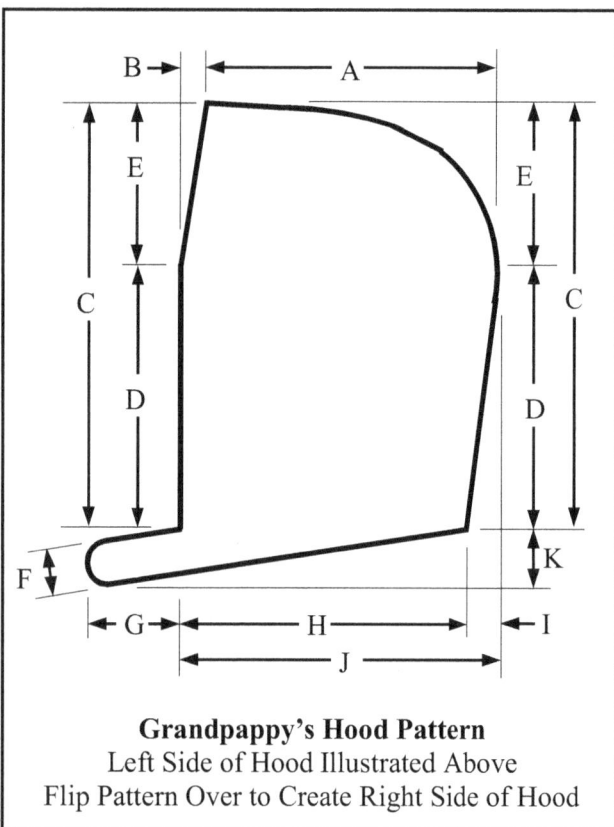

Grandpappy's Hood Pattern
Left Side of Hood Illustrated Above
Flip Pattern Over to Create Right Side of Hood

The bottom front extension can be buttoned under the chin in order to secure the hood to the head so the hood doesn't blow off on windy days.

Measurements:

A = the curved distance from the front center of the neck around the neck to the back center of the neck plus 0.75 inch for a seam

B = 1 inch

C = curved distance from the top center of the head around the side of the head past the ear and down to the shoulder plus 1.5 inches for a seam and a hem

D = straight line distance from the bottom of the neck in the back up to the widest point of the head in the rear plus 0.75 inches for a hem

E = C minus D

F = 2 inches for an adult or 1.5 inches for a teenager or a child

G = one-half the straight line distance from the right side of the neck to the left side of the neck plus 1.5 inches

H = A

I = 1 inch

J = H plus I

K = F plus 0.75 inch for a hem or a seam

How to Sew: Match the left and right patterns together with the hair side of the buckskin on the inside. Beginning at the top of the hood at the face side of dimension "A" sew around the curve down to the bottom of the back of neck and stop at the beginning of dimension "K." Use a double running stitch and an overlapping seam. Then turn the hood inside out so the hair side of the buckskin in on the outside of the hood and the stitches are hidden on the inside of the hood.

Sew a buttonhole stitch around the front face opening of the hood along dimension "C" in front and around the top part of extension "G" and stop at the bottom of dimension "F."

Hem the bottom of the hood along dimensions "G" and "H" and "I" using a double running stitch.

Finally, install a buttonhole near the end of the left front extension and install a button near the end of the right front extension.

There are two ways in which the hood may be worn as follows:

1. If the hood will be worn as a separate garment, similar to a cap, then the hood is now complete. Place the hood over the head and button the hood in front under the chin.

2. If the hood will be attached to a garment then align the bottom of the seam in the back of the hood to the center of the rear of the neck opening in the garment. Sew the bottom of the hood to the neck opening using a baseball stitch for approximately 1/6 of the distance around the neck opening to the right, and approximately 1/6 of the distance around the neck opening to the left. The hood may be allowed to hang down the back of the garment when it is not needed. But when it is needed the hood can be lifted up and placed over the head and buttoned in the front under the chin.

Caps

The flesh side of the hide should be on the inside of the cap and the hair side of the hide should be on the outside of the cap. A cap can be made with the hair still on the hide or with the hair removed from the hide. When I was a young child the television played a series called "Davy Crockett." Davy Crockett wore a coon skin cap and he had a single shot rifle that he called "Old Betsy." The television series was extremely popular and every child wanted a coon skin cap. My family could not afford to buy me a coon skin hat but many of my friends had one. After wearing their new coon skin caps for a few days my friends began to experience serious problems with itching heads and some of their hair started falling out. The raccoon hides had not been properly treated and the children were paying the price for this failure to properly tan those hides. I mention this because there is nothing wrong with creating a cap that does not have any fur or hair on it. It will still keep your head warm and it will probably not cause any type of scalp irritation. Or you may create a hat with the fur still on the hide and the fur will help to keep your head a little warmer, and it will help to shed a little more rain. But a buckskin hat is not waterproof, even with the hair still on it.

Caps are very similar to other articles of clothing. There is no one size cap that will fit everyone. Each cap must be fitted to the individual that will be wearing it.

A cap is worn with the front of the cap above the eyebrows and the front of the cap will be higher on the head than the rear of the cap. When you look at the person wearing the cap from the side you will see that the rear of the cap rests a little lower on the back of the person's head than the front of the cap on the front of the head. This is the natural and comfortable way to way a cap.

A cap should feel comfortable against the top of your head. It should not be too tight nor should it be too loose. It should remain on your head when you bend over and it should not fall off. When you remove the cap from your head you should not see an indentation around your forehead that was left by the cap.

Basic One Piece Cap

This is a basic one piece cap with a seam in the front and a seam in the rear. The sides of the cap will cover both ears and the back of the head.

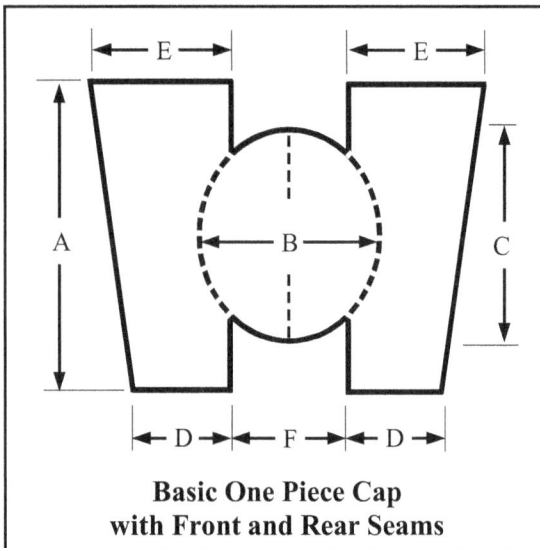

**Basic One Piece Cap
with Front and Rear Seams**

Measurements:

A = one-half the diameter around the head at its widest spot plus 1.5 inches for 2 seams, plus 0.5 inch for shrinkage

B = the straight line distance across the top middle of the head from the left side of the head to the right side of the head plus 0.5 inch for shrinkage

C = the straight line distance across the top center of the head from the back of the head to the front of the head plus 1.5 inches for 2 seams, plus 0.5 inch for shrinkage

D = the straight line distance from the top front of the forehead down to just above the eyebrows plus 0.75 inch for one seam, plus 0.5 inch for shrinkage

E = the straight line distance from the top rear of the head down the back of the head to the bottom of the neck plus 0.75 inch for one seam, plus 0.5 inch for shrinkage

F = 0.62 multiplied by dimension "B"

The oblong circle in the center of the cap (the circle contains some dashed lines) should be centered between the front and the rear of the pattern, and between the left and right sides of the pattern.

The lines drawn at an angle on the left and right sides of the pattern can be drawn last by connecting the ends of lines "E" to the ends of lines "D."

Prepare a paper pattern of the cap following the above instructions and cut it out. Tape the two lines "D" together at the front to form a front seam by overlapping the front seam by 3/4 inch. Tape the two lines "E" together at the rear of the cap to form a rear seam by overlapping the rear seam by 3/4 inch. Then tape the front and rear edges of the oblong circle to the front and rear seams and overlap the circle on the seams by about 3/4 inch. Now place the paper cap on the person's head to determine how well it fits. If it fits good then you can use the pattern without any modifications. If the cap is a little big or a little small then you can adjust the paper pattern to make it fit a little better before you draw the pattern onto the buckskin.

Trace the paper pattern onto the flesh side of the buckskin. Do not draw the dashed lines on the buckskin. Cut out the pattern on the solid lines using some sharp scissors. Either a whip stitch of a double running stitch may be used for most of the seams.

Fold the buckskin down the center of the pattern along the center dashed line in the middle of the oblong circle so the hair side of the buckskin is touching the hair side and the flesh sides are facing out.

Sew the front seam together along lines "D" with a 3/4 inch overlap at the seam. Sew the rear seam together along lines "E" with a 3/4 inch overlap at the seam. Now turn the cap hair side out and place the cap on the person's head and verify that the cap fits comfortably around the top of the person's head and it is not too tight or too loose. If the cap is too tight then undo one or both of the seams and overlap the seam with less material in the seam. If the cap is too loose then undo one or both of the seams and overlap the seam with more material in the seam.

After the cap has been adjusted to fit comfortably around the top of the person's head then remove the cap and turn the hair side in and the flesh side out. Overlap the front of the oblong circle about 3/4 inch onto the front piece of the cap and sew it in place using a double running stitch or a whip stitch. Overlap the rear of the oblong circle onto the rear piece of the cap and sew it in place using a double running stitch or a whip stitch.

Turn the cap hair side out and have the person try the hat on. If the cap fits comfortably then add a 3/4 inch hem around the entire bottom border of the cap and secure it with a double running stitch or a whip stitch.

The cap is now complete and it is ready to be worn.

Basic Two Piece Cap

This is a basic two piece cap with one seam in the rear. It has a top center piece and it has ear flaps that will cover both ears and the back of the head.

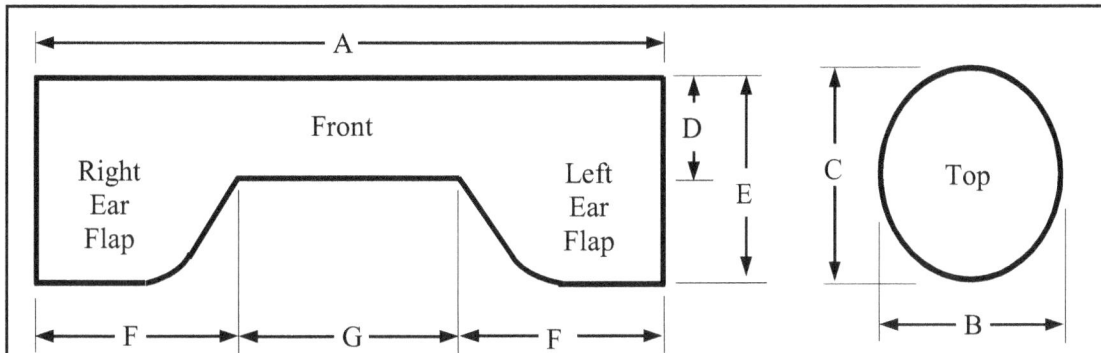

Cap with Ear Flaps and Seam in Rear
Sew the Top of the Cap to the Top Edge of the Cap along "A"
Sew a Seven Inch Long Strap on the Bottom of the Right and Left Ear Flaps
Tie the Straps Under Chin (or Fold Ear the Flaps Up and Tie the Straps Above Head)

Measurements:

A = the diameter around the head at its widest spot plus 0.75 inch for one seam, plus 0.5 inch for possible shrinkage

B = the straight line distance across the top middle of the head from the left side of the head to the right side of the head plus 1.5 inches for two seams, plus 0.5 inch for possible shrinkage

C = the straight line distance across the top center of the head from the back of the head to the front of the head plus 1.5 inches for two seams, plus 0.5 inch for possible shrinkage

D = the straight line distance from the top front of the head down to just above the eyebrows plus 1.5 inches for one seam and one hem, plus 0.5 inch for possible shrinkage

E = the straight line distance from the top rear of the head down the back of the head to the bottom of the neck plus 1.5 inches for one seam and one hem, plus 0.5 inch for possible shrinkage

F = dimension "A" minus 1.25 inches and then multiplied by 0.33

G = dimension "F" plus 1.25 inches

Prepare a paper pattern for the cap and cut it out. Tape the pattern together along seam "E" in the rear of the hat using a seam overlap of 3/4 inch.

Now place the paper cap on the person's head to determine how well it fits. If it fits good then you can use the pattern without any modifications. If the cap is a little big or a little small then you can adjust the paper pattern to make it fit a little better before you draw the pattern onto the buckskin.

Trace the paper pattern onto the flesh side of the buckskin. Cut out the two pieces of the pattern on the solid lines using sharp scissors. Either a whip stitch of a double running stitch may be used for the seams.

Sew the rear seam together along lines "E" with a 3/4 inch overlap along the rear seam. Place the cap on the person's head and verify that the cap fits comfortably around the top of the person's head and it is not too tight or too loose. If the cap is too tight then undo the rear seam and overlap the seam with less material in the seam. If the cap is too loose then undo the rear seam and overlap the seam with more material in the seam.

Turn the hat so the flesh side of the hat is facing out and match the top oblong circle to the center of the cap. Use a whip stitch to attach the flesh side of the oblong circle to the flesh side of the cap with approximately 3/4 inch in the seam. Sew half way around the top piece to the rear seam of the cap. The rear center of the oblong circle should be even with the back seam.

Use a whip stitch to attach the other side of the top circle to the other half of the cap with approximately 3/4 inch in the seam. The rear center of the oblong circle should be even with the back seam.

Turn the cap hair side out and have the person try the hat on. If the cap fits comfortably then add a 3/4 inch hem around the entire bottom border of the cap and secure the hem with a running stitch or a whip stitch.

 Sew a seven inch long strap to the bottom of each of the two ear flaps directly below the center of the person's ears. If the weather is cold or the wind is blowing then you can tie the ear flaps straps together in a bow below your chin. If the weather is not too cold and the wind is not blowing then you can fold the two ear flaps up along the sides and back of the cap and tie the two straps above your head.

The seam should be in the back of the cap because a person will not see or feel the seam on the back of the cap because their hair will cushion the cap against his or her head. After the cap has been worn for several months, and the cap has been washed and allowed to dry several times, then you can adjust the seam in the back of the cap and around the top brim and increase or decrease the size of the cap to more comfortably match the person's head. This will be possible if you allowed a little extra space in the cap in the beginning so that the cap fit just a little loosely at first. Remember that the cap will probably be worn for many, many years so a little minor discomfort in the beginning will be worth it in the long run.

Ski Mask

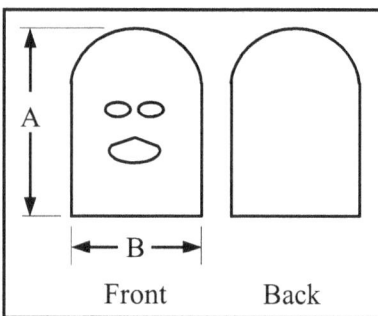

Front   Back

Measurements:
A = straight line distance from top of head to shoulder at neck
B = one-half the diameter around the widest part of the head plus 1.5 inches for two seams, plus 1 inch for comfort

 Place the two halves together with the flesh side on the outside and the hair side on the inside. Sew the two halves together with an invisible or hidden seam and a double running stitch. Then turn the ski mask inside out so the hair side is on the outside and the stitches are on the inside.

The location of the two eye holes and the mouth/nose hole should be determined after the two halves have been sewn together and the ski mask has been fitted to the head so that it is comfortable but not too snug. There are a variety of different ways to cut the mouth and nose opening but the illustrated design will allow for comfortable speech and for easy breathing through the nose. The area between your nose and your lips will be unprotected but in cold weather this is normally an advantage because your nose may run and this design will allow you to wipe your nose frequently so the discharge does not get onto your ski mask or onto your lips.

Sew a buttonhole stitch around the inside edge of the two eye holes and the mouth/nose hole to help these areas retain their original size and shape.

Mittens

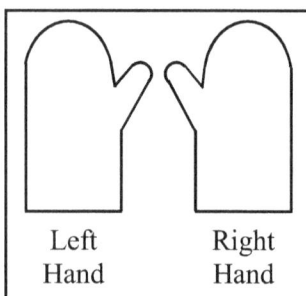

Left   Right
Hand   Hand

 Fold a piece of buckskin in half with the hair side on the inside and the flesh side on the outside and pin it together with straight pins. Place the person's left and right hands on the buckskin and draw around the outside of each hand with the thumb fully extended and all four fingers close together. Draw the wrist straight down on both sides from the outside bottom of the thumb and the outside wrist below the little finger to provide enough space for the hand to enter the mitten. Cut out the mittens leaving one inch of extra buckskin all the way around the pattern. Place the two pieces together so the flesh side is facing out and the hair side is facing in. Sew around the outside of the mittens using a buttonhole stitch but do **not** sew the wrist opening closed. Turn the mittens inside out so the hair side is on the outside and the stitches are on the inside of the mittens. Sew a hem around the wrist opening of each mitten using a double running stitch to help the wrist opening retain its original shape and to minimize stretching.

Gloves

Gloves are similar to mittens but each finger has its own individual opening. The easiest way to make gloves is to draw the outline of the hand (with all the fingers spread far apart) onto a piece of a buckskin folded in half, with 1/2 inch added around all the fingers and the thumb, and with 1/2 inch added from the outside bottom of the thumb straight down to the wrist, and with 1/2 inch added from the outside bottom of the little finger straight down to the wrist. Do not taper the gloves from the thumb and little finger down to the wrist or the hand will not be able to fit inside the glove opening.

There are two ways that gloves can be sewn together:

1. **Without a Center Piece:** Match the two right hand glove pieces together with the hair side of the buckskin on the inside. Use a whip stitch and a hidden seam to sew all the way around the two pieces except do not sew the wrist area closed. Either hem the wrist area or sew a double running stitch around the entire wrist area without a hem. Repeat the procedure for the left hand glove. Finish by turning the gloves so the hair side is out.

2. **With a Center Piece:** Cut four long thin rectangular pieces of buckskin about 3/4 inch wide and twice the length of your fingers. These pieces will be sewn between each of two adjacent fingers and between the thumb and the forefinger in order to join the top and bottom halves of the glove together. Each long piece will be sewn to the glove beginning at the tip of one finger and continuing down the finger, around the tiny curve between your fingers, and up the adjacent finger to the tip of the adjacent finger. Sew the gloves together with the hair side facing in and when you are finished turn the glove inside out so the hair side is facing out and the stitches are hidden on the inside of the glove.

Chapter Thirty-Five

Grandpappy's Moccasin Pattern

Moccasins made from moose hides are relatively comfortable and durable. However, moccasins made from the hides of other animals do not last very long when worn on a daily basis when you must walk several miles each day. Moccasins made from deer hides will last longer than moccasins made from the hides of elk or pronghorns (antelopes).

Moccasins are not waterproof. If your moccasins get wet then your feet will also get wet. The process of getting wet and drying, repeatedly on a regular basis, shortens the life expectancy of moccasins.

Native American Indians considered moccasins to be a disposable item. If they were going to travel a reasonable distance from their camp then the Indians would take one or two spare sets of moccasins with them so they could replace their moccasins when they wore out. Most native American Indians went barefoot the majority of the time. This resulted in the bottom soles of their feet becoming extremely thick and tough and they could walk comfortably over terrain that most "civilized people" could not transverse without wearing some type of footwear.

Although people in civilized countries expect their footwear to have a different shoe for their left and right feet, handmade moccasins are generally not designed that way. Each moccasin is a mirror image of the other moccasin and therefore either moccasin may be worn on either foot.

The front curve of the moccasin should match the front curve of your other footwear. If you will look at any other pair of shoes or boots that you may now own then you will notice that the front curve of the shoe is basically symmetrical. In other words, there is no long toe area on the left side of the left foot, and there is no long toe area on the right side of the right foot. Moccasins are made the same way as other shoes. The front curve on moccasins is also symmetrical from side to side.

If you will closely examine the front lower sole of your current footwear you will notice that the sole curves upward from the bottom of the shoe at the ball of your foot until it reaches the front toe area. The reason for this is based on the design of the human foot. If you will place your foot on the floor in a comfortable manner you will notice that the heel of your foot and the ball of your foot make contact with the floor, but the instep of your foot and the front toes of your foot are curved slightly upwards and they do not make contact with the floor. Therefore, in order for moccasins to be comfortable, the front toe area of the moccasins should curve upwards in the same way your other shoes do. Although the moccasin pattern presented in this chapter shows a flat sole across the entire bottom of the moccasin, the front sole of the moccasin will gradually begin to curve upwards when it is being worn because this is the natural shape of the front of your foot. The reason is because buckskin material is soft and flexible and it will gradually match your foot shape and size.

It is possible to improve the comfort and the life expectancy of moccasins by gluing (or sewing) a very stiff hard piece of leather onto the sole of each moccasin after it has been completed. The hard piece of leather that you add to the sole of the moccasin will enable you to more comfortably walk across terrain that is not smooth or soft and that contains hard or sharp objects such as gravel. The hard piece of leather will also help to extend the useful life of your moccasins. If you use glue then use "Shoo Goo" that is sold in the footwear section of most stores that sell shoes, or you may use any glue that is designed for use with leather. (Note: If you do not have any leather then you may use two pieces of buckskin glued or sewn together and then glued or sewed to the sole of the moccasin.)

Moccasins can be made more attractive by sewing colored beads onto the front of each moccasin.

The inside of moccasins may be lined using any soft material, such as fleece or an old sweatshirt.

Moccasins are more comfortable to wear if you also wear an ordinary pair of socks.

Grandpappy's Universal Moccasin Pattern for Children, Teenagers, Women, and Men
Make a paper pattern first and tape it together to determine if any minor adjustments will be necessary.

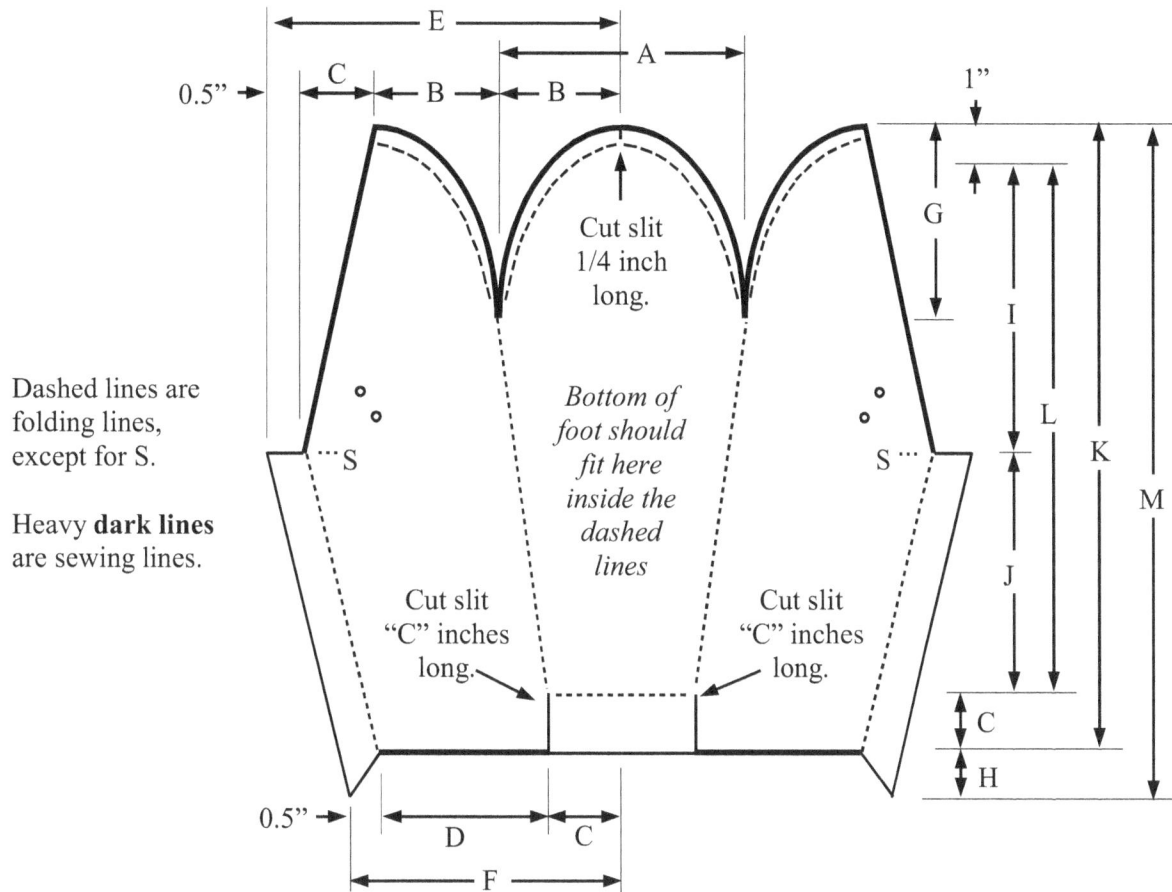

Dashed lines are folding lines, except for S.

Heavy **dark lines** are sewing lines.

Cut slit 1/4 inch long.

Bottom of foot should fit here inside the dashed lines

Cut slit "C" inches long.

Cut slit "C" inches long.

W = Width = Distance across the widest part of the front of foot
L = Length = Distance from the tip of the big toe to the back of the heel

Width Measurements:
A = W + 0.75"
B = 0.5 x A
C = 0.4 x W
D = 0.8 x W
E = A + C + 0.5"
F = C + D + 0.5"

Length Measurements:
G = 0.75 x A
H = 0.1 x L
I = 0.65 x L
J = 0.35 x L
K = L + C + 1"
M = K + H

S = Optional Slit (Read the instructions on page 136 for Step Eleven)

The above measurements will work for most people.

However, our feet are all unique and there are differences between people.

Therefore make a paper pattern of the moccasin using the above dimensions and tape it together and then use it to determine if the person's foot will fit into the paper moccasin. If not then make the appropriate adjustments to the above dimensions and try again.

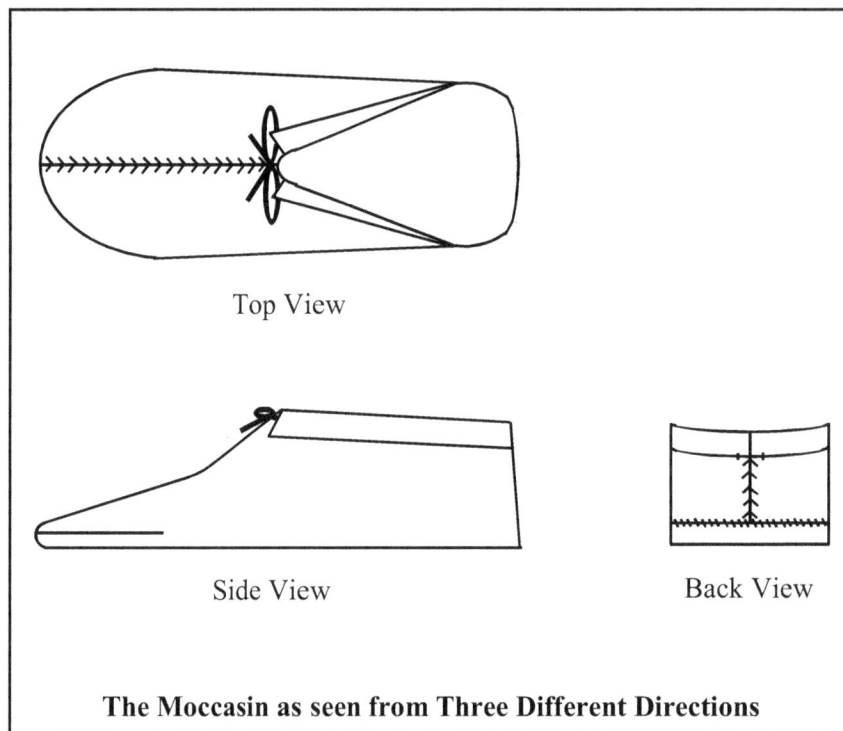

The Moccasin as seen from Three Different Directions

How to Make Moccasins Using Grandpappy's Pattern

Step One: Take two measurements of the person's foot as follows:

W = Width = The widest measurement from side to side at the front of the foot.

L = Length = The measurement from the tip of the big toe to the back of the heel.

Use the above two measurements and the equations shown below the moccasin pattern on page 133 to compute the values for all the required measurements, such as A, B, . . . , K and M.

Step Two: Obtain a large piece of paper, such as a piece of flip chart paper, or brown package wrapping paper, or the inside white surface of gift wrapping paper. If you cannot find any paper that is big enough then you can tape several ordinary pieces of notebook paper together at their edges to make a piece of paper that is large enough for the moccasin pattern.

Step Three: Draw the moccasin pattern on the paper using the appropriate dimensions. Before you cut the paper pattern have the person place his or her foot on the center of the pattern between the imaginary dashed lines where the pattern will be folded and verify that the pattern is big enough for the person's foot and that it is not too big or too small. If the person will place his or her heel on the dashed line between the two slits at the heel of the pattern then there should be approximately 1/4 inch or more on both sides of the person's foot, except at the heel, and approximately 3/4 inch or more extra space at the front toe area. If the pattern meets these specifications then it can be used without modifications. But if it does not meet these specifications then the pattern needs to be redrawn so that it will match these space requirements.

Step Four: Cut the paper pattern around its outside edges. Cut two slits in the rear heel area of the pattern. Cut a very short slit 1/4 inch or less in length in the center of the round toe area. The purpose of the short front slit is to allow the moccasin to more easily conform to the front toe area of the foot after the toe area has been sewn and then turned inside towards the person's toes. Now have the person place his or her foot on the center of the pattern as before and fold the outside edges of the pattern up and verify that the right and left front part of the moccasin will meet along the front top curve of the person's foot. If the pattern will meet along the front part of the person's foot without being too tight then the pattern may be used without any further modifications. Also fold the rear of the pattern around the heel of the person and make sure the left and right sides of the heel will touch from the top to the bottom of the heel. If the paper pattern does not fit correctly then do one of the following as appropriate:

1. **Too Small:** If the pattern is too small and it won't meet in front then you will need to tape a little extra paper (between 1/4 to 1/2 inch) to both of the front sides of the paper pattern to make the pattern just a little bigger.

2. **Too Big**: If the pattern has an excessive amount of extra space around the top of the person's foot then you will need to trim a little paper off both of the front sides of the paper pattern, to make the pattern just a little smaller.

Step Five: Place the paper pattern on the flesh side of the buckskin and use a pencil to trace the pattern onto the buckskin. The length of the pattern from toe to heel should be placed on the buckskin from the neck to the tail of the buckskin because the buckskin will stretch less in this direction. The left and right sides of the paper pattern should therefore be facing the left and right sides of the buckskin because the buckskin will have a natural tendency to stretch just a little from left to right. After you have traced one moccasin onto the buckskin, shift the paper pattern on

Longest Life of Moccasins

Best Utilization of Buckskin

the buckskin and use a pencil to trace the second moccasin onto the buckskin.

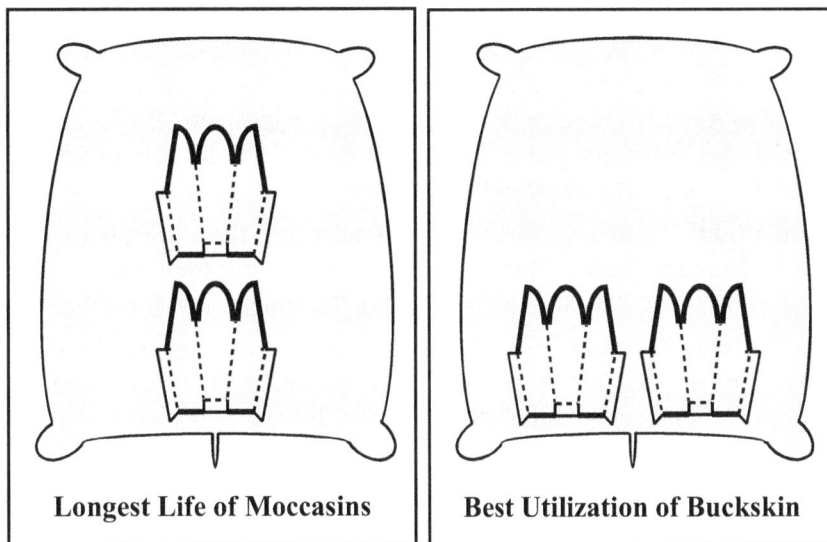

1. **Align both patterns from top to bottom along the backbone:** If you align the pattern for each moccasin down the backbone of the buckskin then you will be making the moccasins from the strongest part of the buckskin and therefore the moccasins will have the longest possible useful life. But you will not be utilizing the buckskin in its most efficient manner.

2. **Align each pattern on the left and right sides of the backbone:** If you arrange the two moccasin patterns side by side on the rear of buckskin you will achieve better utilization of the buckskin. But the useful life of the moccasins will be just a little shorter. The rump of the buckskin is usually stronger than the front of the buckskin so the useful life of the moccasins will not be that much shorter than when the moccasins are made from the backbone area. Therefore, unless you have more buckskins than you need, I recommend placing the moccasin patterns on the rump area on the buckskin (unless the rump area has cuts, or holes, or other imperfections that have been sewn closed).

Step Six: Cut out one of the two moccasins from the buckskin using sharp scissors. Do **not** cut out both moccasins. Only cut out one moccasin and then complete all the steps to sew the moccasin together following Step Seven to Step Eleven below. Then have the person try the one moccasin on and verify that it is indeed a proper fit. If it fits well then you should cut out the second moccasin and sew it together. But if the first moccasin has fit issues then you can determine what needs to be done different and begin again at Step Three above and create a new moccasin pattern that resolves the fit problems. This will limit the loss of some of your buckskin to a single moccasin instead of two identical moccasins that do not fit.

Step Seven: Use scissors to cut the two slits in the heel area of the moccasin and cut the short 1/4 inch slit in the middle of the center front curve of the moccasin. Fold the left side of the moccasin onto the center of the moccasin so the half-curve on the left side of the moccasin exactly matches the left half of the center curve at the top of the moccasin with the hair side of the moccasin touching the hair side of the moccasin. Do not fold on the dashed line down the left side of the moccasin because that dashed line is not used in this step. Instead carefully match the top left half curve to the left half of the center curve. The flesh side of the buckskin should be facing out, and the hair side of the buckskin should be touching the hair side of the buckskin where the moccasin is folded. Start at the top center of the curve and use a whip stitch to sew the left half curve to the left half of the full curve. The needle holes for the stitches should be about 1/4 inch from the outside edge of the curve. The stitches should also be about 1/6 inch apart or about six stitches per inch around the curve. As you get closer to the lower left side of the curve the stitches will gradually need to get closer and closer to the outside edge of the moccasin and then put two short stitches in the edge of the moccasin about 1/8 inch beyond where the curves meet to reinforce that area and to prevent it from tearing. Now fold the right side of the moccasin onto the center of the moccasin so the half-curve on the right side of the moccasin exactly matches the right half of the center curve at the top of the moccasin. Sew the right half of the moccasin the same way you sewed the left half of the front of the moccasin. When you have finished sewing the entire front curve of the moccasin you will need to push the front curve of the moccasin into the moccasin so the flesh side of the moccasin is now on the inside of the moccasin and the hair side of the moccasin is on the outside of the moccasin. When you have finished you should not be able to see the stitches around the front curve of the moccasin from the outside of the moccasin.

Step Eight: Bring the top left side at the front of the moccasin over so that it touches the top right side at the front of the moccasin. Starting at the middle of the front curve use a "baseball stitch" to attach the left and right sides of the moccasin together along the straight line from the toe to the foot opening of the moccasin.

Step Nine: Fold the left heel of the moccasin over against the right heel of the moccasin. Starting at the bottom of the heel use a "baseball stitch" to attach the left and right heels together up to the point where the moccasin flap begins. Stitch all the way to the top of the heel but do not sew the extended left and right flaps at the very top of the heel.

Step Ten: Fold the bottom heel piece (between the two heel slits) up against the heel and sew it to the heel using a whip stitch along the top edge of the heel piece.

Step Eleven: Fold the top left and right flaps down around the outside of the moccasin. Now have the person try the moccasin on and verify that it fits properly. If the moccasin fits well then skip down to Step Twelve. However, if there are fit problems then take corrective action as follows:

1. **Foot Will Not Fit into Foot Opening:** Depending on the size of the person's foot, and the size of the foot opening in the moccasin, it may be necessary to widen the foot opening a little bit on each side in order to make it easier for the person to slide the moccasin on and off. This will involve cutting short slits at the top center of the opening on the left and right sides of the moccasin in the positions indicated by the letter "S" on the original pattern. These short slits should be cut from where the baseball stitch ends at the top front of the moccasin and continue a short ways down the left and right sides of the moccasin in a straight line towards the bottom of the moccasin and the bottom of the foot. Begin with a very short 1/4 inch slit on both the right and left sides of the moccasin in the direction of the letter "S" on the original pattern. The person should then try to insert his or her foot into the moccasin again. If it is possible to easily get the moccasin on and off then do not cut the slits any longer but insert two short stitches at the end of each slit to prevent the slit from gradually become longer when the moccasin is worn. However, if the person still cannot get his or her foot into the moccasin then cut each slit another 1/4 inch and try again. Depending on the size of the person's foot and the size of the foot opening, it may be necessary to cut each side slit 3/4 inch or 1 inch long. If the sides slits have each been cut to a length of 1 inch and the person still cannot get his or her foot into the moccasin then cut a 1/2 inch slit towards the front of the moccasin. Try the moccasin on again. If the moccasin now fits and the person can easily get his or her foot into and out of the moccasin, then reinforce the edges of all the cuts you just made using a buttonhole stitch around the edges of the cuts.

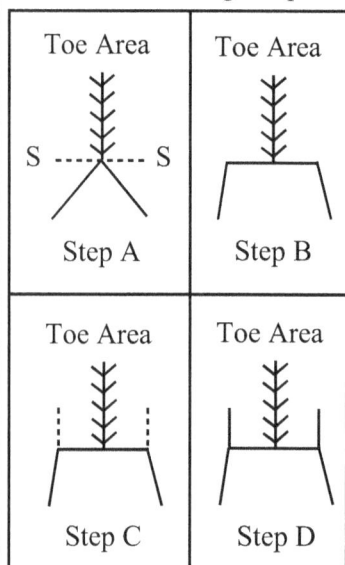

Toe Area	Toe Area
S ----X---- S	
Step A	Step B
Toe Area	Toe Area
Step C	Step D

If the person still cannot get his or her foot into the moccasin then you will need to determine how much extra space is needed for the foot opening and create a new pattern beginning at Step Three.

2. **Moccasin is Too Long:** The person's foot slides back and forth on the inside of the moccasin. If the foot opening is just a little too big, then undo the heel stitches, and trim a little off the entire back edge of the moccasin, and then resew the heel together to make the moccasin a little shorter. However, if the foot opening is just right then turn the moccasin inside out and remove the stitches around the front toe area of the moccasin. Then trim a little material off the entire toe curve and reassemble the moccasin.

3. **Moccasin is Too Wide:** The person's foot slides right and left inside the moccasin. Undo the front top stitches, trim a little bit off the right and left sides of the top of the moccasin, and then resew the front together to make the middle of the moccasin a little narrower.

4. **Moccasin is Too Small:** If you measured the person's foot correctly in Step One, and you tried the paper pattern on the person's foot in Step Four, then the moccasin should not be too small. But if the moccasin is too small then determine where the mistake was made and correct it by starting over at Step One.

Step Twelve: A strip of rawhide, or a shoelace, should now be inserted under the top flaps on each side of the moccasin foot opening. Fold the two top flaps down over the rawhide or shoelace. Add one or two short stitches on the left flap and on right flap at the back heel area to keep the flap down against the moccasin and to prevent the piece of rawhide or shoelace from falling down out of its protective flap at the back of the moccasin. Punch two small holes on the left and right sides of the baseball stitch on the front of the moccasin and push each end of the rawhide strip, or the shoelace, through the first hole into the moccasin and then back up through the second hole about 1/2 inch from the first hole. In other words, there will be two small holes on the left half of the top front of the moccasin on the left side of the baseball stitch, and there will be two small holes on the right half of the top front of the moccasin on the right side of the baseball stitch. After the person has the moccasin on his or her foot, tie the two loose ends of the rawhide or the shoelace into a bow so that some gentle pressure is applied around the top of the moccasin to hold it onto the person's foot when he or she is walking.

After you have completed the construction of one moccasin and you have verified that it fits well, then make the second moccasin the same way.

Right Foot and Left Foot Moccasins

You now have two identical moccasins that can be worn on either foot. However, you should try each moccasin on each foot because you may discover that one of the moccasins feels more comfortable when it is worn on the right foot or the left foot. If this occurs then you now have a right foot moccasin and a left foot moccasin. If your feet can't distinguish any difference between the two moccasins then that is also good because you will know that you created two almost identical moccasins.

Even if both moccasins feel the same when worn on either foot you should still designate one moccasin as your right foot moccasin and the other moccasin as your left foot moccasin. Then somehow mark each moccasin so you can tell which one belongs on each foot. For example, you may add two small stitches on the upper right flap near the front on the right foot moccasin, and two small stitches on the upper left flap near the front of the left front moccasin.

As you wear your moccasins, each moccasin will gradually begin to match the shape of your foot. The toe areas on each moccasin will stretch just a little in the big toe area, and the instep side of each moccasin will gradually curl up a little towards your foot. The front of both moccasins will gradually begin to curve up just a little to match the front curve of your foot at the toes. In other words, even though you did not create a special moccasin for each foot, as you wear your moccasins each one will gradually match the shape of the foot on which it is being worn. Therefore it is a good practice to always put the same moccasin on the same foot.

Chapter Thirty-Six

Buckskin Strips, Ropes, and Whips

Long thin pieces of buckskin can be used as laces, thongs, and straps. In this chapter all of these items will be called "strips" of buckskin. When cutting strips you should use scissors instead of a knife. The scissors should be very sharp and they should have cutting blades that are at least 2.5 inches long. There are a variety of ways to create buckskin strips. However, the two most efficient ways to make strips are to use:

1. the outside edge of a hide, and
2. scraps of buckskin that are left over from a sewing project.

Let's examine both of these options one-at-a-time.

The Outside Edge of a Hide

Frequently there are two outside edges of a hide as follows:

1. **The original outside edge of the hide:** This is the area beyond the small holes you punched around the outside edge of the hide in order to secure it to the stretching frame. Because there are so many holes close to the outside edge of the hide, this piece of material is not used to make clothing. The outside edge of the hide is usually trimmed off by cutting from the edge of one hole to the edge of the next hole all the way around the outside edge of the hide. When you are finished you will have an extremely long strip of buckskin that can be up to 14 feet long. If you followed the instructions in the stretching frame chapter then those holes are approximately 3/8 inch from the outside of the hide. However, the outside edge of a hide will be uneven so the holes will not all be exactly 3/8 inch from the edge of the hide. Therefore if you simply cut through the edges of the holes then you will have a strip of buckskin with one relatively straight side and one uneven side. The way to remedy this problem is to make two cuts around the outside edge of the hide instead of one. The first cut should be at a constant distance away from the holes so that the uneven rough edge of the hide is trimmed off. The second cut will then be through the outside edge of the holes. When you are finished you will have a long strip of buckskin with smooth edges.

2. **The new outside edge of the hide:** Pattern pieces are usually placed on each side of the spine because this is the strongest and most durable part of the hide. Most of the pattern pieces will not extend all the way to the edge of the hide. When the pattern pieces are cut out of the hide there will be a few inches near the outside edge of the hide that is not used. This long thin piece of buckskin can be converted into strips.

Scraps of Buckskin Left Over From a Sewing Project

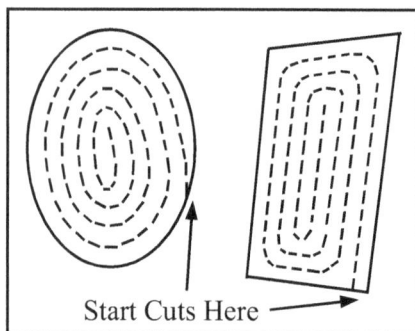

Start Cuts Here

Scraps of buckskin that are at least 4 inches or larger may be used to make buckskin strips. The shape of these scraps is not important because you will be cutting them into long thin strips. This is done by starting at the outside edge of the piece and gradually cutting around the piece in a spiral so that when you finish cutting you are in the center of the piece. This is illustrated using an oval piece of scrap and a four sided piece of scrap. The four sided piece of scrap will need to have its outside sharp corners trimmed off to make the entire buckskin strip the same thickness. The thickness of the buckskin strips can be whatever you require for the project in which the strip will be used.

Coating the Strips: Pull each strip through an old cloth that has been soaked in some warm freshly melted (rendered) animal fat. This will make the strip somewhat water resistant and it will significantly increase its useful life expectancy.

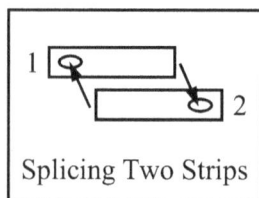

Splicing Two Strips

Splicing Instructions: Push the end of strip 1 through the hole in strip 2 and push the end of strip 2 through the hole in strip 1. Then pull on the far end of both strips at the same time to tighten the splice at the ends with the holes in them.

Instructions for Braiding Strips

The following braiding techniques will produce a strong rope or whip. But do not put 2 or more splices within 5 inches of one another. Space the splices so each strip is spliced to a new strip at a different location along the braid. When you are finished making the braid then tie off (whip) each end of the braid using thin pieces of sinew by wrapping the sinew around the end of the braid several times.

Three Strips: This is the same as braiding someone's long hair. The right outside strip is brought across the top of the center strip and it becomes the new center strip. Then the left outside strip is brought across the top of the center strip and it becomes the new center strip. This process continues to the end of the braid.

Four Strips: The right outside strip is brought behind the two center strips and then it is immediately brought back around in front of and over the left center strip so that it now becomes the new right center strip. The left outside strip is brought behind the two center strips and then it is immediately brought back around in front of and over the right center strip so that it now becomes the new left center strip. This process continues to the end of the braid.

Six Strips: The right outside strip is brought behind the three strips that are beside it and then it is immediately brought back around in front of and over the last strip that it went behind so that it now becomes the third strip from the right instead of the fourth strip from the right. The left outside strip is brought behind the three strips that are beside it and then it is immediately brought back around in front of and over the last strip that it went behind so that it now becomes the third strip from the left instead of the fourth strip from the left. This process continues to the end of the braid.

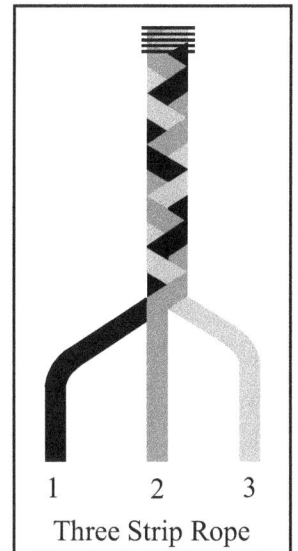

1　　2　　3
Three Strip Rope

Buckskin Ropes

Buckskin strips may be braided together to make a buckskin rope. The thickness of the strips and the number of strips will determine the strength of the final rope. Strips that are 1/4 inch thick will produce a smaller diameter finished rope than strips that are 3/8 inch thick. Long ropes can be made from shorter buckskin strips by splicing the ends of the strips together as shown in the illustration on the previous page.

Leather Whips - For Educational Purposes Only

A leather whip is similar to a braided rope except it has a thick diameter at the grasping end of the whip and it has a thin diameter at the opposite end of the whip. This can be accomplished by using wide strips at the handle end and then gradually splicing in narrower strips as you create the whip. A whip can be braided using three, four, or six strips of leather depending on the purpose of the whip.

Optional Handle End: A 5 inch long tapered wood dowel can be put in the handle end of the whip to create a solid handle for the whip. Begin braiding at the end of the wood dowel and braid around the wood dowel so the wood dowel is completely enclosed inside the leather strips. One method of enclosing the end of the whip handle is shown in the illustration on the right using four strips. After pushing the end of each strip under another strip in the direction of the arrows then put some leather glue between the strips to hold the braid together. After the glue dries cut off the long loose ends with the arrows.

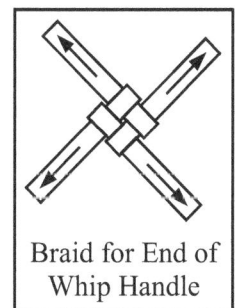

Braid for End of
Whip Handle

Optional Whip End (Cracker): Stop braiding about 6 to 10 inches from the end of the whip and tie off (whip) the braid with sinew. This will leave a few inches of unbraided loose thin strips extending from the end of the whip. Cut each loose strip end into 2 or more very thin strips. When the whip is cracked (snapped) it will make a sharp loud noise if the whip end breaks the sound barrier.

For Educational Purposes Only: To crack a whip allow the end of the whip to lie on the ground in a straight line beside and in front of you. The whip should always be off to your side and never directly in front of your body. Quickly bring your hand straight back beside and behind you and then quickly bring your hand straight to the front and level with your shoulder and then quickly bring your hand straight back behind you again. *This is dangerous. Do not do this unless an experienced whip cracker is present and he is training you.*

Chapter Thirty-Seven

How to Make a Buckskin Sling and How to Correctly Use a Sling for Hunting
For Educational Purposes Only

The basic sling consists of a center pouch that holds the stone. The pouch is then tied to two straps (or thongs) which are held in your hand. The center pouch can be a simple oval shape.

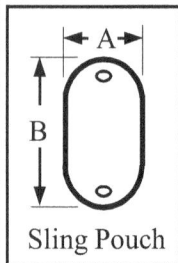

Measurements of Pouch:
A = 3 inches
B = 6 inches

Sling Pouch

The pouch can be made of buckskin, leather, canvas, or heavy denim blue jean material. (Do not use belt leather because it is too thick and it will not function properly.) If a weaker material is used for the center pouch then it may tear and this could result in an injury to the user. Punch or cut a small hole approximately 3/8 to 1/2 inch from each end of the pouch to receive the two thongs.

The straps (or thongs) can be leather (or a strong cord or thin rope) that are between 3/16 to 3/8 inch in diameter. One strap should be about 28 inches long, and the other strap should be about 38 inches long. Tie both straps to the center pouch. Then make a wrist slip loop in the opposite end of the longer strap. Form a large knot in the opposite end of the shorter strap. After tying and forming a wrist slip loop and hand knot then the two finished straps should be between 24 to 26 inches long. (Note: Longer straps will provide more force and distance but at the expense of accuracy.)

The stone projectiles should be relatively round and each one should weigh somewhere between 2 ounces up to approximately 8 ounces. To the extent possible you should select stones of the same approximate size and weight because the weight of the stone will impact the trajectory of the stone on its way to the target. Therefore it is better to practice with stones of the same approximate weight so you can become relatively accurate with stones of that weight.

Stones that have been worn smooth by the passage of water in a stream or creek are an excellent choice. Stones with uneven or rough edges will snag in the center pouch (or on the loose thong when thrown) and they will not fly true to the intended target. Small or light-weight stones will not throw or hit well. Stones about 1.5 inches in diameter, or about the size of a golf ball, or a little larger are ideal.

Slide the wrist loop around the wrist of your throwing arm and adjust it so it is snug and comfortable but not too tight. Then place a stone in the center pouch and fold the center pouch around the stone. Hold the knot end of the shorter thong between the thumb and forefinger of the same hand. If necessary, untie and reform the large knot in the shorter thong so the knot fits comfortably between your thumb and forefinger and the stone inside the pouch hangs evenly at the end of the two thongs.

The proper standing position in relation to your target is approximately the same as when you shoot a bow and arrow. Position your body at about a 45 degree angle to your target with your feet about 18 to 24 inches apart. While holding the loaded sling with the stone in the pouch hanging straight down towards the ground, lean backwards about 6 to 8 inches and bend your knees. Then swing the stone inside the pouch up in front of you at about a 45 degree angle while holding your arm at its full length. Continue the circle up above your head, around behind your body, down towards the ground, and as the stone comes back towards the front quickly release the knot held between your thumb and forefinger and the stone will exit the pouch at high speed and maximum force. This motion is a little bit like throwing a softball using an underhanded pitch.

Do not twirl the swing around the top of your head. Do not use small projectiles. Practice until you know your own personal effective distance and accuracy.

The sling is a powerful and seriously underestimated weapon. Do not make the same mistake Goliath did when he confronted David. The sling is not a toy. Treat it with respect. It is a very deadly weapon.

Chapter Thirty-Eight

How to Make Parchment,
and How to Make Ink,
and How to Make a Feather Pen

Parchment

Although parchment is made from animal skins, the process of creating parchment is different from the process of creating buckskins and leather as follows:

1. Buckskins and leather are tanned but parchment is not tanned.
2. Buckskins and leather are not limed but parchment is limed.
3. Buckskins and leather have most of their natural animal glue removed but parchment does not have as much of its natural animal glue removed.
4. Buckskins and leather are made from thicker animal skins but parchment is made from thinner animal skins.

The Twelve Basic Steps for Creating Parchment

1. Select an animal with a relatively thin skin, such as a domestic sheep or a goat or a very young calf.

2. Remove the hide (skin) of the slaughtered animal using the method described in Chapter 4.

3. Soak the hide in clean water for 24 hours. Stir the hide in the water every four hours during the day. Remove the hide from the water bath and discard the water bath. Rinse the hide in clean water until the water runs clear.

4. Scrape the flesh from the flesh side of the hide using the method described in the Chapter 8. Rinse the hide in clean water until the water runs clear.

5. Create a new water bath using clean water and some lime. Continue to gradually add more lime to the water and stir the lime in the water until the water bath has a thick cloudy appearance similar to fresh milk. Fold the hide in half with the flesh side of the hide on the inside of the fold and the hair side of the hide on the outside of the fold so the entire hair side of the hide is exposed. Place the hide in the lime water bath for four days. Every four hours during the day stir the hide inside the lime water bath. At the end of four days remove the hide and discard the lime water. Rinse the hide in clean water until the water runs clear. (Note 1: If lime is not available then wood ashes may be used as described in Chapter 9.)
(Note 2: In the cold winter months the soaking may require more time. In the warm summer months the soaking may take less time. In other words, the temperature of the water and lime solution will influence the time the hide needs to soak in the water and lime solution. If a hide is soaked too long then it will not be able to withstand the stretching process on the stretching frame. To determine if the hide has soaked long enough you should try to scrape the hair side of the hide. If the hair scrapes off the hide without an excessive amount of effort then the hide has soaked long enough and you should skip to step seven below. However, if the hair requires considerable effort to remove then proceed with step six below.)

6. Create another water bath using clean water and some lime. Gradually add some lime to the water and stir the lime in the water until the water bath has a thick cloudy appearance similar to fresh milk. Fold the hide in half with the flesh side of the hide on the inside of the fold and the hair side of the hide on the outside of the fold so the entire hair side of the hide is exposed. Place the hide in the lime water bath for four days. Every four hours during the day stir the hide inside the lime water bath. At the end of four days remove the hide and discard the lime water. Rinse the hide in clean water until the water runs clear.

7. Scrape the hair from the hair side of the hide using the method described in Chapter 10. Rinse the hide in clean water until the water runs clear.

8. Create another water bath using clean water and some lime. Gradually add some lime to the water and stir the lime in the water until the water bath has a thick cloudy appearance similar to fresh milk. Fold the hide in half with the flesh side of the hide on the inside of the fold. Place the hide in the lime water bath for two days. Every four hours during the day stir the hide inside the lime water bath. At the end of two days remove the hide and discard the lime water. Rinse the hide in clean water until the water runs clear.

9. Soak the hide in clean water for 24 hours. Stir the hide in the water every four hours during the day. Remove the hide from the water bath and discard the water bath.

10. Tie the soaking wet hide inside a stretching frame using the method described in Chapter 19. Scrape the flesh side of the hide to remove any residual membrane. Scrape the hair side of the hide to remove any residual hair membrane. Sand both sides of the hide using a rock or sandpaper using the method described in Chapter 20. Allow the hide to dry in the stretching frame in the shade for two days under pressure. Make sure the hide is stretched tightly inside the stretching frame. There should be no slack anywhere in the hide as it dries. Adjust the cords every morning and every evening as the hide dries to equalize the tension across the surface of the hide.

11. Moisten the hide with water and sand the hide again using the method described in Chapter 20. Tighten the cords after sanding. (Note: If you wish to improve the whiteness and the smoothness of the hide then mix some egg whites and some milk with the water and rub the solution deep into the hide before sanding. This will make the finished parchment whiter and the writing surface smoother. After sanding rinse both sides of the hide with clean water to remove any egg whites and milk that was not absorbed into the hide.)

12. Allow the hide to dry tied inside the stretching frame in the shade until the hide is completely dry and stiff. Adjust the cords every morning and every evening as the hide dries to equalize the tension across the surface of the hide. When the hide is completely dry and stiff, remove the hide from the stretching frame and cut the thin stiff hide into convenient sizes to use as parchment.

How to Make Ink

Parchment is not waterproof. Therefore it will absorb and retain almost any type of ink that is used on it. The three most common types of homemade ink are created using berries, or charcoal, or walnuts.

Berry Ink

The juice inside a berry may be converted into good ink by adding a little vinegar and a little salt. The color of the berry juice will be the color of the ink that you create. Almost any type of berry may be used, including berries that can be eaten and berries that should not be eaten.

Examples of edible berries are: Blackberries, raspberries, blueberries, and huckleberries.

Pokeweed
Berries

Examples of non-edible berries are: Juniper berries (blue-purple) and pokeweed berries (purple). Pokeweed berries are also called "ink berries" because they have been used for many centuries to create homemade ink.

Recipe for Berry Ink:
1 cup of ripe berries
1/2 teaspoon vinegar
1/2 teaspoon salt

Crush the berries in a bowl or inside a zipper plastic bag that has been sealed at the top. Press on the berries until most of the juice has been squeezed out of the berries. Stain the berries through a fine wire mesh screen or an old cloth to separate the juice from the pulp and seeds. Discard the pulp and seeds. Add the vinegar and the salt to the juice and stir. The vinegar helps the ink to retain its original color and the salt helps to prolong the shelf life of the ink by minimizing mold and bacteria problems.

Ink storage and ink consistency are discussed at the end of the instructions for making walnut ink on the next page.

Charcoal Ink

Add 1 ounce (weight) of the cold fine ash from a charcoal fire to 1 ounce (volume) of clean hot rainwater (or distilled water) and stir until the very fine ash dissolves in the hot water. The ink will be very dark and it will stain your hands or clothing if you get it on you. Add one drop of vinegar and stir. The vinegar will help to stabilize the ink and it will help to make the ink permanent when it dries on the parchment.

Ink storage and ink consistency are discussed at the end of the instructions for making walnut ink below.

Walnut Ink

Black Walnuts: The exterior husks of black walnuts contain tannin and other chemicals that will produce an ink that is somewhere between brown and black. Walnut ink will not gradually fade with the passage of time, and it will not gradually fade when exposed to light, and it is permanent. In other words, after writing on a piece of parchment it is almost impossible to remove walnut ink from that piece of parchment.

If you have some old rusty iron nails then you can use them when you make walnut ink. If you do not have any rusty iron nails but you do have some surplus iron nails that you don't need then put about six iron nails outside and leave them in the rain and in the weather for several months so they will gradually rust.

Locate a black walnut tree. During the fall season the black walnuts will fall off the tree onto the ground. The black walnuts will be inside a slimy black husk and if you touch that husk with your bare hands then you will get black stains on your hands. Therefore wear some type of rubber or vinyl gloves when you are collecting and handling the walnuts. Collect as many black walnuts as you desire because the nutmeats may be safely eaten by almost anyone who is not allergic to nuts and who enjoys the taste of walnuts.

Allow twelve of the black walnuts that are still inside their husks to age and dry for about two months. Remove the black walnut from its exterior husk. Remove the nutmeats from inside their shells. The nutmeats may be eaten or used in a recipe that calls for nuts.

You will need a tempered glass cook pot or a metal cook pot. A steel pot may be used but a cast iron pot is preferred. The best pot to use is an old rusted cast iron cook pot. The rusty iron pot will release some of its rust into the ink mixture as it cooks and this will significantly improve the quality of the walnut ink.

Place the exterior husk pieces and the walnut shells from all twelve walnuts into the metal cook pot and cover them with water. If you have a few rusty nails then add them to the pot if you are using a glass pot or a steel pot or an old cast iron pot. Do not put nails in a good cast iron pot or you will scratch the interior surface of the pot and damage the pot. But the rusty nails will not hurt an old rusty cast iron pot because that old pot can't be used for cooking anyway but it will always be a good pot for making walnut ink.

The water inside the pot will immediately begin to absorb some of the dark color from the walnut husks. Begin to simmer the contents in the pot over very low heat. The water will immediately begin to darken. Gently stir the mixture occasionally but be careful to not scratch the pot with the rusty nails that are in the mixture. Continue to simmer the mixture until the color is deep enough to be used as ink and the consistency of the solution is thick enough to be used as ink. The mixture should not be too thin (runny) or too thick (pasty). Turn off the heat and allow the mixture to cool. Wait 8 hours for the mixture to continue to absorb the chemicals and color from the contents in the pot. Then strain the mixture through a very fine mesh screen, or an old cloth, to remove the husks and shells (and the optional nails). Discard the husks and shells (but save the optional nails for the next batch of ink).

Ink Storage and Ink Consistency for Berry Ink, Charcoal Ink, and Walnut Ink

Ink Storage: Save the ink inside a small clean **glass** jar with a screw on lid. Some examples would be: a baby food jar, or jelly jar, or pickles jar. Keep the jar tightly covered in a dark place when you are not using it. Shake the ink bottle just before you begin using the ink to mix the contents inside the bottle.

Ink Consistency: When you begin using the ink after it has been in storage for awhile, the ink may be the perfect consistency, or it may be too thin or too thick. If the ink is too thin then boil the ink to remove just a little water and test the ink again. If the ink is too thick then add just a little water and boil the ink for about 30 seconds, and stir the ink and water to mix them together. Then test the ink again.

How to Make a Feather Pen (Also Known as a Quill Pen)

History of the Quill Pen: Quill pens were used by scribes and authors until the 1820s. The Septuagint (Greek translation of the Old Testament around 132 B.C.) and the British Magna Carta (1215 A.D.) and the United States' Declaration of Independence (1776 A.D.) were all written using quill pens.

Feather Selection: Any long feather may be used to make a feather pen. The feather should be a wing feather from a reasonable size bird. Swan feathers are the best choice, followed by goose feathers, and then the wing feathers from a crow, eagle, hawk, owl, or turkey. Right-handed scribes traditionally preferred a feather from the left wing because the left wing feather curved slightly to the right and therefore it was a little more comfortable to hold in the right hand. The center shaft of the feather should be between 3/16 inch to 1/4 inch in diameter (thick) and it should be round and not crushed. A feather shaft smaller than 3/16 inch in diameter (thick) is usually not wide enough to be used as a quill pen.

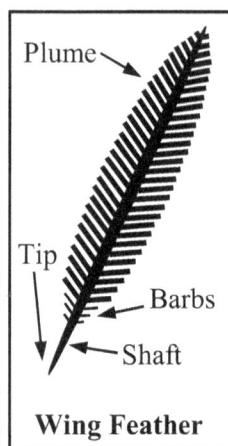

Wing Feather

Feather Barbs and Plume: Carefully cut off (trim) the barbs (small pieces of feather) and part of the plume from at least the lower half of the shaft (barrel or tube) of the feather so it will fit comfortably in your hand. Prior to the 1820s the barbs and the entire plume were removed from the shaft of the feather because they served no purpose. However, to quickly and visually illustrate that a person was writing with a quill pen, Hollywood movies began using huge decorative feathers with most of the plume on the upper 3/4 of the feather. If you wish to remove all the barbs and the plume then use some scissors to trim the shaft from the top end of the feather towards its tip. If you use a knife then shave the shaft from the tip end of the feather toward its top end.

Hardening: The lower shaft of the feather will need to be hardened to make it stronger and more flexible. There are three methods for hardening the lower shaft of a feather:

1. **Hot Sand:** Fill a metal can with sand to a depth of approximately six inches. Put the can of sand into an oven at 350°F (or 177°C) for fifteen minutes. Carefully remove the hot can of sand from the oven and push the tip of the feather into the hot sand so the entire lower 1/3 of the feather is below the surface of the sand. The top 2/3 of the feather should be in the open air. Wait for the sand to gradually cool off and then remove the feather. This is the preferred method for hardening the tip end of the feather shaft.

2. **Hot Campfire Ashes:** Use the lower 1/3 of the feather to stir some hot campfire ashes. This is a reasonable option if all the feather barbs and the entire plume have been removed from the feather because the heat of the campfire ashes could easily ignite these items.

3. **Boiling Water:** Bring some water to a boil and then turn off the heat. Submerge the lower 1/3 of the feather into the hot water and wait for the water to gradually cool before removing the feather.

After hardening the tip of the feather using one of the above three methods, allow the tip of the feather to cool off before trimming its shaft into a writing point. (Note: If you have trouble cutting a straight slit in the shaft then you may need to harden the shaft after cutting the slit instead of before cutting the slit.)

Hollow Shaft: The inside shaft of a feather may contain some dried membrane. Depending on the age of the feather there may or may not be any dried membrane inside the shaft of the feather. As the feather ages the inner membrane gradually dries up and disappears. However, if there is some membrane still inside the feather shaft, then when the tip of the pen is cut to form a writing point this membrane will need to be scraped out of the bottom of the shaft to form a hollow tube. The membrane can be removed using a very thin knife, or a craft needle, or some very thin tweezers. The hollow cavity will function as a reservoir to hold ink and the ink will gradually flow to the split tip of the quill pen as a result of capillary forces.

Quill Knife: To gain access to the hollow cavity inside the feather shaft a small piece at the tip of the feather will need to be removed with a sharp knife. Traditionally this was done with a special knife that had a sharp thin blade and it was called a "quill knife." The short thin narrow blade of a quill knife had one flat side and one slightly curved (convex) side. Beginning in the 1820s the quill pen was gradually and systematically replaced with a metal pen that had an ink reservoir and a steel tip. But the "quill knife" survived and its name was changed a few times until it eventually became known as the "pen knife" or "pocket knife" of today. The primary difference is that both sides of a pen knife are flat and neither side is curved. Almost any sharp thin narrow blade knife may be used if it has a straight sharp cutting edge and not a serrated edge. The tip of the quill shaft will usually be relatively hard and you will need to **gradually carve** the correct curve into the tip of the quill shaft instead of cutting the curve with a single stroke of the knife.

At the beginning of the year 2012 there are two ways to cut a writing tip into the shaft of a feather pen. There is the traditional method that is currently described in all the available literature on this topic that explains how to make a quill pen. And there is my way that eliminates the cutting of the first curve at the tip of the shaft. Cutting the first curve is superfluous (unnecessary) because you cut the entire first curve off when you cut the second curve. Therefore I will begin by describing the method I currently use to create a quill pen and then I will explain the traditional method for accomplishing this same task.

Grandpappy's Seven Steps for Cutting a Writing Tip into a Feather Shaft

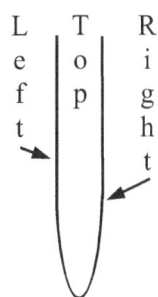

Step One: Look at the shaft of the feather. It will be curved. The shaft should be held so the shaft curves downwards towards the parchment. The side that faces up towards you will be referred to as the top of the feather shaft. The opposite side of the shaft will be the back and the left and right sides will be defined when looking at the top side of the shaft from its point. The point of the shaft should curve slightly downwards to the flat surface and this is the best angle for writing because it will allow the ink to flow to the point of the shaft before the ink makes contact with the parchment.

Step Two: Use some sharp scissors to cut the tip off the end of the shaft in a straight line. This will expose the interior cavity of the shaft. If there is any dried membrane in the shaft then scrape the dried membrane out of the interior of the shaft using the tip of your knife, or a quilting needle, or some very thin tweezers.

Grandpappy's Seven Steps for Cutting a Writing Tip into a Feather Shaft

| 1. Rotate shaft so the tip curves down to the surface. | 2. Cut straight across the tip with scissors. | 3. Cut a 3/16" long slit in the top at the tip of the shaft. | 4. Rotate shaft and cut curve from the back to the top. | 5. Rotate shaft so the back of the shaft is facing you. | 6. Trim the right and left sides of the shaft to form a point. | 7. Rotate shaft and inspect the pen point. |

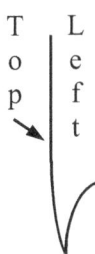

Step Three: There are two ways to do Step Three:

1. Cut a slit into the top of the shaft by inserting one tip of your scissors into the shaft a little less than 1/4 inch deep and then gently cut a very short straight slit in the shaft.
2. Cut the slit with the tip end of your knife beginning at the bottom of the scissor cut you made in Step Two by applying very gentle pressure. It may help if you make a small scratch 1/4 inch long on the outside of the shaft where you want the slit to appear.

If the shaft suddenly separates and the slit is longer than 1/4 inch then use your scissors to cut the tip off the end of the shaft so that only a 1/4 inch long slit remains.

Step Four: Rotate the shaft so the left side of the shaft is facing you.

Step Five: Use a sharp knife to gradually carve a curve in the back side of the shaft. Begin carving about 1/2 inch above the bottom of the slit that you cut in Step Three. Do not attempt to cut the curve with one stroke of the knife. Instead gradually carve small pieces off the shaft until the curve is the shape you desire. Then remove some more of the dried membrane from inside the hollow shaft.

Step Six: Rotate the shaft so the back of the shaft is facing you and you can see the hollow shaft cavity and the rear of the slit you cut in Step Three.

Step Seven: The illustrations are not drawn to scale because the tip of the shaft would be too small to see clearly. Therefore when you begin cutting the tip of the feather you will not be able to see the detail that is shown in the illustrations. Gradually trim the right and left sides of the shaft to form a curved pen point that stops a little to the right and a little to the left of the slit in the end of the shaft. If the end of the tip is too narrow then it will wear down quicker. If the end of the tip is too wide then it will spread ink over a wide area. The two curves on each side of the slit do not have to be identical but it is important that the slit be centered between the bottom of the two curves where the tip will make contact with the parchment. My personal experience is that it is easier to trim the curves on each side of the slit with some sharp scissors instead of trying to gradually carve the curves with a sharp knife.

Step Seven: Rotate the shaft so the top of the shaft is facing you and inspect the writing point of the pen. The critical issue is not the appearance of the tip but whether or not the tip will work as a writing pen. Before you trim too much material off each side of the tip of the shaft you should test the tip of the pen with some ink and determine if it works or not. If it does not write well then trim the tip some more and try to write with it again. If necessary, you can cut a new straight tip across the end of the shaft and start over.

* * * * * * * * * * * *

The Traditional Nine Steps for Cutting a Writing Tip into a Feather Shaft

Step One: Look at the shaft of the feather. It will be curved. The shaft should be held so the shaft curves downwards towards the parchment. The side that faces up towards you will be referred to as the top of the feather shaft. The opposite side of the shaft will be the back and the left and right sides will be defined when looking at the top side of the shaft from its point. The point of the shaft should curve slightly downwards to the flat surface and this is the best angle for writing because it will allow the ink to flow to the point of the shaft before the ink makes contact with the parchment.

Step Two: Rotate the shaft so the left side of the shaft is facing you. Use a sharp knife to carve a curve from the top side of the shaft towards the back side of the shaft. This will expose the interior cavity of the shaft. If there is any dried membrane in the shaft then scrape the dried membrane out of the interior of the shaft using the tip of your knife, or a quilting needle, or some very thin tweezers.

Step Three: Rotate the shaft so the top side of the shaft is facing you and you can see the hollow cavity in the shaft.

Step Four: Insert the tip of your knife blade into the hollow shaft cavity with the sharp edge facing up and then pry the knife upwards using the inside of the shaft for leverage in order to cut a slit between 3/16 inch to 1/4 inch long in the top center of the curve you just cut in Step Two. The knife blade must be extremely

The Traditional Nine Steps for Cutting a Writing Tip into a Feather Shaft

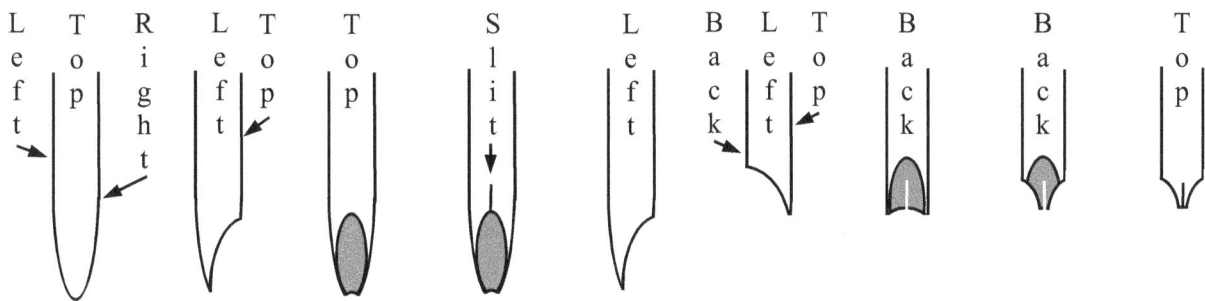

Left · Top · Right · Left · Top · Top · Slit · Left · Back · Left · Top · Back · Back · Top

1.	2.	3.	4.	5.	6.	7.	8.	9.
Rotate shaft so the tip curves down to the surface.	Rotate and cut curve from top side to back of shaft.	Rotate shaft so the top side of the shaft is facing you.	Cut a 3/16" long slit at the top of the curve.	Rotate shaft so the left side is facing you.	Cut from back to top. Stop at tip of the slit.	Rotate shaft so the back of the shaft is facing you.	Trim the right and left sides of the shaft to form a point.	Rotate shaft and inspect the pen point.

sharp and the knife blade should do the work and not the muscles in your hand. If the slit is cut too long then you can make it the correct length in Step Six by cutting the extra length off the bottom of the slit.

Step Five: Rotate the shaft so the left side of the shaft is facing you.

Step Six: Use a sharp knife to carve a curve in the back side of the shaft. Begin cutting about 1/2 inch above the top of the first curve that you cut and continue cutting the curve through the shaft to the top side of the shaft until you reach the lower tip of the slit that you cut in Step Four. Then remove some more of the dried membrane from inside the hollow shaft.

Step Seven: Rotate the shaft so the back of the shaft is facing you and you can see the hollow shaft cavity and the rear of the slit you cut in Step Four.

Step Eight: Gradually trim the right and left sides of the shaft to form a curved pen point that stops a little to the right and a little to the left of the slit in the end of the shaft. If the end of the tip is too narrow then it will wear down quicker. If the end of the tip is too wide then it will spread ink over a wide area. The curve on each side of the tip needs to quickly become wider as shown in the illustration. The two curves on each side of the slit do not have to be identical but it is important that the slit be centered between the bottom of the two curves where the tip will make contact with the parchment.

Step Nine: Rotate the shaft so the top of the shaft is facing you and inspect the writing point of the pen.

* * * * * * * * * * * *

How to Use a Feather Pen: Dip the tip of the shaft in some ink and wait for some of the ink to enter the hollow cavity in the shaft. Write on the parchment until the color or thickness of the ink strokes begins to become a little lighter. Dip the shaft in the ink again. Write some more. And so on.

Writing Pressure: Do not press down hard on the feather pen when writing. The tip of the feather pen should glide across the surface of the parchment

Ink Blobs: If the pen is leaving blobs of ink on the parchment then the curvature on each side of the slit is probably too straight. The curve on each side of the slit should be more rounded.

Ink Splatters or Sprays: If the tip of the pen is shooting thin sprays of ink in every direction then the tip of the pen is probably too narrow. Trim a straight line across the very tip of the pen so there is a little more surface area on each side of the slit to make contact with the parchment.

Ink Doesn't Feed Properly: This could be due to either or both of the following:

1. The slit may look like a slit but it might be nothing more than a tight crack in the shaft and it will not allow the ink to flow. Carefully and gently use your knife to make sure the slit is open along its short length.

2. The opening in the hollow cavity of the shaft needs to be cut a little higher. Use your knife to trim a little material off the back of the shaft a little higher above the writing point to open up a little more of the hollow cavity so ink can more easily enter the shaft when it is dipped into the ink, and the ink can more easily exit the shaft along the slit when writing.

Line Thickness: A medium thick ink line is easier to read when compared to a very thin ink line or a very thick ink line. If you trim the shaft to a sharper point then you will create a thinner line and the letters and words may not be easy to read. You will need to experiment by trimming the tip of the shaft to a slightly different degree of sharpness and then drawing lines (or letters) of different widths to determine the proper line width to use for the letters in the average word to make your writing as easy to read as possible.

Periodically Sharpening the Tip of the Feather Pen: The tip of the shaft will be dipped in some ink and the tip of the shaft will get wet. As the ink is transferred from the shaft onto the parchment the tip of the shaft will become dry. This process of wetting and drying, and wetting and drying, gradually causes the split in the tip of the shaft to become wider and the pen becomes less effective as a writing instrument. This will usually occur somewhere between three to six pages of writing depending on the size of the letters in your words, the size of the parchment pages, and the smoothness (quality) of the surface of the parchment. Before your lettering becomes noticeably unacceptable, the tip of the pin will need to be sharpened by cutting and forming a new point on the shaft a little above the current dull writing point. This involves cutting the original center split a little deeper and then reshaping and cutting the tip to remove the old point and create a new point. This can be done about four times and then the opposite side of the point will need to be split to form a new point. The tip of a feather can be reshaped into a functioning pen point until you reach the area where the main plume of the feather originally began. From that spot and above the shaft of the feather is not as easy to convert into a functional pen tip.

Feather Mites: Feathers will sometimes contain tiny mites that cannot be seen by the unaided eye. To kill the mites put the feathers in a plastic freezer bag and then put the bag of feathers into the freezer for 24 hours and the mites will freeze and die. If you don't have a freezer then put some small shavings of soap inside a small plastic bag with three or four feathers for seven days. The fumes from the soap will kill the mites that are trapped inside the small plastic bag. Or place the feathers in a small plastic bag with two or three moth balls and leave them closed up for seven days and the mites will die.

Writing Errors

If you make a writing error (a mistake) on parchment then you have three options:

1. **Scratch Through:** Draw a straight line through the mistake and then write the correct spelling beside or above the word you marked through.
2. **Wash Damp Ink Off:** Depending on the type of ink you are using you may be able to carefully dissolve the damp ink on the parchment and wipe it off with a clean cloth. Wait for the parchment to dry and then write the correct spelling in the area you just cleaned.
3. **Scrape Dried Ink Off:** If the dried ink has not penetrated deep into the parchment then scrape the mistake off the parchment using the sharp edge of a small knife. In other words, scrape a very thin layer off the parchment to remove the ink and to expose the clean parchment beneath. This requires careful control of the edge of the scraping knife so you do not scrape a hole through the parchment.

Chapter Thirty-Nine

A Simple but Extremely Practical Smokehouse

A simple smokehouse is strongly recommended for smoking meat and for smoking hides. The following minimum materials would be required to build a simple smokehouse:

1. Five sheets of 4 feet by 8 feet plywood that is between 1/2 inch to 3/4 inch thick.
2. Eight 8 feet long 2x4 boards to build the interior frame for the smokehouse.
3. Some 3 inch long nails to build the interior frame.
4. Some 1.5 inch long nails to nail the plywood to the interior frame.
5. Some waterproof sealant for the wood and a paintbrush.
6. One metal latch (gate latch) that can be used to open and close the front door.
7. Two heavy-duty hinges (gate or door hinges) for the front door.
8. Two medium-duty door hinges for the lower side wall door.
9. One oven or meat temperature gauge with a scale that will read between 100ºF to 200ºF (or higher).
10. One Dutch oven or a heavy-duty steel pot with a lid.
11. A flat rock or a patio stone to place beneath the Dutch oven inside the smokehouse.
12. Some wires that can be strung between the walls on the inside of the smokehouse.

How to Build the Interior Frame of the Smokehouse

Do **not** use pressure treated wood to build the interior frame of the smokehouse. Pressure treated wood contains chemicals that will contaminate any meat that is smoked inside the smokehouse. Use ordinary interior grade 2x4 lumber for the interior frame. Also use interior grade plywood for the walls that will be nailed to the interior frame.

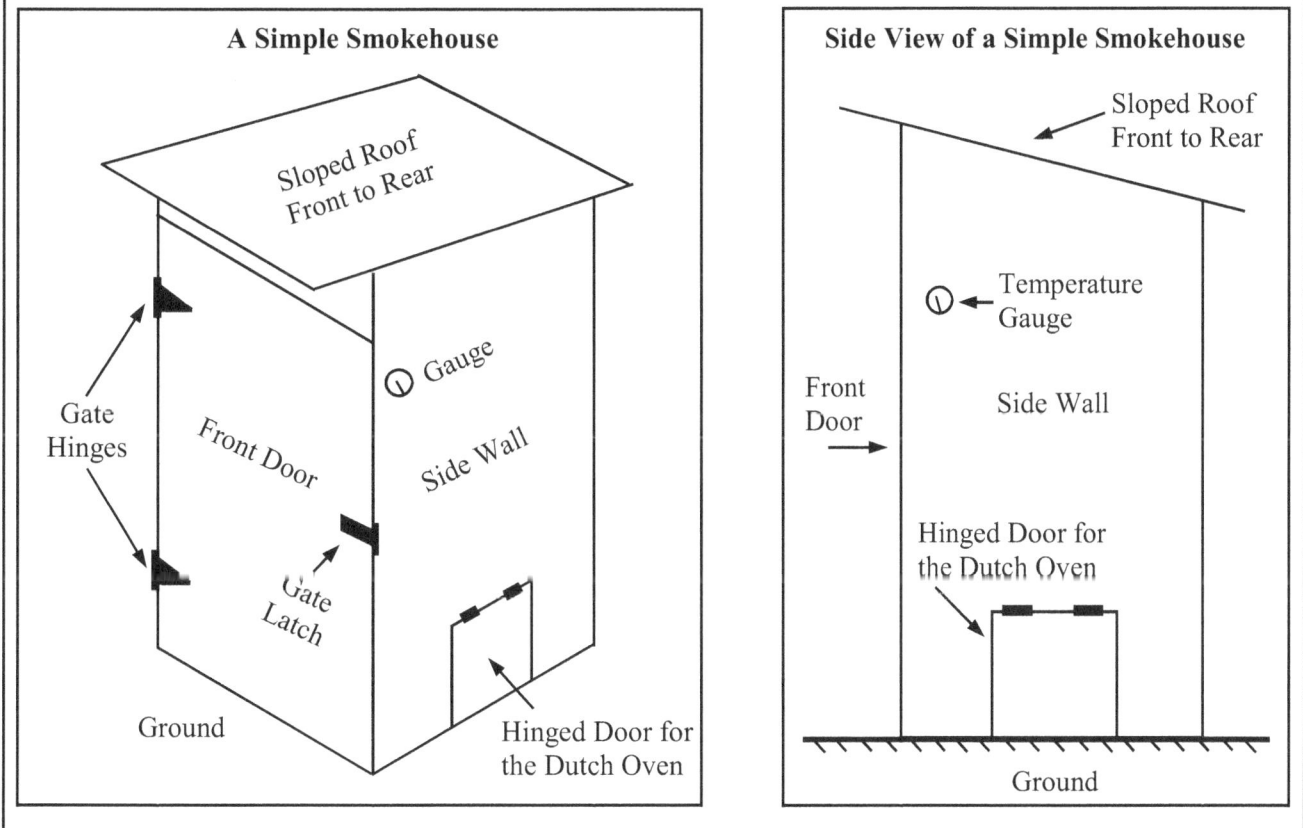

A Simple Smokehouse

Side View of a Simple Smokehouse

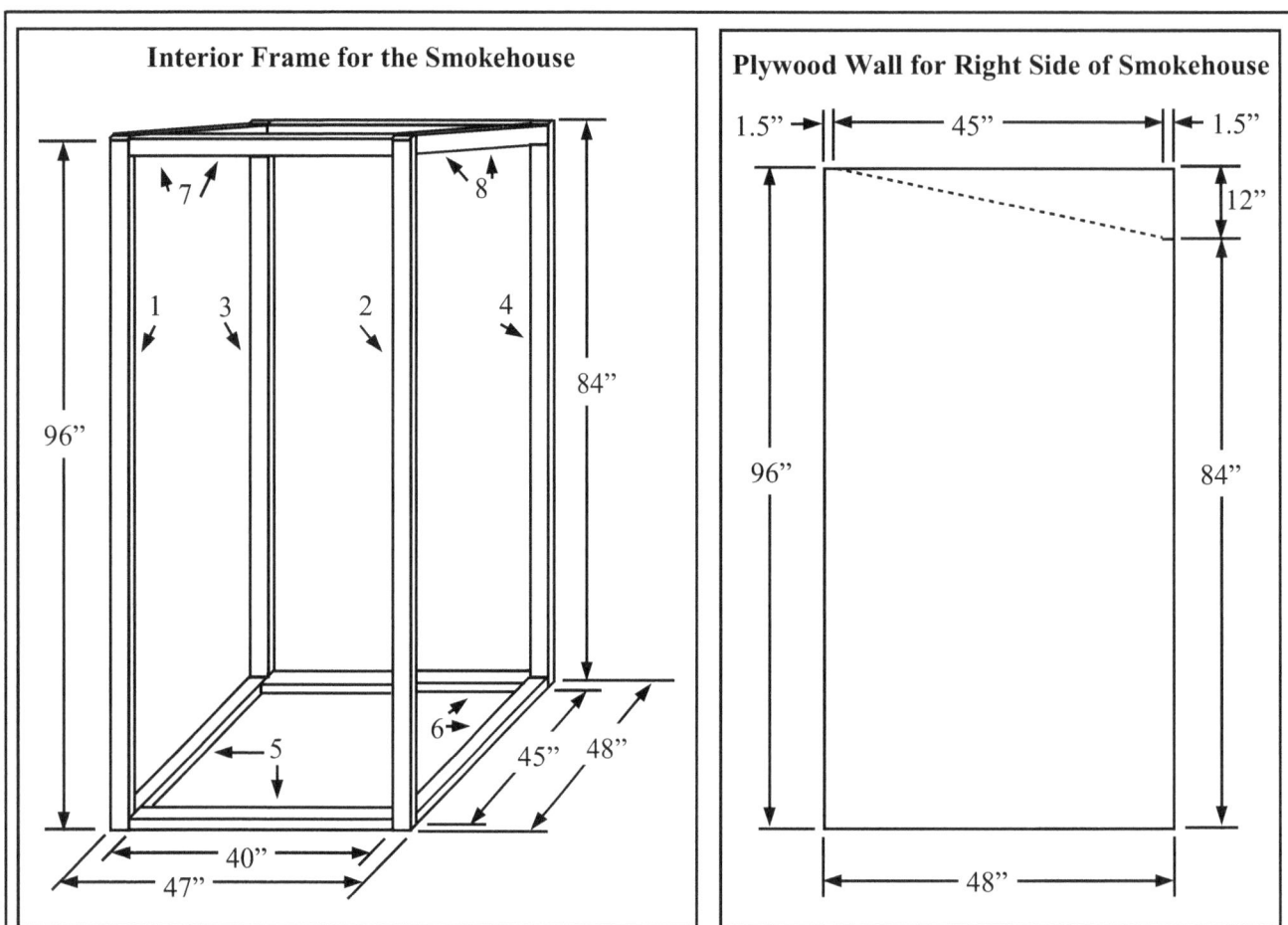

Interior Frame for the Smokehouse

Plywood Wall for Right Side of Smokehouse

The five sheets of plywood will need to be cut as follows:

Plywood Front Door: Cut the plywood 78" high. Leave the plywood 48" wide. Save the 18" piece of plywood that you cut off in addition to the 78" high door.

Plywood Rear Wall: Cut a straight line so the plywood is 83.75 inches tall instead of 84 inches tall. The 1/4 inch will allow the roof plywood to rest on the 2x4 interior frame for support instead of the rear plywood wall.

Plywood Right Side Wall: Lay the plywood on the ground with the good side of the plywood facing up towards you. Use a pencil to mark the top edge of the plywood as shown in the illustration on the above right. The first 1.5 inches at the top left will be nailed to a 1.5 inch wide 96 inch tall 2x4 board so it will remain straight. The 1.5 inches on the right side of the plywood that is 12 inches below the top of the plywood will be nailed to a 1.5 inch wide 84 inch tall 2x4 board so it needs to be straight to match the top of the 2x4 board. Now draw a straight line between the two 1.5 inch wide marks. Cut the top right of the plywood along the 1.5 inch right mark to a depth of 1.5 inches and stop. Now cut the top of the plywood along the straight line that you just drew beginning 1.5 inches from the left edge of the plywood and cutting down until you reach the 1.5 inch long straight cut that you made 12 inches down from the top of the plywood.

Plywood Left Side Wall: Lay one uncut piece of plywood against the piece of plywood you just cut so that the good side of both pieces of plywood are touching one another. Use a pencil to mark the uncut piece of plywood across its top using the cut piece of plywood as your template. Then cut the new piece of plywood in the same manner as before along the lines you just drew.

Plywood Roof: Cut the plywood 78" long. This will allow the roof plywood to extend off the front and the rear of the smokehouse so rainwater will flow off the rear of the smokehouse onto the ground.

The interior wood frame should be built using 8 feet long 2x4 lumber and some 3 inch long nails. Each piece of 8 feet long lumber should be cut to the following lengths:

The dimensions given for boards 5 through 8 below are based on 1/2 thick plywood. The plywood on the front and rear walls will extend 1/2 inch past the edge of each of the two side walls and cover the edges of the plywood on the two side walls. Therefore the side walls will be 49 inches from front to rear because they will include an additional 1/2 inch in the front and in the rear for the plywood on the front and rear walls.

If you use plywood of a thickness other than 1/2 inch then adjust the 40 inch cuts below as follows:

3/8" thick plywood walls: Cut 40.25" not 40".
5/8" thick plywood walls: Cut 39.75" not 40".
3/4" thick plywood walls: Cut 39.50" not 40".

Board 1: Do not cut. Leave at 8' (96") long.
Board 2: Do not cut. Leave at 8' (96") long.
Board 3: Cut 84 inches long for rear wall.
Board 4: Cut 84 inches long for rear wall.
Board 5: Cut 40 inches and 45 inches.
Board 6: Cut 40 inches and 45 inches.
Board 7: Cut 40 inches and 45 inches.
Board 8: Cut 40 inches and 45 inches.

The four boards on the bottom of the frame that will be in permanent contact with the ground should be coated with waterseal sealant using a paintbrush. This will help to protect and preserve those boards so they will last longer.

The four boards on the bottom of the frame (cut from boards 5 and 6) should be laid flat with their 3.5 inch wide surface touching the ground. Then the four upright wall boards (boards 1, 2, 3, and 4) should be positioned in each of the corner locations as shown. Coat the bottom surface of the upright wall boards with some waterseal sealant to help protect and preserve them. However, do not coat the entire upright board from top to bottom. Only coat the bottom 2 inches of the board with some waterseal sealant.

Nail the bottom of the frame together and nail the bottom of the four upright boards to the bottom of the frame as shown in the illustration.

The top four boards of the frame will be positioned with their 3.5 inch wide surface facing up and down. This is exactly opposite to the way the four bottom boards were attached to the frame. The four bottom boards were positioned with their wide side facing the ground but the four top boards will be positioned with their wide side facing into the interior of the smokehouse.

At the bottom of a side wall there should be a swinging door that you can open to add wood to the fire pot.

Smokehouse Equipment

1. A meat thermometer should be inserted through the wall of the smokehouse so you can read the temperature dial from the outside of the smokehouse to let you know when to add more wood to the fire. Or you can use a charcoal grill or a gas grill thermometer instead of a meat thermometer.

2. A cast iron Dutch oven (size at least 6 quarts) should be used to contain the fire. The lid will allow you to control the burn by letting more or less air to the burning wood. The Dutch oven should be placed on top of a large flat rock, or a flat patio stone, about 12 inches inside the small door opening at the bottom of the smokehouse.

3. Wires should be strung horizontally (level) from front to rear, or from side to side, inside the smokehouse near the ceiling to hang the hides on.

The Fire

Start a small fire inside the Dutch oven using some small extremely dry sticks. Gradually add a few chucks of dry wood. Continue to add small chucks of dry wood until you have a nice bed of red hot coals about one inch deep in the bottom of the Dutch oven. Now you may add some very dry decayed wood, or any wood that smokes well, on top of the hot coals inside the Dutch oven and immediately place the lid on top of the Dutch oven so there is only a small opening on one side of the lid to allow air to enter the oven and heat and smoke to exit the oven.

It is now time to leave the smokehouse and close the smokehouse door behind you.

You may notice some of the smoke (and heat) escaping from the smokehouse around the edge of the roof where it is attached to the smokehouse.

The smoke should gradually become thick and dense inside the smokehouse. The thicker the smoke the better. You want maximum smoke and just the right amount of heat but no moisture.

Precautions

Do not smoke meat for human consumption at the same time you are smoking hides.

The smokehouse should not be air tight. The smokehouse should allow some of the heat to escape. Too much heat will cook your meat and your hides and ruin them.

Different Types of Wood

Avoid moisture in the wood and in the fire.

Freshly cut wood is called "green wood" because it still contains moisture and it has not dried yet. Wood that contains moisture will smoke extensively when it is burned. For this reason most firewood is allowed to season, or dry, before it is used in a wood burning fireplace because dry wood will produce more heat and very little smoke.

Avoid any wood that contains pitch, such as pine, because the pitch will be in the smoke and the pitch will therefore get into the hide (or meat) and the hide will feel sticky and somewhat stiff after smoking.

The best wood to use to create smoke is semi-rotten wood. Semi-rotten wood is called "punky" wood. Dry corncobs or dry leaves or dry sawdust may also be used to create smoke.

Different types of wood yield different amounts of heat and smoke. In other words, some types of wood burn hotter and some woods create more or less smoke than other types of wood. Therefore it is not possible to establish the exact amount of time that a hide needs to be smoked.

The thickness of the wood chips should be between 1/2 inch to 3/4 inch. The width of the chips should be between 1 to 2 inches. The length of the wood chips should be based on the size of your Dutch oven. The wood chips should be at least one inch shorter than the minimum inside diameter of your Dutch oven.

Save the sawdust you create when you are cutting your wood and your wood chips. A little dry sawdust dropped onto hot coals will produce a good quantity of smoke for the smoking process.

The more time that a hide is smoked the darker in color the hide will gradually become. If the hide is relatively white to begin with then it will gradually turn yellow, then orange, and then light brown as the smoking time is increased.

Optional Painting of the Exterior of a Smokehouse

A coat of exterior house paint that is applied to the exterior of a smokehouse will achieve two objectives:

1. **Protection:** It will protect the smokehouse from the weather and extend its useful life expectancy.

2. **Temperature Control:** It will either increase or decrease the temperature inside the smokehouse when the sun is shinning, even when there is no fire burning inside the smokehouse. The two basic color choices are black and white:

a. **Black:** Black will absorb the heat from the sun and the temperature inside the smokehouse will be warmer than if the smokehouse was not painted. If you live in the northern United States, or in any area where the winters are relatively long and cold, then a black color will absorb the sun's energy and increase the temperature inside the smokehouse on a bright sunny day.

b. **White:** White will reflect the heat from the sun and the temperature inside the smokehouse will be cooler than if the smokehouse was not painted. If you live in the southern United States, or in any area where the winters are relatively short and mild, then a white color will help to reflect the sun's energy and minimize the temperature inside the smokehouse on a bright sunny day.

Temperature control is an extremely important factor when smoking meat and when smoking hides. In both situations the temperature inside the smokehouse needs to be kept within a narrow range so that the meat or the hides are properly smoked and they are not cooked.

Smokehouse Location

The smokehouse can be built in one day, if the area where the smokehouse will be constructed is ready to receive the smokehouse. The smokehouse requires a space of approximately 4 feet wide from side to side and 5 feet deep from front to rear. For safety reasons it should be at least ten feet away from any other structure on your property. It should also be at least ten feet away from any trees or shrubs. Finally, the area around the outside of the smokehouse should be short grass, or dirt, or gravel, or stone.

Smoking Meat for Immediate Consumption

A smokehouse is **not** designed to cook meat for immediate consumption for three reasons:

1. The meat needs to be thoroughly cooked and it must also remain moist and tasty. A smokehouse is not designed to provide the moist cooking environment required to smoke meat for immediate consumption.

2. The quantity of meat is relatively small, usually ten pounds or less. This is enough meat to feed a small family or a small group of people for one day.

3. Since the quantity of meat is relatively small, a large smokehouse is not needed. A smaller smoking chamber will accomplish the task more efficiently using less smoke and it is easier to control the temperature inside a smaller smoking chamber.

The easiest way to smoke small quantities of meat and fish for immediate consumption is with a commercial quality smoker, or a combination charcoal grill and smoker. These units are available in the camping or gardening department of some stores, at some hardware stores, and at some Army/Navy stores. Some of these smokers are on wheels and some are not. But most of these smokers are portable and they can be stored inside a shed or a garage when they are not being used.

Meat and fish that is properly smoked for immediate consumption will be safe to eat for several hours without the need for refrigeration. However, if all the smoked meat is not consumed in a short period of time then the leftovers must be refrigerated. If the leftover meat is not refrigerated then it will gradually become unsafe for human consumption.

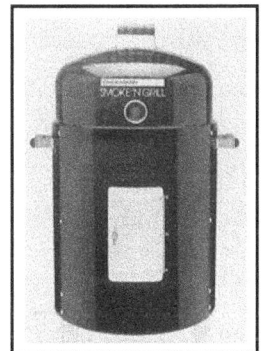

Chapter Forty

How to Smoke Meat and How to Create Meat Jerky

(Some of the information in this chapter is also in my book:
Grandpappy's Recipes for Hard Times)

There are some major differences in the methods that are used to smoke meat for immediate consumption, and to smoke meat to extend is useful shelf life, and to smoke hides to create buckskin clothing. If you are aware of these differences then you will be less likely to make the mistake of trying to smoke everything the same way.

The variables of smoke, moisture, and heat need to be controlled differently for each of the following three applications:

1. **Smoking Meat so You can Eat it Now:** Requires some smoke, some moisture, and good heat.
2. **Smoking Meat for Long-Term Storage:** Requires some smoke, no moisture, and less heat.
3. **Smoking Animal Hides:** Requires thick smoke, no moisture, and almost no heat.

In this chapter we will be describing how to smoke meat for long-term storage so we will be trying to produce a reasonable amount of smoke, but no moisture, and just the right amount of heat.

Instructions for Smoking Meat for Long-Term Storage

1. Slice the meat into strips in the same direction as the muscle. Each strip should be about one inch wide and 1/4 inch thick. The length isn't important. Trim off all the fat because the fat won't cure properly and it will spoil the meat.

2. **Optional** "brine" solution of salt and water: -- If you wish you may soak the meat strips in one quart of water that contains 1/8 cup pure salt (not iodized salt). Soak the sliced meat in the salt solution for 30 to 60 minutes, depending on the thickness of the meat strips. Stir the meat strips inside the salt solution every 15 minutes to achieve a good distribution of the salt mixture onto all the surfaces of the meat. Several pounds of fresh thin meat strips can be processed in the salt and water solution at the same time. If your only objective is to preserve the meat then a salt brine soak is a very good idea because the salt and water solution will saturate into the meat and help to protect it. After removing the meat from the salt bath you may add your favorite seasoning to the meat, if you wish. However, seasoning is not needed if you smoke the meat because the smoke will overpower the seasoning.

3. **Optional** "string of meat" -- If you wish to create a string of meat, then push a clean thin wire, or a needle and some strong nylon thread, or a needle and some strong fishing line, through one end of each piece of meat. Each piece of meat should not touch itself or another piece of meat on the string of meat.

4. Dry the raw meat using any one of the following four methods.
   a. **Sun Drying Method:** Dry the raw meat using the heat of the sun, but not in direct sunlight. Support the meat by hanging it over a clean straight pole. Or hang a string of meat between two poles. Protect the meat strips with cheesecloth or screen wire so the birds can't eat them and the flies can't lay eggs on them. This is the method that was used by some Native American Indians. This method takes the most time and it does not put a protective smoke coating on the meat and it does not add the aroma and taste of the smoke to the meat.
   b. **Fire Pit and Smoke Method:** Dig a hole in the ground and start a fire in the hole. Or use some cement blocks or bricks to create a temporary small fire area that is protected from the wind. Put a metal grill on the blocks to support the meat. If you don't have a grill surface then support the meat by hanging it over a clean straight pole. Or hang a string of meat between two poles driven in the ground. Don't burn soft wood such as pine because the pine pitch will taint the meat. When the fire has burned down to hot coals then place the meat above the hot coals. The air should feel hot to your hand but it should not burn your hand. Do not cook the meat -- only dry the meat. Add some decayed wood or sawdust to the coals to make smoke. The smoke will put a protective coating on the meat. The heat and the smoke will keep the birds and flies away.

c. **Smokehouse Method:** Hang a string of meat in the smokehouse. Start a fire inside the Dutch oven in the smokehouse following the instructions in chapter 39. Add some decayed wood or sawdust to the coals to make smoke. Maintain the temperature inside the smokehouse between 170° to 185° F (77° to 85° C) for 6 to 10 hours. The smoke will put a protective coating on the meat. The heat will destroy any harmful microorganisms in the meat. Do not cook the meat. You only want to dry the meat.

d. **Oven Method:** Spread out the meat strips on aluminum foil on a cookie sheet and dry the meat inside an oven at a temperature between 170° to 185° F (77° to 85° C) for 6 to 10 hours. The heat will destroy any harmful microorganisms in the meat. Do not cook the meat -- only dry the meat. Turn the meat strips over every two hours so they dry evenly on both sides. This method does not put a protective smoke coating on the meat and it does not add the aroma and the taste of the smoke to the meat.

5. Periodically bend the meat jerky strips to test for dryness. Properly dried meat jerky will crack or snap when bent. If it bends without cracking then it still contains too much moisture. If it crumbles then it is too dry. It will still be edible but it will have lost some of its nutritional value.

6. Store the dried meat jerky in a container to protect it from insects. Properly dried meat jerky is safe to eat for up to one year. It may be eaten dry but **it tastes better if it is dipped in water for a short time just before eating.** Or use the meat jerky in a stew.

How Much Time is Required to Dry The Meat?

It is not possible to predict the amount of time required to dry the meat because there are four different methods that can be used, and there are too many different variables that impact the actual time that will be needed.

For example,
1. The thickness of the meat strips.
2. The amount of moisture in the meat strips.
3. The size of the original fire, if drying above a fire.
4. The type of wood used to build the original fire, if drying above a fire.
5. The distance the meat strips are placed above the coals of the fire, if drying by a fire or in a smokehouse.
6. The amount of heat generated by the red hot coals in the fire pit or in the smokehouse.
7. The air temperature ten feet away from the fire or outside the smokehouse (30° F, 70° F, 105° F, etc.).
8. The normal humidity in the air about ten feet away from the fire, if drying above a fire.

Therefore to determine if the meat is done you must bend each strip of meat. If it cracks or snaps it is done. If it bends easily it is not done.

1. The meat directly above the very center of the fire will usually dry faster than the meat near the outside edges of the fire.
2. The meat near the outside edges of the fire will usually take a little longer to dry properly.
3. The **thinner** meat strips will usually dry a little faster.
4. The **thicker** meat strips will usually take a little longer to dry properly.

You will probably discover that you will not be removing all the meat strips from above the fire, or from the smokehouse, or from the oven, at the same time. Instead you will be selectively removing specific meat strips as they become dry enough and you will be leaving some of the other meat strips above the fire, or in the smokehouse, or in the oven, for a slightly longer period of time.

Index

Index

159

About the Author

Robert Wayne Atkins, P.E. (Grandpappy)

Born in 1949. Accepted Jesus Christ as Savior in April of 1976.

B.S. Degree in Industrial Engineering & Operations Research, Virginia Polytechnic Institute and State University, Blacksburg, Virginia, June 1972.

Master of Business Administration, Major in Marketing, Georgia State University, Atlanta, Georgia, March 1985.

Licensed Professional Engineer (P.E.), Florida 1980, Georgia 1982.

Ordained Deacon in Christian Church, Ocala, Florida, 1980.

Member of The Gideons International continuously since 1979.

Author of Nine Computer Software Games, including "**The Lost Crown of Queen Anne**," 1988-1991.

Contributing Author to "**Maynard's Industrial Engineering Handbook**," 5th Edition, p. 5.10, 2001.

Contributing Author to "**Maynard's Industrial & Systems Engineering Handbook**" 6th Edition, p. 102, 2023.

Listed in "**Who's Who in America**," 64th Edition, 2010.

Listed in "**Who's Who in the World**," 29th Edition, 2012.

Recipient of "**Who's Who**" Lifetime Achievement Award, 2019.

Picture Taken in 2004.
Grandpappy Age 55.

Robert is a descendant of the early European settlers in Virginia who married American Indian Cherokee wives.

In the year 2003 Robert began writing down what he had learned from the Holy Bible after more than 25 years of reading it on a daily basis. But he suspected his children might not read what he wrote if he put it into a sermon format. Therefore he began writing short Christian poems because he hoped that his children, grandchildren, and his other future descendants might take the time to read a short poem even if it was Christian oriented.

Later it occurred to him that some of his knowledge might be of interest to other people. Therefore he began publishing some of his writings on his website. Based on the favorable email feedback he received he continued to freely share his knowledge on his website. After several years, and at the request of many of his readers, he eventually consolidated some of his writings into the books below.

Other Books by this Same Author:

1. Handbook of Industrial, Systems, and Quality Engineering (English and Spanish).
2. Introduction to Engineering Management.
3. Engineering Statistics and Applications.
4. Engineering Economy and Financial Analysis.
5. Introduction to Quality Engineering.
6. Introduction to Industrial and Systems Engineering (and Instructor's Manual).
7. Work Measurement and Ergonomics (and Instructor's Manual).
8. Facilities Design and Plant Layout (and Instructor's Manual).
9. Practical Small-Scale Electrical Energy Systems.
10. Practical Strategies for Long-Term Survival.
11. The Practical Prepper's Survival Handbook.
12. Self-Defense Weapons: Traditional and Modern.
13. How to Maximize Your Eating Pleasure and Your Life Expectancy.
14. The Common Sense Diet.
15. The Food Book.
16. Grandpappy's Gourmet Cookbook.
17. Grandpappy's Recipes for Hard Times.
18. Grandpappy's Campfire Survival Cookbook (English and Spanish).
19. Grandpappy's Survival Manual for Hard Times, Third Edition.
20. The Most Important Survival Skills of the 1800s.
21. How to Live Comfortably for Several Years in a Hostile Wilderness Environment.
22. The New Heaven and The New Earth (English and Spanish).
23. Some Difficult Questions Answered Using the Holy Bible.
24. Religion and Christianity in the Twenty-First Century.
25. Grandpappy's Christian Poems.
26. Grandpappy's Stories for Children of All Ages.
27. Ancient Board Games and Solitaire Games from Around the World.
28. The Four Pillars of Prosperity: Governments, Businesses, Religions, and Banks.

www.ingramcontent.com/pod-product-compliance
Lightning Source LLC
Chambersburg PA
CBHW081230090426

42738CB00016B/3243